WHAT IS THE BIBLE?

IS VOLUME

60

OF THE

Twentieth Century Encyclopedia of Catholicism

UNDER SECTION

VI

THE WORD OF GOD

IT IS ALSO THE

1ST

VOLUME IN ORDER OF PUBLICATION

Edited by HENRI DANIEL-ROPS of the Académie Française

WHAT IS THE BIBLE?

By *HENRI DANIEL-ROPS*

Translated from the French by J. R. FOSTER

HAWTHORN BOOKS · PUBLISHERS · *New York*

First Edition, September, 1958   *Fifth Printing,* August, 1959
Second Printing, October, 1958   *Sixth Printing,* November, 1959
Third Printing, October, 1958   *Seventh Printing,* June, 1960
Fourth Printing, January, 1959   *Eighth Printing,* January, 1961
                  Ninth Printing, February, 1962

NIHIL OBSTAT

Johannes M. T. Barton, S.T.D., L.S.S.

   Censor Deputatus

IMPRIMATUR

E. Morrogh Bernard

   Vicarius Generalis

Westmonasterii, die XXV APRILIS MCMLVIII

The Library of Congress has catalogued this publication as follows:

Daniel-Rops, Henri, 1901–
    What is the Bible? Translated from the French by J. R. Foster.
[1st ed.] New York, Hawthorn Books [1958]

    128 p. 21 cm. (The Twentieth century encyclopedia of Catholicism, v. 60. Section 6: The Word of God)

    Includes bibliography.

---

   1. Bible—Introductions.   I. Title.
                          Real name: Henri Jules Charles Petiot.
 BS475.D273   220.6   58–11591 ‡

CONTENTS

CONTENTS

CHAPTER I

THE BIBLE, THE BOOK
OF BOOKS

THE FOUNDATION OF OUR CIVILIZATION

There is a unique and inexhaustible book in which all there is
to say about God and man is said. God's presence pervades it
and in it are revealed all those aspects of his mysterious being
that we are allowed to glimpse; in it he appears, he speaks and
he acts. Man can also see himself in it, in all his potentialities,
his grandeur and his weakness, from his sublimest aspirations
down to those obscure regions of consciousness in which each
of us bleeds from the wound of original sin. It embodies above
all a religious doctrine, the doctrine of the revealed truth; but
human knowledge and intellectual activity also find in it rich
and never-failing nourishment. It is as vain to claim to understand the principles of ethics and law as of sociology, economics
and even politics if one is unaware of the message contained in
this book.

Art and literature are still more obviously dependent on it.
But for this book, the sculptors of Chartres, the mosaic-workers
of Ravenna, Michelangelo, Rembrandt and El Greco would
not be the artists we admire. Still more important and significant than the number of the works which owe their themes to
it is the existence, also due to the Bible, of an art that transcends the laws of aesthetics and acquires a spiritual meaning.
It is the same with literature. This book praised by Montaigne
and Racine, by Shakespeare and Goethe, even by Nietzsche and

Anatole France, has done more than provide innumerable subjects for dramatists; from it flows the stream of living water that
feeds the roots of masterpieces. But for the Bible, would there
ever have been a Dante, a Racine, a Pascal or a Dostoyevski?

Paul Valéry wisely pointed out that western civilization rests
on three foundations: Greek intellectual curiosity, Roman order
and Judaeo-Christian spirituality. Let one of these collapse and
the whole edifice is threatened with destruction. And of these
three foundations the third, and really the most important because it endows the whole structure with its true meaning, is the
unique and inexhaustible book which gives it its character and
initial impetus. Without it the West would not be what it is.

But to link this book with the existence and development of
western civilization alone is to falsify its meaning and limit its
range. We can see more and more clearly, as efforts are made to
render its message universal, that, by its underlying premises as
well as by the modes of expression it employs, it is perfectly
suited to mentalities very different from those of Europe, that
Asia and Africa can welcome it perfectly naturally and that
their genius is even, in a sense, allowed for in it. If the white
man must to a large extent thank the Bible for the rôle of guide
that history grants him, the coloured races owe to it their
awakening to greater light.

Such is *the Bible*, the book of books, the book of man and
the book of God.

THE HOLY BOOKS; THE BOOK

The very name we give this book sums up and indicates all
its exceptional characteristics. The word goes back beyond its
Greek etymology—*biblos* or *biblion*, book—to those distant
days in the second millennium before Christ when the Phoenicians of Byblos had made their port the greatest papyrus mar-
ket of the time and imposed the name of their town on the
product that they sold. Its use in the sense we give it, however,
only goes back to the fourth century of our era, to the days of
St Jerome, who gave currency to the expression "the Holy

Books" or simply "the Books"; in Greek, *ta biblia*. Low Latin turned the word into a feminine and declined it *biblia, bibliae*. And so in everyday usage this plural became a singular, and this collection of seventy-three books was referred to by a word which implies its underlying unity, its supernatural harmony. The synonym that has often been used to describe it, *Scripture* —a term that in fact translates *"the Holy Scriptures"*—expresses in different words the same idea, namely that all the heterogeneous elements of which it is formed coalesce into a higher synthesis.

Scripture, Holy Books, Book, Bible; the different words all correspond to one and the same intention. We are clearly dealing with the unique book, the book *par excellence*, the book that surpasses all other books. It is the absolute in books, because the message it contains is itself the absolute.

THE MOST WIDELY READ BOOK IN THE WORLD

The Bible is also, of all the works of the spirit, by far the most widely read in the world. It is only possible to guess at the number of copies in circulation; the figure of one to two thousand million has been mentioned, and it grows every year by some two million. Even in antiquity the book had begun to spread. The traditional story of Ptolemy Philadelphus asking the High Priest Eleazar to send him the seventy-two best scholars in Israel to endow the library of Alexandria with a Greek translation of the Hebrew scriptures has symbolic value; it proves the fame that the work already enjoyed. The Bible became still more widely diffused when the Christians, having added to the Jewish section the part containing the supreme revelation brought by Jesus, strove to spread it. The Bible was copied in monasteries; the great ones of the earth wanted to have copies. When Gutenberg invented printing, he turned to Scripture for the first text to which he applied the new technique.

Today, the Bible can be read in almost every language of any

importance in the world. Estimates of the number of translations vary from seven hundred and thirty to eleven hundred
and forty. It exists in Japanese and Arabic, in Breton and
Flemish, even in Eskimo and Senegalese. We might perhaps
single out for special mention the year 1817, when it appeared
for the first time in an African language—Malagasy, in point of
fact—whilst Morrison was working on the first Chinese version.
The public for the Book never ceases to expand. In the century
of the "death of God" this success is significant; it confirms the
sovereignty of the Word, of that Word of which it was said that
it would not pass away.

CATHOLICS AND THE BIBLE

Yet it must be admitted that for a long time Catholics lagged
behind in this field. For nearly three hundred years their attitude towards the Book of Books was one of anxious mistrust.
This was one of the consequences of the terrible crisis that
shook the whole Christian world in the sixteenth century and of
the split that is marked in the annals of the Church by the
Protestant revolution. Yet it would not be correct to say that
when Luther, shut up in the Wartburg castle that hid him from
the eyes of his enemies, undertook his great work, the German
translation of the Bible, Catholicism as a whole was showing
no interest in the Scriptures. Between the invention of printing
(1450) and the year (1520) in which the former Augustinian
monk set to work, one hundred and fifty-six Latin editions of
the Bible had appeared and, to mention only Luther's own
country, seventeen versions in German. There can be little
doubt, however, that these publications were intended almost
solely for specialists, that the common people had scarcely any
access to them and that the Book "which ought to have been,
night and day, in the hands of devout men, lay only too often
buried in dust". The simultaneous decline of interest in the
Bible and the liturgy from the end of the thirteenth century
onwards corresponded closely with that break-up of the ideal
of Christendom of which the rise of nationalism in politics, the

development of nominalism in theology and the relaxation of morals were other symptoms. Save for that decline, Luther's attack would have had no significance and its results would not have been what they were.

But when Luther and, with him, the other "reformers" gave back to the Book its supremacy and lustre, they committed the irreparable mistake of separating it from the tradition which had guaranteed its text and contributed so much to its elucidation. Having become man's only source of faith and spiritual life, the Bible provided a means of doing without the Church, its social organization, tradition and hierarchy. The Catholic Church was quick to see the danger of this break in the historical evolution of the Christian message and of this conversion of belief into a matter for the individual conscience. It reacted with the protective measures taken by the Council of Trent. The most important of these forbade the faithful to read Scripture in vernacular translations which had not been approved by the Church and were not accompanied by commentaries in conformity with Catholic tradition. Excessive caution, perhaps, combined with an influence not untinged with Jansenism, endowed this prohibition with an absolute character that it never possessed. It became common to hear it said: "The Bible is on the Index", or "A Catholic must not read the Bible". The Modernist crisis at the beginning of this century, when imprudently directed studies called in question the authenticity of Scripture, helped in no small measure to strengthen this suspicious attitude.

All this involved a serious loss for Catholics. How could one be fully Christian after cutting oneself off from the very roots which have allowed the Christian faith to live and blossom? It has been the especial merit of popes in the last sixty years to measure the extent of the loss and to remedy it. Three great encyclicals restored the rights of the truth—and of the Bible: *Providentissimus Deus* of Leo XIII in 1893; *Spiritus Paraclitus* of Benedict XV on the occasion of St Jerome's fifteenth centenary in 1920; and the illuminating message of Pius XII in 1943, *Divino afflante Spiritu*, which was the starting point of the present biblical revival. At the same time several bodies were either created by the Holy See or founded with its encouragement. Among them were the *Pontifical Biblical Commission* (1902), which lays down the teaching of the Church in matters of Scripture,[1] and the Pontifical Biblical Institute (Jesuit) and the Biblican School of Jerusalem (Dominican), which are responsible for pursuing and directing studies in this field. The Benedictine monastery of St Jerome, in Rome, was given the task of revising the Latin translation of the Scriptures, the most important one as it is in Latin that the sacred texts are used in the Roman rite.

From now on, the Catholic Church says to her children, "Read the Bible!" And in every country in the world in which her authority is recognized considerable efforts are being made to obey this injunction. In France alone, six translations, one sixty years old but recently brought up to date, one twenty years old and four other more recent ones share a public that grows daily greater.[2] One of them, recommended by Cardinal Liénart, has sold more than three hundred thousand copies in four years. Today, therefore, it is perfectly easy for Catholics to obey

---

[1] A few words about the decrees of the Biblical Commission. Its decrees have lately been republished (*Enchiridion Biblicum*, 1954); at the same time its secretary and deputy-secretary published a note emphasizing (i) the *historical* bearing of the decrees (they must be interpreted according to the circumstances of their publication) and (ii) their specific nature (a distinction must be made: "We have in mind two kinds of decisions. It is possible that a decree is connected with faith and morals; in so far as it is so connected, it naturally retains all its authority and remains binding. But very often the decisions of the B.C., by the very nature of their subject, have no connection with faith and morals. The Commission has generally intervened in questions of a historical or critical nature. In questions of this kind new evidence may re-open a question which might have seemed settled. . . ."). (Article by Dom Jacques Dupont, O.S.B., "A propos du nouvel Enchiridion' Biblicum", in *Revue Biblique*, July 1955, pp. 414–19.)

[2] For details of modern English translations of the Bible, see the bibliography at the end of this book. The most important are Mgr Knox's version (from which, unless otherwise indicated, quotations in the text are taken), the Westminster Version and the new American translation, known as the "Confraternity version", now in course of publication. [*Trans.*]

the instruction of Canon 1391 and to read the Bible only in authorized editions. As for the number of publications devoted to the Bible, it is staggering: nearly two hundred works and a host of articles in French alone in 1954.

These efforts and their results have their significance. The sacred text is no longer a prey to the whims of free examination and private judgement. Handed on to the faithful by Mother Church herself, who interprets it according to the wisdom of a tradition that stretches back twenty centuries, Holy Scripture has once more assumed its rôle of living link and inexhaustible source. Reading the Bible is no longer, as it may have appeared to some of the sixteenth-century heresiarchs to be, a personal adventure, a revolt against authority, tradition, the hierarchy and established dogma; it is a lofty act of faith and loyalty.

Thus Holy Writ appears as a decisive factor in the twentieth century's choice between faith and the refusal to believe. Henceforth there is one section of humanity which lives by Scripture, by the Book of Books, and another which rejects it, because henceforth there is one section of humanity which can conceive of a life without God and another that makes him, as the Bible does itself, the *Alpha* and *Omega*, the beginning and end of all things.

CHAPTER II

FROM THE SPOKEN WORD

TO OUR "BIBLES"

THE BOOK WAS FIRST THE SPOKEN WORD

How were these books, which together form the Bible and which we regard as the foundations of our faith, composed and handed down to us? Our modern "bibles" hide under their uniform appearance not only the amazing diversity of their component parts but also the mystery of their origins. Who thinks, as he thumbs the closely printed pages, of the time when these words and sentences were not fixed in cold print but chanted or intoned to audiences by the voices of the Heralds of God?

Long before it was a written text, by far the greater part of the Bible was oral teaching. In the form of more or less stereotyped narratives, rhythmic and assonant poems, and pithy proverbs and sayings, its elements were handed down from generation to generation by the spoken word before the use of writing became general. This rather special kind of genesis, of which other oriental books (the Koran, for example) provide examples, is intimately related to the cultural, spiritual and linguistic patterns of the people among which the Bible grew up, patterns of a simple and communal type in which literary creation was much less individual and intellectual, and more living and spontaneous, than among us. To understand properly how the Bible arose, we must forget the habits we have acquired as modern men and members of a paper civilization. Reading and writing have become such automatic operations that it is difficult for us to realize that some societies have been able to manage almost entirely without them. Our memory has become bloodless and barren, and our faculties of improvisation have more to do with mere words and rhetoric than poetry and prophecy. In ancient Israel, right up to the time of Christ, it was very different. The ability to speak with fluency, art and a gift for aphorism was the mark of those who today would be "writers". The trained memory was a superb tool. "A good disciple," said the Jewish Scribes, "is like a well-made cistern; he does not let a single drop of his master's teaching escape."

Transmission by memory and the spoken word was greatly facilitated by the technique applied to it. There was an art of learning by heart that formed part of the art of composition. This oral style has left a visible mark on the text; the written version to a large extent preserves its patterns. The regularity of the rhythm, the repetition of certain words and the use of alliteration assisted memory. We have only to read aloud many passages in the Gospels to become aware of the oral phrasing behind the written text. In the verses

> You would not dance when we piped to you,
> You would not mourn when we wept to you,
> (Luke 7. 32)

we are obviously confronted with a rhythmical fragment, a sort of refrain.

Sometimes we know for certain that the teaching existed before it was written down; the prophecies of Jeremias were *spoken* twenty-two years before they were committed to writing. All the prophetical books, all the psalms and all the poetical parts, especially the Song of Songs, which is a collection of wedding hymns, obviously possess this character. Even in the historical books we may suspect from the tone and from various turns of phrase that we are dealing with spoken chronicles, rather like those with which Homeric bards and medieval minstrels alleviated the boredom of the nobility.

This does not mean that written elements did not exist. The

Bible itself alludes to collections, like the *Book of the Wars of Yahweh* and *The Book of the Just*, which must have been familiar to everyone, to judge by the way in which they are mentioned. "Is it not written in the Book of the Just" (Josue 10. 13) how Josue, to win time to make his victory complete, ordered the sun to stop and was obeyed? Today, after the innumerable discoveries of archaeology from Sinai to Ras-Shamra, no one denies the existence of very old biblical writings earlier in date than the tenth, perhaps even than the twelfth, century. At the time when Moses' Hebrews were in Egypt, writing had been in general use on the Nile for fifteen centuries. However, these written elements were for long only aids to memory before they were incorporated in the compilation that we possess.

Curiously enough, the process was the same with the New Testament books, or at any rate with the Gospels; the Acts of the Apostles, the Epistles and the Apocalypse are written documents presented as such. Some, like St Paul's letters, were dictated, and in these the "oral style" reappears. The Gospels were certainly first "spoken" before they were written down. The first generations of Christians attached enormous importance to this oral teaching. Imagine a child of today being told by his grandmother that her own grandmother used to talk to her, when she was a little girl, about Napoleon, and tell her how she had seen troops marching past just before Waterloo; surely that direct memory would seem much more concrete and real than anything he could read in his history book? For at least four or five generations Christians heard the Gospel as a story handed down, by word of mouth, by unimpeachable witnesses. About A.D. 130—that is, at a time when the four evangelists had long published their books—St Papias, Bishop of Hierapolis in Phrygia, declared that what he preferred to anything else, where tradition was concerned, was "the living and enduring word". A little later St Irenaeus, at Lyons, recalled the days when he used to listen to St Polycarp, the great Bishop of Smyrna, telling what he had heard himself from St John the Apostle. The

Gospels preserve the tone of these living witnesses; that is what is so moving about them.

However, the need to guide those who handed on the Gospels and the wish to avoid deviations, errors, exaggerations and distortions eventually made it necessary to have recourse to writing. Behind the final text of the four little books the reader can still sense the "notes" that the evangelists used at first.

THE TRIUMPH OF WRITING

The transition from oral to written transmission poses a number of problems. The first is that of date: at what point did the text assume its written form? For the Old Testament, only a cautious reply can be given to this question. There were, it seems, three periods of intense literary activity. In the time of Ezechias the oral or written records of the Southern Kingdom were probably collected, put into order and compared with those of the Northern Kingdom, which Samaritan scholars who fled to Jerusalem in 722 B.C. brought with them (cf. Prov. 25. 1). In the reign of Josias the famous "discovery" of Deuteronomy took place and the first complete version of the Pentateuch may have been put into writing. The work seems to have been completed soon after the return from exile, when Cyrus, in 538, allowed "the remnants of Israel", the exiles in Babylon, to return to their country and to set up a sort of little state under Persian protection. Just as Nehemias, in about 445, rebuilt the walls of Jerusalem, so another great man erected the spiritual citadel, the Bible: the wise scribe Esdras, lawyer and theologian combined, was reputed to have miraculously dictated ninety-four holy books and to have made his whole people follow their precepts. So it was apparently in the fifth century that the old fragmentary versions were collated, the orally transmitted parts written down and these various elements arranged in a coherent whole. A century earlier, at Athens, Pisistratus had lent his name to a similar operation on the Homeric poems. To this original Bible was subsequently added a small number of texts referring to the centuries that followed and recording fresh spiritual attainments.

The facts concerning the second part of the Bible, the New Testament, are better known. It has already been mentioned that the Acts of the Apostles, the Epistles and the Apocalypse make it clear in so many words that they are written or dictated texts; so far as they are concerned, therefore, no problem arises. As for the four Gospels, the transition from word of mouth to writing took place at various dates, for different reasons and under different conditions. Without going into the details of learned discussions, the composition of the Gospels may be summarized as follows. Papias says: "Matthew was the first to put down the sayings of the Lord, in the Hebrew tongue." So the first of the "evangelists" was apparently the former tax-gatherer of Capharnaum, who probably wrote his Gospel between 50 and 55 in the language spoken by the Jews at that time, that is, Aramaic. Soon afterwards St Peter, who was in Rome, was joined by Mark, a young Jew who knew Greek; as he listened to the Prince of the Apostles, this intelligent young man noted down what he heard, compared his notes with the little aids to memory already in circulation, and between 55 and 62 produced his Gospel. It was in popular Greek and obviously addressed to the Christian lower classes of Rome all round him. Almost at the same time a well-educated doctor, Luke, who had been St Paul's companion on his travels, arrived in Rome. He had learned much from the Apostle of the Gentiles and during his stay at Jerusalem had gathered first-hand information, perhaps from the Virgin Mary herself. In due course he wrote his Gospel, in excellent Greek and in the first place for the rather more distinguished people who gathered round Paul. Either the success of these two new accounts or even that of his own Aramaic one induced Matthew to complete and translate his own work, probably soon afterwards, between 64 and 68. As for the fourth Gospel, St John's, it was written at Ephesus by the beloved apostle at the end of his long life, some considerable time after the first three. It is a mixture of reminiscence, documentation and spiritual meditation and is usually reckoned to date from the last few years of the century, perhaps from about 96–98.

This brief summary has shown in what languages the Bible was written. There were three. Hebrew, the original, sacred language of God's people, is used in the vast majority of the parts that are the fruit of the Jewish tradition; it was to remain the liturgical language of Israel up to our day, and the Dead Sea discoveries have proved that the Essenes were still using it round about the beginning of our era. Aramaic, a related Semitic language, was always gaining ground at the expense of Hebrew in everyday use, so much so that it may have been this that forced Esdras to fix the text of the Scriptures; in Christ's day everyone used it. But there are only a few books in Aramaic in the Bible: Matthew's original Gospel, as we have seen, and certain parts of Esdras, Daniel and Jeremias. Greek was little used before the time of Christ—only the second book of Machabees and that of Wisdom were written in this tongue— but when our era began its use was so widespread that to all intents and purposes all the sacred books of the Christians were written in Greek—popular Greek, by the way, which was by no means always identical with the language of Homer or Plato.

There remain two practical questions: on what material and in what writing was the text of the Bible recorded? Two materials were used. One, which was cheap, consisted in the fibres of the papyrus, the Egyptian reed, crushed and held together by a coating of varnish; this was the origin of paper. The other, which was much dearer, was parchment, that is, the carefully tanned and pumiced skin of an animal. Originally the leaves of papyrus or parchment were fastened end to end in rolls; the Jewish liturgy has remained faithful to this practice. The custom of sewing the leaves together in groups of four pages—each group was called a *quaternion*, from which is derived the French word *cahier*, copybook—which were then assembled in a volume, dates from the second century before Christ and was popularized by the Christians.

As for the scripts employed, they varied enormously during the course of the centuries. Early Hebrew was not written in the massive, square letters that it employs today; this script only took shape in the centuries immediately before Christ. The archaic letters were more like the Phoenician alphabet. Neither form of writing included the signs and dots which in present-day Hebrew indicate the vowels. Greek was more or less as we know it today, except that the old copyists did not separate the letters or use any punctuation, which often makes it difficult to read. Needless to say, in both languages the writing varied in quality. Sometimes it is the careful calligraphy of the "publishing firms", at others cursive and rapid, with the words all joined together. This kind of writing does not make any easier the ticklish problem of the transmission of the texts down the centuries before the invention of printing, that is to say, the notorious problem of the manuscripts.

MANUSCRIPTS OF THE BIBLE

It is hardly necessary to say that we do not possess any original manuscript of the books of the Bible, any more than we do of Homer or Pindar. We know them only in copies. Thousands of manuscripts of the Bible exist; they are far from being catalogued. In 1780 a Hebrew scholar by the name of Kennicott boasted that he had personally collated 261 manuscripts of the Jewish Bible and examined 349 others; whereupon one of his rivals, the Italian de Rossi, retorted with the assertion that in his own library alone he had 310 copies that the Englishman had never seen. As for the value of these extremely numerous manuscripts, their interest obviously varies tremendously according to their date and the care taken in copying them.

In speaking of an ancient text one must never lose sight of the elementary fact that until the invention of printing the written word was handed down by a succession of copies. Each time it was copied the text ran all kind of dangers; the scribes might be careless, ignorant or so eager to do a good job that they "emended" the original in accordance with their own ideas. As for the "revisers" who intervened from time to time to restore the text to its original purity, it often happened that their boldness or lack of comprehension produced further blunders. Consequently, our chances of possessing an accurate copy of an ancient text diminish with the passage of time. It is not generally known that in the case of the great classical writers the interval between composition and the first known manuscript is almost always enormous: fourteen hundred years in the case of the tragedies of Sophocles and the same for Aeschylus, Aristophanes and Thucydides; sixteen hundred years for Euripides and Catullus, thirteen hundred years for Plato and twelve hundred for Demosthenes. How great is this interval in the case of the Bible?

So far as the Hebrew part is concerned the reply until recently was fairly pessimistic. No manuscript earlier than the ninth century was known. The oldest seems to be that of the synagogue at Karasubazar, near Simferopol in the Crimea, which has been dated at A.D. 830. The Leningrad Bible, also discovered in the Crimea, is dated in "the year 1228 of the era of the Seleucids". Antiochus the Great reigned in Syria from 223 to 187 B.C., so this manuscript would date from about 1000. The divergencies between different copies of the Hebrew Bible are in any case very slight, because in very early medieval times the Rabbis gave careful attention to the task of fixing the text and its pronunciation by the addition of vowel points. The result of their labours is known as the *Massora*.[1] As many as possible of the manuscripts earlier than this Massoretic revision were destroyed and only small fragments of them are still extant.

The situation has been modified by the recent discoveries in the neighbourhood of the Dead Sea. It is well known that in 1947 rolls containing many biblical texts were found hidden in jars in a cave. The subsequent exploration of neighbouring caves brought still more rolls to light. It is generally agreed

---

[1] *Massora* means tradition in Hebrew. The work of the Massoretes extended from the sixth to the tenth century. Up till then vowels had not been indicated in the Hebrew text of the Bible. [*Trans.*]

that they formed the library of a nearby Hebrew monastery belonging to the strict sect of the Essenes and were hidden in these caves during the terrible events of the Jewish War of A.D. 66–70. It goes without saying that the texts must be earlier than this date, and some of them seem to be a great deal earlier, dating perhaps from the third or even fourth century B.C. For the parts of the Bible which occur in the "Dead Sea Scrolls", therefore—notably two complete copies of Isaias and parts of Genesis, Deuteronomy and Exodus—we now have copies extremely close to the original. The question arises whether comparison with previously known manuscripts will lead to important modifications in the received text. First reports suggest that it will not. The text of Isaias is apparently almost identical with ours.[1]

When we come to the books of the New Testament the problem is much more complicated. We are confronted with innumerable copies of every age differing greatly in character. They may be divided into three classes: minuscules, uncials and papyri. The minuscules are all later than the ninth century; by this time the text had been standardized and, apart from a few details, they reproduce the "received text". The most famous manuscripts are those copied between the fourth and ninth centuries in that noble script known as uncial. At least two date from the fourth century: the *Codex Vaticanus* (at the Vatican) and the *Codex Sinaiticus*, which was found at the monastery of Sinai among old parchments that had been cast aside, taken to Russia and sold by Soviet Russia to the British Museum. The *Codex Bezae* at Cambridge dates from the fifth century. It fell into Protestant hands at Lyons and was given to the University of Cambridge in 1581 by Theodore of Beza, Calvin's famous disciple. So the interval between the originals and the copies of the Christian books is one of only three or four centuries; of the great classical writers, only Terence and Virgil are in this happy position.

---

[1] See *Les Manuscrits hébreux du Désert de Juda*, by A. Vincent (Paris, 1954) (or *The Dead Sea Scrolls and their Significance*, by H. H. Rowley (London, 1955) [*Trans.*]).

What is more, the sands of Egypt have yielded papyri (which were often used for wrapping mummies) covered in writing. Among these invaluable documents are several fragments of the Gospels and Epistles. The most noteworthy papyri are the Egerton papyrus, the Chester Beatty papyri and those acquired by the University of Michigan. The biggest fragment gives us St Paul's letters almost in their entirety. The most precious of all is the Rylands papyrus, which is to be seen at Manchester. It contains a passage from chapter 18 of St John's Gospel and dates from about A.D. 130, that is, it is almost contemporary with the original. The case is unique in the whole history of ancient texts and proves how swiftly the Gospel spread.

By comparing all these manuscripts with one another it is possible to arrive at a text that may well be completely authentic. It should be added that we have another indirect check at our disposal, that provided by translations.

ANCIENT TRANSLATIONS OF THE BIBLE

Today we read the Bible in translation. Only professional biblical scholars go back to the original text, to the great Hebrew edition by Rudolf Kittel of the Stuttgart Biblical Institute (Stuttgart, 1937) or to the Greek editions of the New Testament by Nestle (Stuttgart, 1898–1941) or A. Merk and the Pontifical Biblical Institute (Rome, 1948). The Bible was translated into other languages at a very early epoch, and the interest of these old translations is considerable, for they enable us to reconstruct the texts used by the translators, which are often earlier than those preserved by our manuscripts.

The first in date of these translations, and one of the most famous, is the Septuagint. We have already seen that it was made in Egypt—in the third and second centuries before our era—according to the legend at the request of an enlightened pharaoh, in fact because the Jews of Alexandria, ill-acquainted with Hebrew, needed a translation. This Greek version was an outstanding success. The first Christian communities used it and almost all the translations into other languages were made from it. Some of the Fathers of the Church, St Augustine for example, thought that it was "inspired". Modern scholarship, however, has subjected this illustrious work to close examination and, while emphasizing its great interest, pointed out that some of the translators made mistakes or paraphrased the text. However that may be, the fame of this translation ousted all the other Greek versions, for example those of Aquila (c. A.D. 140) and Theodotion (c. A.D. 180), of which Origen thought highly.

The Gospels had scarcely been published before translations of them were made, particularly into the two languages most used (together with Greek) by the primitive Christian communities, Syriac and Latin. The Latin versions are obviously of prime importance, first because they occur in a large number of very old manuscripts, and second because it was through the medium of Latin that holy Scriptures became part and parcel of western civilization. One is famous above all others, the Vulgate of St Jerome. But before the great scholar set to work numerous Latin versions had been made, especially of the Gospels, often differing considerably from each other and no doubt based on very early texts. Only about fifteen manuscripts of these earlier versions are extant. The two most famous are in Italy. One is at Vercelli (it belonged to Eusebius, who was bishop of this city and died in 371) and the other at Trent, the Palatinus, which also belongs to the fourth century. The triumph of the Vulgate caused the older translations to be discarded.

St Jerome lived from 347 to 420, first at Rome and afterwards in a solitary hermitage at Bethlehem. On the advice of his friend Pope Damasus, he resolved to endow the Church with as perfect a translation as possible of the holy books. For the New Testament, he limited himself to a careful and detailed revision of the existing text; for the Hebrew Bible, he undertook the monumental task of making a translation direct from the originals. St Jerome's Vulgate, living, warm and often picturesque, has had a profound effect right up to the present day on the reading of the Bible by Christians. It even eliminated from everyday use versions which had their value, like the revision made by St Augustine. Copied from generation to generation, until the invention of printing, the Vulgate suffered the common fate of texts copied by hand. After the Council of Trent an official edition was compiled, on the orders of Clement VIII (1592–1605). The Benedictine monks of the Abbey of St Jerome in Rome are now at work on a more scientific revision.

Recent translations of the Bible into modern languages almost all take into account the Septuagint and the original Hebrew or Greek as well as the Vulgate.[1] In the last fifty years an immense amount of energy has been devoted to the task of sifting the text. We certainly possess a more "authentic" Bible than the Christians of days gone by.

TEXTUAL CRITICISM

This task is governed by textual criticism, a meticulous science with exacting laws of its own. Amid the multiplicity of variants, that is, more or less divergent readings, it is no easy matter to arrive at the truth. Some idea of the complexity of the problem may be gained from the knowledge that, in the four Gospels alone, there are upwards of a hundred thousand variant readings. Most of them, of course, only affect details, sometimes a word or even only a syllable or letter, but that does not make collation any easier.

Textual criticism employs methods which, when all used simultaneously, form a touchstone of authenticity. External criticism studies and compares the manuscripts. It has to decide whether the better of two variants is the one given by a hundred manuscripts that may all have copied the same original, which itself perhaps contained a mistake, or the one given by one single manuscript that seems better guaranteed. So for each text

[1] Of modern versions in English, Mgr Knox's is a translation from the Vulgate. The Westminster Version and the Confraternity Version of the Old Testament are translations from the original tongues. For further details of these versions, see the bibliography. [*Trans.*]

an attempt must be made to reconstruct the history of its transmission. This is not always possible. In that case we must turn
to internal criticism, which tracks down obvious errors by
making use of the context. It tries to detect whether such-and-
such a reading interrupts the train of ideas, has been influenced
by another text (this is quite frequent in the Gospels), or conflicts with the author's genius and modes of thought and
writing. It can easily be imagined that the whole science is an
extremely delicate one and that its results are often only con-
jectural. Thanks to its patient efforts we can rely on having as
faithful a text as possible. But it should be emphasized that, on
the whole, these variants only affect very small points, tiny
details even, and that it is rare for discussion of them to call in
question important truths. Taken as a whole, the text of holy
Scripture as we possess it today is quite sufficiently sound and
well guaranteed to form a basis of faith.

CHAPTER III

THE "CANON" OF THE
TWO TESTAMENTS

A COMPLEX AND APPARENTLY HETEROGENEOUS BOOK

It must be admitted that the reader's first impression on opening the Bible and turning over its pages will be one of amaze-
ment. Chateaubriand confessed as much in a famous passage
of his *Genius of Christianity*. What is the meaning of this
heterogeneous collection of books differing from each other in
kind, in tone and in intention? It is as if the *Song of Roland*, a
code of canon law, Joinville's *Chronicles*, *Cyrano de Bergerac*,
some interesting bits from Michelet's *History of France*, two or
three of Voltaire's *Philosophical Tales* and some anthologies of
poetry had all been strung together.[1] Any attempt to detect a
less formal kind of unity, to discover a style common to all the
books or even to all the authors would be futile. Some parts of
the book flash with the sparkle of genius, others are undeniably
platitudinous and dull. Yet the astonishment aroused by a
merely superficial glance at the Bible is nothing, as we shall see,
compared to that produced by a consideration of its contents
or any attempt to take them all literally.

The reader must overcome his initial discomfiture and seek

[1] An equivalent list from English literature would juxtapose items
like *Beowulf, the Anglo-Saxon Chronicle, Henry the Fifth*, selections
from Macaulay's *History of England*, two or three essays from the
Spectator and the *Golden Treasury*. [*Trans.*]

the aid of introductions and commentaries (there are many good ones today) which will prevent his losing his way in this maze. Above all, he must try to grasp the grand idea binding all these diverse books together. To regard the Bible as a collection of heterogeneous texts ranging from cooking recipes to the highest mystical speculations is to condemn oneself to complete incomprehension. On the other hand, everything appears in a fresh light and falls into place when you realize that, taken as a whole, the Bible is a history, the history of a unique people whose destiny followed a divine plan. From the literary point of view it is absurd to talk of the "plan" of the Bible; yet everything in it, even the mostly unlikely looking passages, has its part to play in God's plan.

HOW TO FIND A BIBLICAL REFERENCE

When a text from the Bible is quoted, it is normally followed by a reference consisting of letters and figures, in most cases an abbreviated word, a roman numeral and an arabic numeral (but sometimes two arabic numerals, which is not so clear). We might come across, for example, Jer. vii, 15 (Jer. 7. 15) or Mt. ix, 7 (Matt. 9. 7), which mean, "Book of the Prophet Jeremias, chapter seven, verse fifteen" and "Gospel according to St Matthew, chapter nine, verse seven". These simple indications immediately point to an interesting fact: the division of the Bible into books, chapters and verses. This division is certainly useful, for its triple nature enables us to pin-point immediately any given passage, but it is questionable whether the breaks it involves, whose artificiality is obvious as soon as we start to read continuously, do not form a tiresome interruption to the train of ideas and even occasionally make the narrative hard to understand.

The division into books designated by a title (Book of Kings, Exodus, Epistle to the Romans, or Apocalypse), by the name of their author (Jeremias, Isaias, Matthew, Mark) or by that of the principal character in them (Tobias, Job, Ruth) is bound up with the conditions under which the Bible grew up, that is, with the problem of choice, which we are going to tackle in a moment. The other divisions are of lesser importance and in any case of much more recent origin.

The chapters, which are of approximately equal length, only go back to the beginning of the thirteenth century. The credit for this innovation belongs to Stephen Langton, a professor at the University of Paris and later Archbishop of Canterbury and a Cardinal. It was a great success; Parisian scribes made it fashionable and from 1226 onwards it spread everywhere. The Jews themselves adopted it with only small differences. The present chapter divisions are still those made by the learned English cardinal.

As for the division into verses, it is comparatively recent, just four hundred years old. The celebrated Parisian printer Robert Estienne introduced the famous little figures that mark—and sometimes chop up—the sentences when he brought out an edition of the Bible in 1551. The method governing the division defies rational analysis; sometimes a clause is cut in two, at others two quite unconnected statements are put together. Very often it looks as though purely typographical reasons were at the bottom of it. However, the procedure has been so long sanctified by usage that in practice it is impossible to abolish it.

THE TWO "TESTAMENTS"

The first and most important division in the Bible is the one which divides its books into two portions of unequal length known as the Old Testament and the New Testament. At first sight the word "testament" looks ambiguous; in French and in English it has a very precise meaning which it seems difficult to apply to the books of the Bible. Yet, rightly understood, it confronts the reader immediately with the mystery at the very heart of Scripture, that of the covenant between God and man through the intermediary of a people, that is, it confronts him with the divine plan.

For testament simply denotes *alliance*, the Hebrew word

berith applying to the Covenant which existed, from the time of the call heard by Abraham, between the Almighty and the People which he had appointed to be his witness and mouthpiece. *Berith* was rendered in Greek in the Septuagint by the word *diatheke*, which lays emphasis on the idea of treaty or document sanctifying the alliance (the term *suntheke* would have been more appropriate and was in fact used by other less illustrious translators). In Latin, *diatheke* was translated by *testamentum*, a term which denoted "a written document of an official character", that is, treaty of alliance as well as will.

In the former sense it describes first of all the special relations of God with his people, but it can also refer to the union which God himself, putting on a human form, sealed with man by the sacrifice of Christ. So there is an Old Covenant and a New Covenant, as the Gospel often repeats. And surely the latter includes the second meaning of the term. For, as the Epistle to the Hebrews says (9. 15–22), it is by the testator's death that the heirs enter into possession of his goods, and it is by Christ's death that the children of God gain access to their eternal heritage. In the most tragic sense of the term, testament expresses man's right to the divine adoption secured for him by the sacrifice of Calvary; the New Covenant is sealed with blood.

THE "CANON", THE RULE OF FAITH

In each of the two main parts of the Bible there are a certain number of texts or Books. Why are they there? Because the Church declares that they express authentically and properly the Alliance of God with man in its two forms. This is the idea denoted by the usual term Canon and not, as is often thought, simply that of "list" or "catalogue".

The word is Greek, but probably borrowed from some Semitic tongue; in Hebrew *qaneh* means a measuring reed, the one of which Ezechiel speaks (40. 3, 5). It was employed by the Alexandrian grammarians for the corpus of classical works worthy of serving as models, by Cicero in the same sense, by

Pliny, with reference to the sculptor Polyclitus,[1] to denote the right methods to follow in making statues, and by Epictetus to describe the moral rules of the good life. The Fathers of the Church in large numbers, from St Clement of Rome to St Hippolytus, used the word to denote anything fundamental to religion: the rule of tradition, the rule of faith or the rule of truth. Quite naturally the sense was extended to cover any writing that laid down a rule; a text was called "canonical" when it fixed rules of belief or action; hence, by extension again, the sense of "collection of writings laying down the rule". When in 350 St Athanasius said of the *Shepherd of Hermas*, "It is not part of the Canon", it was in this sense that he understood the term. From that time onwards it became current; St Jerome, St Augustine and St Gregory Nazianzen all use it.

It is in this sense that down the centuries many of the official documents of the Church have taken it, among the most important being the decisions of the Council of Trent in 1546 and those of the Vatican Council in 1870. So the "canon" of Scripture comprises all the books proclaimed by the Church as "regulating faith"—and at the same time "inspired", a qualification which depends, as we shall see, on another criterion. The list is henceforth unalterable; let us see how it was settled.

THE CANON OF THE OLD TESTAMENT

The list of "canonical" books is the one drawn up by the Council of Trent at its fourth session. It comprises forty-five books: Genesis, Exodus, Leviticus, Numbers, Deuteronomy (these first five together form what is known as the Pentateuch), Josue, Judges, Ruth, two books of Samuel, two books of Kings, two of Chronicles, Esdras, Nehemias,[2] Tobias, Judith, Esther,

---

[1] One of his most famous statues, the *Doryphorus*, a youth carrying a spear, was in fact known as "The Canon" or standard. [*Trans.*]

[2] Some of these books have alternative names: 1 and 2 Samuel and 1 and 2 Kings are also called 1, 2, 3 and 4 Kings; Chronicles are called Paralipomenon and Nehemias is also known as 2 Esdras. These are the names used, for example, in the Rheims-Douay and Knox versions. [*Trans.*]

Job, Psalms, Proverbs, Ecclesiastes, Song of Songs, Wisdom, Ecclesiasticus, Isaias, Jeremias (with Lamentations), Baruch, Ezechiel, Daniel, Osee, Joel, Amos, Abdias, Jonas, Micheas, Nahum, Habacuc, Sophonias, Aggeus, Zacharias, Malachias (these last twelve are known as the Minor Prophets) and two books of Machabees. The Jews (followed by the Protestants) only recognize thirty-eight of them; even in the time of Jesus they were not agreed on the canonicity of all the holy books, some—the most numerous and strictest—accepting only those in Hebrew, the others wishing to include seven other books generally preserved in Greek, Tobias, Judith, Wisdom, Ecclesiasticus, Baruch and the two books of Machabees, not counting some parts of the book of Esther only extant in Greek. For a long time now, or at any rate since the thirteenth century, Catholics have divided the Old Testament into four main parts: the Pentateuch (which the Jews call the Law, the Torah), the Historical Books (Josue to Esther together with Machabees), the Poetical and Sapiential Books (Job to Ecclesiasticus) and the Prophetical Books (Isaias to Malachias).

The next question that arises is how the canon of the Old Testament was formed, that is, how the religious leaders of Israel, the chief priests and doctors of the Law, decided what was "canonical". There is absolutely no doubt (the fact is attested by the Jewish historian Flavius Josephus, who lived from 37 to about A.D. 100) that in the time of Christ, apart from the differences mentioned above between strict Jews and more liberal, hellenizing Jews, there existed a properly drawn-up list of the scriptures, a "canon"; it contained the thirty-eight books, a figure which was sometimes artificially reduced to twenty-two, the number of letters in the Hebrew alphabet. But as for the criteria and methods that the rabbis used in making their choice and the dates when they made it, these are questions to which we can give no precise answers. It seems to have been King Josias (639–609 B.C.), in whose reign the high priest Helcias "found the Book of the Law in the house of Yahweh", who first established a still very short and rudimentary canon. Anyway, from the fifth century onwards there was a list of sacred books read in the synagogues; Esdras drew it up about 444 B.C. The prophetical group seems to have been fixed somewhat later, perhaps about the third century B.C. The Book of Psalms, which enjoyed great prestige because of its attribution to the royal poet David and its use since time immemorial in the liturgy, must have long formed part of the canon by natural right, as it were. The other, so-called "hagiographical", books were put together by scribes and scholars during the third and second centuries, and the list must have been finally settled after the famous persecution of Antiochus Epiphanes (175–164 B.C.), when Judas Machabeus ordered a search for the sacred rolls that had escaped destruction in order to collect them together. So by and large it does not look as though there was ever an official verdict, comparable to the decision of a General Council, declaring the Old Testament as a whole canonical.

The canon did not pass into Christian use without numerous discussions and hesitations. The general principle was to regard as canonical the books quoted by Jesus and the Apostles, but in practice this did not work. It would be true to say that the Fathers of the Eastern Church tended to favour the smaller Hebrew list, while the Western Fathers admitted the deutero-canonical books that the Jews had finally excluded. In the fourth century the situation was still fluid; St Hilary refused to grant the seven books in question the title of "canonical", but considered them nevertheless as part of Holy Scripture. It seems to have been St Jerome and St Augustine who, by rallying to the cause of the wider canon, secured its triumph in the Church. The councils of Hippo (A.D. 393) and Carthage (A.D. 397), and a letter of Innocent I in 405, prove that by that time the canon was fixed as we know it today.

THE CANON OF THE NEW TESTAMENT

So far as the New Testament is concerned, Protestants are more or less in agreement with Catholics, except that they are not so categorical in their attributions; for example, the Epistle to the Hebrews, to which Catholics affix St Paul's name, remains in their eyes of problematical authorship. But the number of books is the same for both: twenty-seven. They are divided into three sections: the historical books (the four Gospels and the Acts of the Apostles), the didactic books (the fourteen epistles of St Paul and seven other epistles with the signatures of St Peter, St John, St James and St Jude) and finally one prophetical book, the Apocalypse.

It should not be thought that this new canon was rapidly fixed by an *ex cathedra* decision. It was much more a matter of common assent, amid the inspired fervour of those primitive churches which were close to the revelation and still nourished the flame of the Holy Spirit. The decision arose from practice, quite naturally and calmly. There were certainly hesitations, second thoughts and perhaps discussions. Eusebius tells us that Serapion, bishop of Alexandria, confronted with a Gospel according to St Peter, at first authorized it to be read, then, having examined it closely and found traces of the Docetist heresy in it, forbade its use. The Shepherd of Hermas, that attractive early second-century book, was for some time considered to be inspired; then it was removed from the canon by the West, but remained in favour in the Egyptian Church.

What is certain is that the Church used extremely rigorous methods in making its choice. Tertullian tells us, about A.D. 200, that some thirty years earlier, in the province of Asia, a book known as the Acts of Paul had appeared, telling how the Apostle converted a young pagan girl called Thekla, who then began to preach the Gospel admirably. Tertullian goes on to say that the story looked suspicious, its authorship was investigated, and the writer, a priest more well-intentioned than wise, immediately deprived of his position. In any case, we have only to read the so-called "apocryphal" books and to compare them with the canonical writings in order to see where good sense, moderation and wisdom are to be found and how tactfully Scripture fixes and limits the bounds of the supernatural and the marvellous.

The two criteria which decided the choice were essentially catholicity and apostolic nature. A text was admitted to the Canon when, in the Christian communities as a whole, it was recognized as faithful to the true tradition and the true message. As the liturgy crystallized, the custom of reading pages from the Epistles and Gospels during Mass exposed their contents to a public test; when the Christian conscience, illumined and guided by ecclesiastical authority, had recognized a certain number of them as bearing the mark of the Holy Spirit, the choice was made. And as in these primitive communities the apostolic connection was fundamental, those writings were retained which living testimony established as emanating directly from the disciples of Jesus.

In any case, towards the close of the second century the choice had been made. We possess an extremely precious document that proves it, the Muratorian Canon, so called after Muratori, librarian of the Ambrosian Library at Milan, who discovered and published it in 1740 in the version preserved in a manuscript of the sixth or seventh century. This document simply reproduces a catalogue or list of the Scriptures compiled at Rome about A.D. 200. It shows that at that time the Roman Church had the same canon as the Christian Church of today (except for the Epistles of St James and St Peter), and that it rejected the Shepherd of Hermas (which it authorized to be read, however) and more categorically certain writings of gnostic tendencies. Some hundred and fifty or two hundred years later, between 359 and 400, catalogues of the canon grew more numerous; they have been found in Africa, Phrygia, Egypt and at Rome. The Council of Carthage in 397 drew up a definitive list. "The first article of our faith", said Tertullian, "is that we are to believe nothing beyond what is contained therein." The decree of the Council of Trent at its fourth session in 1546 only confirmed this list, to which Eastern Orthodox Christians decided to subscribe in 1672.

A STRANGE WORLD: THE APOCRYPHA

So the canon is the result of a choice willed and guided by
the Holy Spirit, and it becomes clear that the Bible is the
residue of a considerably larger literary production which we
are far from knowing in its entirety. The recent discoveries in
the neighbourhood of the Dead Sea have revealed to us the
existence of a non-biblical religious literature of strikingly high
quality; some of the fragments already published—the Commentary on Habacuc, the Psalms of Thanksgiving, the Manual
of Discipline, the War of the Sons of Light and the Sons of
Darkness—would not be unworthy to take their place by the
side of many books in the Old Testament.

The books excluded from the Canon are known as *apocrypha*;
the word originally means "hidden, secret, esoteric", but as the
heretics of the gnostic sects had a passion for the esoteric, a
tendency to which the genius of Christianity was hostile, anything based on any kind of so-called secret became suspect, and
"apocryphal" came to mean "condemned by the Church".[1]

There are Old Testament apocrypha, compiled between 300
B.C. and A.D. 100, that is, at a time when the Jewish community
was painfully enduring the tyranny of various pagan con-
querors. Originating in an atmosphere of anguish, they reflect a
state of intense spiritual fermentation; some persist in giving
a distracted commentary on the Law; others are appeals to a
purer, loftier moral life, a rebirth of souls; the last, and the most
numerous, offer the escapism of *Apocalypses* (*apokaluptein* in
Greek means to uncover), by revealing the approach of the end
of the world, when the elect of God will receive justice; the
Psalms of Solomon, the *Ascension of Isaias* and the *Sibylline
Books* are among the best known of these.

As for the New Testament Apocrypha, they form a curious

---

[1] Protestants do not employ the same terminology as Catholics. They
use the word *apocrypha* to denote the seven books retained by the
Catholic Bible and called by Catholics *deutero-canonical*, that is, later
than the Jewish canon. They call the Apocrypha *pseudepigrapha*, because they almost all borrow the names of famous people as
pseudonyms.

world in which snippets of truth float on a sea of delirium. These books, which arose in the primitive Christian communities from the earliest days up to the sixth or seventh century, are the products of pious curiosity about anything to do with our Lord, the fondness of the masses for a good story and sometimes of suspicious heretical intentions. We have so-called gospels according to St. James, St Matthew, St Peter and even according to Nicodemus, infancy gospels full of details about the first years of Jesus, accounts of the Assumption of Mary, and pseudo-acts of the Apostles and apocalypses attributed to Peter or Paul. The Middle Ages were very fond of these stories; art made use of them and many were collected in Jacques de Voragine's *Golden Legend*. They would scarcely have any more than historical interest if it were not that many present-day customs had their origin in them; for example, that of putting a donkey and an ox on each side of the crib in which the infant Jesus sleeps.

CHAPTER IV

THE BOOK IN WHICH

GOD SPEAKS

INSPIRED BY GOD

The Catholic Church (and conservative Protestants, too) attributes to all the books composing the Bible the special character of being inspired. That is an essential premise, a premise of faith: the whole Bible is an inspired book. "As sons of the Church", writes Lagrange, "we must believe this with divine faith. If the Church imposes this belief on us, it is because she has the power to do so, and it is only by her authority that we can have certain knowledge on this point." The idea is in any case contained in the various expressions used to describe the Bible: Holy Books, Holy Scripture, "divine literature" (Tertullian), "divine library" (St Jerome), Holy Bible. And the first words of the most recent encyclical on the biblical question, that of Pius XII in 1943, say just the same thing: "Divino afflante Spiritu", "Inspired by the Divine Spirit, the sacred writers composed the Books which God wished to give to the human race . . .".

So the Bible is the Word of God addressed to men, the Word in writing. The Church received this certainty from Israel, where it had existed from time immemorial. Since the Hebrew people knew that it had been chosen by God, that there was a Covenant between the Almighty and itself, and that its whole history formed part of a divine plan, it was natural that the book in which, together with this history, the instructions and appearances of God were recorded should be regarded as inspired. Had not God revealed himself to Abraham in his unique divinity? Had he not commanded Moses to write down his words and thus fix the law? Had it not been the same with the Prophets? Yahweh's words to Jeremias were true of all of them: "Into thy mouth I put my words" (Jer. 1. 9). So the Jewish historian Flavius Josephus is summing up what was nothing less than a dogma when he emphasizes that all the authors of the Book wrote "inspired by God".

Christians have always said, and continue to say, the same thing. Formulas affirming the same faith are continually on the lips of Jesus and the Apostles. It was really God who spoke to Moses (Mark 12. 26; John 9. 29; Acts 7. 44; Rom. 9. 15); it was he who expressed himself through the Prophets (Luke 1. 70; Acts 3. 18); he even spoke through the mouth of the royal poet David (Acts 1. 16; 4. 25). The elliptical phrase in the Epistle to the Corinthians is categorical and significant: "God has told us so" (2 Cor. 6. 16). "Everything in the scripture has been divinely inspired", proclaims St Paul again to his friend Timothy (2 Tim. 3. 16), and St Peter teaches: "It was never man's impulse, after all, that gave us prophecy; men gave it utterance, but they were men whom God had sanctified, carried away, as they spoke, by the Holy Spirit" (2 Peter 1. 21). It is pointless to quote the Fathers and Doctors of the Church; texts repeating and affirming the idea are too numerous. The *Enchiridion Biblicum*, published at Rome in 1935, collects quotations from the popes and councils stretching over nearly two thousand years. What Leo IX wrote in 1053 corresponds exactly to what Pius XII wrote in 1943; what the Council of Lyons proclaimed in 1274 is identical, word for word, with the decrees of the Council of Trent in 1546 and of the Vatican Council in 1870. The teaching of the Catholic Church has never wavered.

WHAT INSPIRATION MEANS

It is clear, however, that the term inspiration needs to be defined. Nothing could be more mistaken than to imagine the

Bible as a miraculous work originating somewhere or other in some mysterious fashion and suddenly appearing even more mysteriously among men. Opponents of Christianity have sometimes reduced the doctrine of inspiration to this bare outline in order to ridicule it. "The Bible", says Mgr Weber, the Bishop of Strasbourg, humorously but wisely, "is a divine book, but it did not fall from Heaven ready made."

The precise definition of inspiration is to be found in St Thomas Aquinas: "The Holy Spirit is the principal author of the Scriptures, men were his instruments" (Quodl. 7, art. 14), a statement which has been expanded in Leo XIII's encyclical *Providentissimus Deus*: "Inspiration is a supernatural impulse by means of which the Holy Spirit excited and moved the sacred writers to write and helped them whilst they wrote in such a way that they could conceive exactly, wished to report faithfully and expressed with infallible accuracy, all that God commanded them to write and nothing else." A wise and penetrating definition which, in the production of the sacred books, leaves room for God's power on the one hand and man's intelligence and will on the other.

The Lord did not write the Bible himself in the same way that his visible hand outlined on the wall of Balthazar's palace the famous warning words: *Mane, Thecel, Phares*. He did not dictate it to a succession of mediums in trances, as the Greeks thought was the case with the Pythia[1] of Delphi. Even the paintings which depict an angel whispering in an evangelist's ear the text which he is in the process of writing, although admissible in a symbolic sense, run the risk of giving a false idea of the phenomenon. To bring the Bible into existence the Holy Spirit used as his instruments men; and each of them retained his personality, his distinctive characteristics, his talent or genius, his habits of thought and his stylistic ability. He did not destroy or infringe on the faculties of those whose function it was to put his message into words.

It should be emphasized that one of the most important

[1] The priestess of Apollo, who replied, usually in incoherent or ambiguous words, to the questions put to this famous oracle. [*Trans.*]

results of pontifical teaching in the last sixty years, from *Providentissimus Deus* to *Divino afflante*, is to have made possible a clearer conception of the rôle played by man as God's instrument in the phenomenon of inspiration. Many so-called difficulties, absurdities or contradictions which "free" criticism claims to meet in the study of the Bible disappear when one takes account of this rightful division between the divine work and the human task. Today, Renan would have considerable difficulty in enumerating those famous conflicting truths of the Bible which alienated him from the faith.

IF THE LORD SPEAKS, WHO SHALL RESIST?

Let us consider the three phases of the phenomenon, as defined so well by Leo XIII. God *excited and moved* the sacred writers to write; they did not buckle down to the task of their own free will, as profane writers do (although literary "inspiration", so often referred to, is to some extent the secular reflection of authentic inspiration).

This aspect of the phenomenon is particularly striking in the case of the Prophets and everything connected with prophetic inspiration. There are innumerable passages in Scripture showing the irresistible effect of the Spirit on anyone possessed by him. The Spirit "pounces" on him, says the book of Samuel, and "enters into" him. The person inspired can only say what Yahweh dictates to him. God "opens his eyes" or ears. The prophet cannot escape the task he is inspired to perform. As Amos, Jeremias and many others said from personal experience, "If the Lord speaks, who shall resist?" We all know how Jonas paid for refusing to carry the word of the Lord to Nineveh. There we have a struggle between the will of God and the will of man which must ultimately be regarded as a mystery of faith.

Scriptural inspiration is similarly, if less clearly, dependent on the divine will. It does happen that sacred writers refer to their sources, exactly as a modern historian would (1 Kings 11. 41; 14. 19, 29; Prov. 30. 1), or even admit that their literary labours have been painful (in the Prologue of Ecclesiasticus, for example, or in 2 Mac. 2. 24, 32); the Jewish tradition and with it the Church's belief declare that the action of the Holy Spirit was just as decisive in this case as in that of the commands thunderously dictated to the Prophets, different though the method employed may have been.

GOD CANNOT ERR

In the second place, according to the Encyclical, God enlightened the intelligence of those whom he chose as his mouthpieces; and he did it in such a way that, while giving full play to their human faculties, he conferred on the work divine value. This supernatural enlightenment must be understood in two ways. On the one hand, God revealed "secrets" to those who had to transcribe his message; this is recorded of Samuel, Daniel, Amos and many others; St Paul in a famous passage even said that he had learnt things "which man is not allowed to utter". This divine illumination does more than open fields of knowledge to the human mind; the inspired writer's judgement, while remaining his own judgement in so far as he is a man, has also become divine judgement through God's supernatural action indissolubly united to man's action.

This is a doctrinal point of capital importance, for with it is bound up the dogma of *biblical inerrancy*, which Fr Benoît, of the Biblical School at Jerusalem, defines in these words: "God cannot be deceived or deceive us. His word is always truth. So if he moves a man to write in his name, he cannot allow him to teach what is false. The charisma[1] of inspiration is necessarily accompanied by the privilege of inerrancy. That is an article of faith which the Church has always professed."

As for the limits of this "inerrancy", it is not enough to say that, taken as a whole, Scripture teaches us the truth. Inerrancy must be understood as an integral property of the whole Bible,

[1] I.e. spiritual gift. Charisma is a Greek word meaning *grace* or *favour*; in the New Testament it has the particular meaning of *a free gift of God's grace*. See especially 1 Cor. 12. [*Trans.*]

since the Bible is the work of God and God is truth itself. This inerrancy exists both *de facto* and *de jure*, and every part of Scripture enjoys it. The Biblical Commission, in a decision of June 18th, 1915, came to this conclusion: "What the sacred author asserts, enunciates or conveys indirectly must be regarded as asserted, enunciated, or conveyed indirectly by the Holy Spirit." So a Catholic is absolutely forbidden to hold the belief that inspiration, and consequently inerrancy, is limited to certain parts of the Scriptures, for example to the dogmatic and moral parts, and that, so far as the rest is concerned, we are at liberty to exercise our critical judgement. He is also forbidden to hold the belief that there can be errors of fact in the perspective adopted by the sacred writer; for example, that in one of the biblical books presented as history there can be historical errors. Such is the doctrine of the Church in all its clarity and force.

THE SCRIBES OF GOD

Yet "side by side with this doctrine, an obvious fact, which we can all observe, forces itself on our attention: the Bible, as well as being a divine book, is at the same time an authentically human book" (Mgr Weber). That is, it is a work written by men of flesh and blood like ourselves, living at a definite point in time, against a well-defined historical background, with all the reactions, modes of thought and even prejudices of their civilization. The question arises whether inspiration affects everything about them, even the smallest details of their style. If the essential premises, the basic concepts proceed directly from the Holy Spirit, can it be said that he also determined the choice of words, expressions and sentences? In discussing purely human literature it is, of course, extremely difficult to separate the pure thought from its expression. God must be present at the formulation, the committing to writing of his message; that is what is called "verbal inspiration", which was admitted in general by theologians and exegetes, but not universally, and in any case has never been defined as dogma in an official document of the Church.

Papal teaching takes very much into account the human conditions under which the message was written down. Obviously "an error must not be imputed to the sacred author where copyists, in carrying out their work, have made some slip" (*Divino afflante*); but it is also essential to take into account the conditions under which the sacred writers lived and their personal habits of thought and expression. The Lord spoke through a man, so it is permissible and even necessary to make ourselves familiar with this man. This is the direction that the great majority of biblical studies have taken at the moment; it is well known that it was part of the genius of Fr Lagrange, the celebrated founder of the Jerusalem Biblical School, to have foreseen that therein lay the solution of innumerable difficulties. Serious study of the Bible can henceforth no longer be separated from that of the period and place in which the book was written.

So inspiration is seen to be a divine operation, a sort of grace which permeates the sacred writer's whole being, illumines and guides him, helps him throughout his mental work, from the impulse to write, the original idea, to the literary execution and sometimes even the formal expression, but leaves scope for the reaction of the writer's personality on the work. "The book of God and the book of man", says Mgr Weber of the Bible, and the phrase aptly summarizes the whole question.

CHAPTER V

THE BOOK DELIVERED

TO MEN

THE LAND OF THE BIBLE

To understand the sacred text, then, it seems to be essential to know the conditions in which men, inspired by God, wrote the Bible. Let us look first at the geographical conditions, those of the country in which the episodes of the Old and New Testaments took place. "Geography and chronology are history's two crutches", asserts an old university saying, and that applies to sacred history, too, and the whole study of the Scriptures.

The land of the Bible is above all Palestine, that tiny piece of territory no bigger than Brittany, easily crossed in a car from north to south in one day, where the modern traveller is amazed to find the distances so short. It is that strip of land along the shore of the Mediterranean which is so narrow and yet divided by its geology and contours into three very different parallel zones, the maritime plain, the mountains (not very high, but craggy and rugged) and the trench—the *ghor*—in which the Jordan descends to the Dead Sea, some 1200 feet below sea level. It is that region with a half-Mediterranean, half-desert climate, where spring is short but delicious and the summers blazing hot, where the rain falls, between October and May, for whole days at a time in a heavy downpour and yet only too often in insufficient quantity. It is the land where the red anemones grow, the "lilies of the field" of Scripture, where the

Aleppo pine, the cypress, the holm-oak, the carob-tree and the olive cover the plains or mark out the hills, and the rearing of sheep and goats holds a preponderant place in rural economy. But the land of the Bible is also much more than Palestine; it is the "fertile crescent", that band of rich plains encircling the Syrian desert from Galilee via the land of Aram, at the foot of the Anti-Taurus,[1] to the Mesopotamian basin, the huge arc followed by Abraham on his inspired migration.

Geography and the habits of life imposed by it are so intimately bound up with the sacred writings that it is very often impossible to understand the latter without reference to the former. When the Gospel shows us Jesus taking pity on the crowd which has come to hear him and has nothing to eat, we must visualize that region of steppe-like hills overlooking the Lake of Tiberias from the west, where there was certainly no food to be found. When Scripture says, "The rain fell and the floods came and the winds blew . . ." (Matt. 7. 25), to explain the causes of the catastrophes that carry away houses, we must think of the terrible storms which, in that region where all the river-beds are of pebble, do in fact cause raging torrents to overflow their banks. In the bay of the Lake of Tiberias, between Ain Tabgat and Magdala, where the cold waters of the Herman and the warm waters from the springs of Capharnaum meet, a great abundance of fish is to be observed; it seems likely that this is the site of the miraculous draught. When Christ gives the clue, "A man will meet you, carrying a jar of water" (Mark 14. 13), it means nothing to us Westerners, but a detail like that puts the seal of truth on the story, for in Palestine it was, and still is, the housewife's job to fetch the water from the fountain. When he reproaches the Pharisees for giving the tithe of *aneth* and scorning higher obligations, it should be realized that this plant, bitter fennel, was so common in Palestine that no one thought anything of it; today we should say, "give a tithe of weeds". Perhaps Renan goes too far when he declares that Palestine is "the fifth Gospel"; but we must cer-

---

[1] I.e. the south-eastern end of the Taurus mountains in eastern Asia Minor. [*Trans.*]

tainly pay attention to the evidence given by the Promised Land on the events it witnessed.

THE AUTHORS

If the geographical background has left its mark on the text of the Bible, the same is true to an even greater extent of the personalities of its authors. The problem is not quite the same as it would be today; the Ancients had no sense at all of literary ownership, and any piece of writing, being in their eyes the property of the community, could be revised, modified or continued. It is therefore not always possible to discover one man behind a biblical text, and certain parts of the Bible give the impression of expressing the collective conscience and of being also a collective work, in which each of the writers suppressed his own personality in favour of the task to be accomplished.

There are, however, numerous cases where the Bible visibly bears the deep impression of the men who wrote it. The impression is sometimes pleasant, sometimes less so: inspiration does not prevent the author of Leviticus from being the most boring of lawyers, the compiler of Chronicles from being totally devoid of talent or the author of the Apocalypse from making many syntactical mistakes in his Greek. On the other hand, we frequently meet powerful personalities expressing themselves in a very personal style, in fact real literary geniuses. The "King David" who wrote the Psalms is a sublime poet; the author of Job is at the same time one of the profoundest and boldest thinkers the human race has produced and a stylist with a striking turn of phrase; the prophet Isaias is a real genius, to be placed on a level with the loftiest lyric poets; and St Paul spontaneously throws out combinations of words and ideas like flashes of lightning. Each of these masters of biblical literature allows us to form an impression—even when he is anonymous —of his personal character. In the New Testament it leaps to the eye: Mark is a simple, unspoiled spirit, near to the people, Luke a cultivated, sensitive man of an inquiring disposition,

John essentially a mystic and Matthew an honest and reliable narrator.

The social surroundings to which these authors belong influence them. Ezechiel and Jeremias, born into priestly families, do not possess the same reactions as Jesus Ben-Sira, a middle-class citizen of Jerusalem, to whom we owe Ecclesiasticus. The author of Job was probably a great sheikh of the desert regions or at any rate on familiar terms with one of these lords of the tent. A provincial like Micheas does not hide how much he hates the big city, which he sees as the very seat of Judah's iniquity. A useful comparison may be made between the imprecations of Isaias (3. 16–24) and those of Amos (4. 1, 3) in the denunciation of female coquetry and luxury; the violence is the same in both cases, but the prophet Isaias is well-born, and remains polite even in his invective, while that ill-educated cowherd Amos allows himself to refer to the fashionable women of Samaria as "cows"—"cows of Bashan", in point of fact—and to inform them that they will be carried off naked and cast into the dung-pit. It is obvious, too, that the place and the date of writing can be very important; the book of Judith reflects the fanatical epoch of the Machabees, and that of Esther corresponds to the mentality of the Jews dispersed throughout Persia, the empire which was to produce the tales of the *Arabian Nights*, of which the story of Esther often reminds us.

Finally, it is surely clear that the style of the biblical writers was liable to vary according to the audience they were addressing. This is particularly striking in the New Testament. Jesus talking to the peasants of Galilee and the fishermen of the lake used a vocabulary familiar to them; he referred to plants, animals and customs they knew. When Luke wants to hand on the message to Roman circles, he has to complete the Master's words here and there, to explain certain details; for example, he has to make it clear that the Jordan is a river and that the Lake of Tiberias is as big as a sea. When St Paul speaks to the Corinthians, who were mad on the Isthmian games, he borrows his comparisons from the sports of the time, wrestling and running; but to the Christians of Phrygia he speaks of the religious speculations. St Athanasius noticed this long ago: "We must note the occasion on which the Apostle spoke, to whom and for what reason he wrote; we must give these circumstances scrupulous and devoted attention, lest by being unaware of them or failing to understand them properly we miss the real sense."

TRADUTTORE, TRADITORE?

It goes without saying that one of the most important factors to take into account in any consideration of the conditions in which the text was written is the language used by the author. Nothing could be more futile, or in a sense more absurd, than arguments turning on the actual words of Scripture in English or some other modern language, when the basis of the discussion is a translation, and often a translation of other translations. The famous verse in the Gospel about the camel and the eye of the needle provides a good example of these interminable but useless discussions. Each of the three languages used by the chosen people, literary Hebrew, conversational Aramaic and popular Greek, known as the *koine* (which was employed in the first Christian communities) had its own genius, its own turns of phrase and expressions, which very often cannot be translated into our modern western languages. The old proverb *Traduttore, traditore* holds good in this case, too; even when he goes straight back to the original, the translator of the Bible always runs the risk of being false to the text.

Apart from anything else, numerous purely idiomatic Jewish terms, translated word for word, can only remain obscure to a westerner of the twentieth century, while they were perfectly clear to a Semite of the time of Christ. How many people today know that throughout the Bible the heart is regarded not as the seat of the emotions but of the intellect; the feelings were reckoned to reside in the loins. So "God searches loins and hearts" means "God sees into the feelings and thoughts of men". Similarly the horn was the symbol of strength; so when, in St Luke (1. 69), the priest Zacharias prophesies that "God has raised up for his people a horn of salvation", he means to announce that a powerful Saviour is going to appear.

More generally, it is the genius of the language which often makes it difficult to understand the sacred text. The most common stylistic tricks of the Semitic languages, parallelism, juxtaposition of propositions and antithesis, are fundamentally different from ours. All three correspond to the dialectic peculiar to the Semitic genius, which is a stranger to the syllogism dear to Greek thought and does not seek to abstract, but aims at seizing the idea in its reality and its unity, even if the result is apparently complex and contradictory. The symbol, which holds an important position in it, does not perform the purely superficial function which it does in our western languages, in which it is scarcely more than a stylistic ornament, or at the most a means of making oneself understood; for the Semites, the symbol is a real sign, which effectively contains within itself a higher reality. When we read that Israel "brings forth the Messias", the word must be understood in its strongest sense; it signifies the whole Promise made to the chosen people and its whole vocation.

LITERARY FORMS OR GENRES

The Bible must be understood according to the language—that is to say, actual tongue and style—in which it was written, but also according to the point of view adopted by the sacred writer; the effort to grasp this point of view is perhaps even more important, and its successful accomplishment in recent years has resulted in the solution or disappearance of a large number of so-called difficulties in the Bible. The most useful contribution to scriptural studies was probably the official recognition by the Church of the existence of literary *genres* and of the necessity for taking account of them.

Anybody with the smallest experience of the written word knows perfectly well that a poet, a novelist, a philosopher and a historian do not use the same registers. The reader instinctively adapts himself to the kind of book he is reading; we do not sit down to read a novel in the same frame of mind as a historical work, and obviously we do not demand from a verse epic the strict accuracy of a military report. It may happen that the same writer uses entirely different registers according to his subject-matter; obviously Shakespeare does not write *The Comedy of Errors* in the same tone as *King Lear*. Each kind of literature has its own laws and customs.

It is the same in the Bible, in which the most diverse *genres* appear side by side; the primitive, popular history of Genesis, the political history of Kings and Machabees, the apologetic history of Chronicles, the moralizing history of Ruth, Tobias and Esther, the collected maxims of Proverbs and Ecclesiasticus, the philosophical essay in dramatic form of Job, the poetry of the Song of Songs and the still more elevated poetry of the Psalms; all these *genres* co-exist in the Old Testament. In the New Testament, we have only to think of the difference between the three Synoptic Gospels and that of St John or between one of St Paul's Epistles and the Apocalypse. If the biblical writers, charged with the task of passing on what had been revealed to them, did so in accordance with the particular genius of the *genre* which they each employed, then the first duty of anyone reading the Bible is to know what kind of literature confronts him. Poetry and song are just as valuable evidence as the historical narrative or the philosophical essay, but they are not the same thing and must not be confused with them, as St Thomas Aquinas warned us. Obviously when we read that, in their Messianic joy, "the hills leap up like sheep", no one takes this poetic formula as the expression of a historical reality.

The question becomes more complex when we come to deal with kinds of literature which the West simply does not possess. For example, a first reading of the Prophets or of the Apocalypse—and even the tenth or hundredth reading in the case of the latter—certainly leaves us feeling somewhat baffled. In Israel, a rather special *genre* was very popular, the *midrash*, a sort of moral fable which was expected not so much to report accurately concrete facts as to exemplify some inner, transcendent truth; to apply to this kind of writing the rules of historical criticism is to risk going seriously astray. The chapters with which the Bible begins, the book of Genesis, obviously belong to a complex species of literature in which history, popular tradition and folklore, moral teaching and cosmogonical revelation are all mixed together and borne aloft on the wings of admirable poetry. As for the actual history to be found in the Bible, it is perfectly obvious that it does not obey the often ridiculously artificial criteria of the "historical science" of today.

The conclusion that emerges from a study of the different kinds of literature in the Bible is that the whole Bible is true, absolutely true, every part of it, but that it is true in the sense in which each kind of literature bears witness to the truth.[1] On this very point the encyclical of Pius XII, *Divino afflante Spiritu* —and more recently, with regard to Genesis, *Humani Generis* in 1950—sheds fresh and piercing light. "It is absolutely essential", says the papal document, "for the exegete to go back to some extent in thought to those distant centuries in the East, so that, making use of the resources of history, archaeology, ethnology and the other sciences, he can discern and recognize what varieties of literature the authors of those ancient times meant to employ and in fact really did employ."

[1] This reference to literary *genres* authorizes liberties which, fifty years ago, would have amazed exegetes and theologians. Dom Célestin Charlier, a Benedictine monk of Maredsous, in *La Lecture chrétienne de la Bible* (Maredsous, 1951), a work published under the Imprimatur of the Bishop of Namur with a preface by Mgr Weber, Bishop of Strasbourg, does not hesitate to write: "The books of Ruth, Tobias and Esther and also, though in a different way, the book of Jonas, belong to the category of works of edification and include obviously fictitious elements" (he prudently adds, it is true, "but for all that we are not entitled to treat them purely as novels in the modern style"). Elsewhere, again, he writes: "The stopping of the sun by Josue is told in a miniature epic poem and looks very much as though it is only an eastern hyperbole."

CHAPTER VI

THE BIBLE AND HISTORY

THE RECORD OF A PEOPLE

That a document of this sort should affirm the usefulness of historical science for the knowledge of the Bible is something quite new and extremely important. Only a hundred years ago the historical problem did not even arise with regard to Holy Scripture, believers limiting themselves to seeking in it religious and moral instruction and unbelievers treating it as myth; today a tremendous effort is being made to discover and establish clearly the historical foundations of the Bible. That is one of the two aims pursued by biblical studies at the moment: to situate the sacred text against its background and to relate the events reported in it to those of profane history. And at once, supported and buttressed by chronology—history's other crutch, the reader will remember—the great episodes of the Bible cease to be the more or less mysterious stories they were reckoned to be not so long ago and become chapters in a history as precise and well-defined as that of the Pharaohs or the Roman Republic.

So the Bible is in the first place a history. It is the record of a people, in fact the most remarkable record a people has ever left, for future generations, of all it did, suffered, believed, thought and hoped. It is the record of a family, Abraham's, kept for about two thousand years, the record of a family that from the Patriarch to Jesus can be followed in its human destiny as well as in its providential mission. That is what gives unity to the Bible and all its heterogeneous parts.

Now it happens that this family, which became a clan and

finally a people, was caught up in the vast series of historical events of which the eastern Mediterranean, Asia Minor and Mesopotamia were the scene. Several times Israel was on the march, from the banks of the Nile to those of the Euphrates; and Palestine, a corridor where the roads from north to south and from east to west cross, was often invaded. All the peoples we know from the ancient history of the East, Chaldaeans, Hittites, Phoenicians, Egyptians, Assyrians, Greeks, Scythians and Romans, were successively in contact with the People of the Promise. The question that comes to mind can therefore receive a reply based on documents outside the Bible itself. And the question is, what is the historical value of this record? Can its evidence be taken seriously?

THE ARCHAEOLOGISTS' REPLY

The reply is given by the archaeologists, those advance guards of the army of historians. Hollot used to say to his pupils at the French School in Athens, "Ancient history is written with a pick-axe". Since, a hundred and fifty years ago, Emile Botta, French consul at Mosul, thought of digging into the oblong "tells" of sand and clay scattered all over the Mesopotamian plain and brought to light the dead towns sleeping under them, the archaeological horizon has never stopped widening. In our day, Fr Poidebard has put the aeroplane at the service of historical science, and aerial photographs taken in the evening when the setting sun casts long shadows reveal undulations invisible from the ground. Even Geiger counters lend their precision to measure the passage of time. The secrets of the buried past are revealed in greater numbers every day.

The modern historian of the Bible draws material from two fields of inquiry. On the one hand, he investigates as an archaeologist the actual sites of events described in the Scriptures, for example the remains of Jericho or traces of the Hebrews' journey through Sinai. Among the most illustrious achievements are those of the Biblical School at Jerusalem, founded in 1890 by Fr Lagrange, whose pupils are carrying on his work. Some of the discoveries in Palestine itself are of the first importance; the uncovering, for instance, in the foundations of the convent of Our Lady of Sion, of the "Lithostroton", the actual paving of the courtyard in the fortress of Antonia in which Jesus waited to be judged by Pilate. The discoveries of the Dead Sea manuscripts are another example.

On the other hand, other branches of history and archaeology can throw light on parts of the Bible; Egyptology provides information in connection with the episodes of Joseph and Moses, and we turn to Mesopotamian archaeology in order to gain a better idea of Abraham and the deportation of the Chosen People to Babylon by Nabuchodonosor. The four hundred years preceding the birth of Christ could only be studied in the Bible—which has little to say about them—by reference to Greek and Roman history; but now the discovery of the spiritual treasures of the Essenes in the Dead Sea caves has thrown new light on these last centuries of the Jewish community.

The result of all this work has been summarized by Sir Charles Marston in the title of his book *The Bible is True*.[1] Not everything in this book can be accepted without reserve, but in its general intention it remains valuable. We see that the sacred text is a document as worthy of interest and study as the various chronicles and histories bequeathed to us by the other peoples of antiquity. There can be no doubt that it is this fact, daily becoming clearer, that largely explains the interest shown in the Bible by people today.

HOW HISTORY THROWS LIGHT ON THE SACRED TEXT

The contribution made by the historical study of the Bible to the knowledge and comprehension of the sacred text is so immense that we can do no more here than give a few brief illustrations. Various precise details, customs and even proper

[1] *The Bible is True. The lessons of the 1925–1934 excavations in Bible lands summarized and explained* (London, 1934).

names which could formerly be regarded as legendary now reappear against a clearly defined historical background. For example, when we found Abraham buying from a Hittite king the cave of Machpelah to bury his wife in, or when Uriah, the unfortunate husband of Bathsheba, the victim of King David's criminal adultery, was described as a Hittite, the term meant nothing until Perrot's first investigations, Winckler's excavations at Boghaz-Keui and Hrozny's decipherment of the tablets discovered there revealed the great destiny of this Hittite people which for nearly five centuries dominated Asia Minor and its approaches. Those famous Philistines whom Samson fought so joyfully are emerging into the light of history now that it seems almost certain that they are to be connected with the first waves of the Aryan invasion; scenes, painted in the time of Ramesses III, of the invasion of the "Sea Peoples" have been found in the Valley of Kings, and Mycenae and Tiryns have shown us fortresses similar to those that Josue and his successors had to attack. Goliath, the tall, blond Aryan, may be a cousin of Homer's Hector.

Certain customs which, in the Bible, might seem strange or even shocking, are confirmed and illuminated by history and its auxiliary, archaeology. An episode like Abraham sacrificing Isaac, which implies the existence of human sacrifice, has become much more comprehensible since, in the tombs of Chaldaea and on the high places of Palestine, skeletons have been found which are clearly those of children and servants put to death as a sacrifice. As for the famous "ram caught in a thicket" which the Angel of the Lord substituted for young Isaac, a perfectly identifiable statue of it has been found at Ur. The vow of *herem* or anathema, that is, total destruction of a captured city, astonishing as such an act may appear when carried out by poverty-stricken tribes who must have delighted in their conquests, can henceforth be seen to derive from a ritual of immemorial antiquity that was followed everywhere. In the foundations of Jericho the marks of a fire have been found; perhaps it was the one started by Josue.

More generally, we find that certain important episodes in

the Bible, when placed in the political and psychological context of their age, acquire in this new light a sort of unexpected depth. The departure of Abraham and his clan from Ur of the Chaldees for Palestine can be understood from a psychological point of view which recent events in the modern world help us to grasp. Supposing a species of polytheistic totalitarian dictatorship had been imposed on Mesopotamia, with all the minutely detailed regulations revealed in the Babylonian codes of law, it would be natural for the monotheist Abraham to want to escape by "choosing liberty"; the voice of God and the voice of his own conscience were at one: an attractive lesson, that has much to teach us.

It is impossible to understand without reference to historical events the amazing change in the attitude of the Pharaoh to be observed at the beginning of the story of Moses. In the previous chapter Joseph, as vizier of the Egyptian monarch, has obtained for his brothers the right to settle in the land of Gessen, not far from the Delta; we turn the page and what do we find? Persecution, the Hebrews subjected to forced labour and the massacre of their new-born children. What has happened? History provides the answer by telling us about the invasion of the Hyksos or Shepherd Kings, Semitic in origin, who occupied the land of the Nile for more than a century. The Pharaoh who appointed Joseph as his chief minister was probably a Hyksos. The Hebrews were cousins of these invaders and worked with them. As a result, when the "leprosy of Asia" had been ejected by the nationalist movement led by the priests of Thebes, they found themselves treated, as collaborators of the occupiers, with the severity of which we read.

If we continue to follow the course of events in the Bible, we find the explanation of another mystery. Josue and his bands attack the land of Canaan and encounter a great many difficulties; they need no less than two or three miracles from Yahweh to enable them to gain a foothold. After all, they can only have been a wretched troop of bedouins, with no military equipment, mediocre weapons and few fighting men. How did these wretched invaders manage, in a mere hundred years, to gain possession of Palestine? If we notice that these events were taking place at the end of the twelfth century before our era, and if we remember that at the same time the Aryan invasion was in full flood, the explanation seems to be clear. The onslaught of the invaders forces the great empires to withdraw the garrisons they maintained in colonial regions; Palestine has no more Egyptian, Mesopotamian or Hittite occupiers, but only native kinglets and princelings. But for this providential event, it seems unlikely that the Judges would have succeeded in their enterprises of conquest.

Even the early chapters of Scripture, those of Genesis, so long regarded by freethinkers as legend pure and simple, have been illuminated in recent times by archaeological evidence. We now know that these ancient stories, collected by Jewish tradition, are closely bound up with the civilization that Abraham knew; that we must go back to at least 3000 B.C. to find the cultural context of the story of the creation of man; that the biblical Flood is obviously the monotheistic version of an account of the same event which occurs in the polytheistic epic of Gilgamesh; that the excavations at Kish have even revealed the occurrence of a deluge of catastrophic proportions at a time when there was already a civilization on the Euphrates; and that the Tower of Babel shows a remarkable likeness to the "Ziggurats", the terraced towers of the Mesopotamian religion of the stars, which the Hebrew monotheists naturally saw as symbols of the mad pride of man, who makes himself idols with his own hands instead of giving himself to the one and only true God.

INFLUENCES ON THE BIBLE?

This historical and archaeological investigation of the Bible does more than illuminate and buttress its text. It would be absurd to hide the fact that it also discloses what Mgr Weber calls "resemblances in composition between the Bible and neighbouring literatures". In some cases it is a question not only of literary but also of factual and doctrinal similarities;

for example, after the sojourn in Egypt the Hebrew people adopted a clerical organization, unknown to its ancestors in the desert, which it had been able to observe at close quarters within the extremely clerical borders of the land of the Pharaohs. Similarly there can be no doubt that the importance assumed by the cult of angels owed something to the "cherubim" of Mesopotamia and also to the celestial beings of Persian tradition. There is no need to be amazed or scandalized at this if we remember the exact definition of the divine inspiration of the Bible; if God made use of men, why should they not have been sensitive to human influences, as we all are?

In some cases the resemblance between the biblical text and these "sources" is so marked that people have sometimes wondered if the inspired author used a pagan model, or if the two texts, the pagan and the inspired, were based on a single source. This is particularly striking in the case of Genesis and especially of the Flood, which is one of the outstanding features of the whole Mesopotamian tradition. The code of Hammurabi, which can be seen at the Louvre, a handsome black slab on which this Babylonian king of the beginning of the second millennium engraved his collected laws, contains ordinances similar to those of Moses. Moreover the Mosaic laws also bear resemblances to the commandments to be read in the Book of the Dead from ancient Egypt. The Song of Songs is related to some wedding hymns found on the banks of the Nile, and the compiler of the section of the book of Proverbs (22–4) often called "Sayings of the wise men" may have been influenced by the Egyptian sage Amenemope or have influenced the latter himself. The same problem of attribution arises with regard to Psalm 104, which is almost modelled on the hymn composed in honour of his only God, the Sun, by the interesting revolutionary Pharaoh Amenophis IV, also known as Akhenaton; unless it was the biblical text that influenced the Egyptian. The Greek book of Wisdom employs the vocabulary of the Alexandrian philosophers and to some extent reflects their doctrines. This kind of resemblance can be discovered even in the Gospel;

Dioscurides'[1] treatise on medicine had been so well studied by the doctor Luke that when the latter came to write his Gospel he more or less borrowed his opening sentences from Dioscurides.

To all of which should be added, in Mgr Weber's words:

> To avoid any scandal that might be caused by these remarks, it should be emphasized that these comparisons, which shed a powerful light on the biblical texts and enable us to understand them, also throw into relief the profoundly human and at the same time transcendental character of the sacred books; for nowhere do we find what often disfigures ancient works: complicated and extravagant notions, immorality or at least sensuality, and above all the polytheism or at any rate pantheism in which pagan documents are literally drenched. *Yet* [our italics] *our Jewish or Christian books are the product of a people at a far lower stage of cultural development than the empires which dominated the Near East in the centuries before Christ, or than Greek circles.*

In this essential difference we can see the whole point of these comparisons and of the search for resemblances; we can see the transcendence of a will that gives history its whole meaning and import.

THE LIMITS OF HISTORY

For indispensable as it is to fix the Bible properly on its foundations and defend it against adversaries who can see nothing but myth in it, and to study the sacred text in accordance with history, it would nevertheless be a grave mistake to stop there. The most precise—and the most pious—of "sacred histories" would still be only an introduction to the study of the Bible. That is why, together with the historical approach, another approach must be—and in fact is being—employed; its aim is to explain and deepen the permanent religious value of Scripture. Gripping and illuminating as it often is, historical

---

[1] A Greek who served as a doctor in the Roman army and probably wrote his *Materia Medica* in the reign of Nero. [*Trans.*]

research must not make us lose sight of the real goal. Study of the political, archaeological, sociological and literary factors which constitute the human framework of Revelation must in no wise remain an end in itself. The ultimate goal is to hear the Word of God, to understand that his will is at work among men and rules the fate of worlds. We can never attain to a full understanding of the Bible unless we really believe that it contains the Message of Life, that it is, above all, the Book of the Acts of God.

CHAPTER VII

THE BOOK OF THE ACTS

OF GOD

GOD ACTS IN HISTORY

The expression "Acts of God" must be understood in both senses of the word "act", that is, legal document and action. As an inspired book, the Bible is the expression of the Word; but it is something else as well: the manifestation of God in deeds. All through Scripture the Lord speaks, but he also acts, and this action is no less revealing for man, no less exemplary and formative. No doubt the whole of human history, "that long chain of the immediate causes that make and unmake empires", as Bossuet[1] says, "is dependent on the secret orders of Providence", but the formal and very precise plan of the Bible is to show men explicitly that "their whole history, everything that happened to them from day to day, was only a continual fulfilment of the oracles delivered to them by the Holy Spirit". The lesson repeated over and over again in the books of the Bible—unlike the one suggested by Greco-Roman paganism—is that man, in the events of history, is not the plaything of a blind fate but in the hands of a Power, a Principle, a personal God on whom all depends and who wishes to lead him to his true goal.

That is what gives the Bible its very special meaning and

[1] This famous seventeenth-century bishop was tutor to Louis XIV's son, and wrote, primarily for his pupil's benefit, a *Discourse on Universal History*. [*Trans.*]

what was already known by its inspired authors, who, in all they wrote, had but one purpose: to bring home to men the action of God in the world and in the dimension of time. To reproach them with lack of the famous modern "objectivity" is pointless. For them, history is written at God's dictation as part of his designs: the moral writings seek to elevate man to the likeness of God; poetry in its various forms exalts the glory of the Most High and furnishes believers with the means of associating themselves with his work through prayer; and the *midrashim*[1] bring home the infallibility of his actions.

What gives the historical study of the Bible its whole import and puts the Bible as a history book in a class by itself is that this slice of events cut out of time and space reveals the divine action; in fact, it is the divine action, directed towards Revelation. An indissoluble union of human realities—some of them a painful, even a lamentable sight—and transcendent and divine realities; that is the very substance of the Bible; that is what constitutes its greatness, but also its difficulty.

THE PROBLEM OF MIRACLES

God's action has on occasion taken the form of direct, outward, perceptible interventions called miracles. The Council of Trent described them as "arguments demonstrating the infinite omnipotence of God and also sure signs, suited to all intelligences, of the divine Revelation". For a believing Christian it is obvious that there can be no question of denying the reality of the miracles reported in the Bible. From the moment we assume that God created and controls the world it becomes perfectly comprehensible that he should produce symbolic manifestations of the supernatural efficacy of his action in deeds, matter and bodies. A miracle is simply a perceptible token of the Revelation contained in the Bible as a whole.

Nevertheless it would be futile to deny that for modern minds, conditioned, sometimes unconsciously, by an atmosphere of rationalism and often sordid realism, miracles constitute a stumbling block. As Mgr Mignot wrote half a century

[1] For the meaning of this term, see above, p. 51.

ago: "At the present time miracles are for many people an obstacle rather than a road to belief. The modern mind, fashioned in the so-called scientific mould, is ill at ease when confronted with a miracle. Even in those not frightened by the supernatural there is a hint of embarrassment, of hesitation, of uncertainty, of doubt."[1] How is this difficulty, which clearly does exist, to be met today by the reader of the Bible, who enjoys the benefit of papal teaching and the illumination of the numerous commentaries on the subject?

First, in accordance with the invitation of *Divino afflante Spiritu*, he will take into account the existence of different "literary *genres*", that is to say, he will put the provisional question whether the biblical writer, when he reported something extraordinary or supernatural, wished to present it as a historical fact. The *midrash* of Jonas or the epic poem about Josue's mighty deed are obviously not written in the same register as the chapters in the Gospels which tell us of Christ's Resurrection; the credence given to this last event is not of the same order as that accorded to the stopping of the sun or the swallowing of the prophet by the sea monster.

As for the miraculous incidents which figure in the strictly historical books, they can be placed in three categories. Some look simply providential; others consist in a concatenation of apparently natural events whose mere accumulation seems to proceed from a divine intention; and the rest, which show God's direct action thwarting or replacing an apparently natural cause, are more precisely miracles in the full sense of the term. With regard to the incidents in the first two categories, we must look at them objectively without overestimating (or underestimating) their marvellous character. Some of them can even be placed in a basically natural context; the supernatural factor is then their occurrence in conditions reported by the Bible and reflecting God's will. For example, the crossing of the Red Sea by the Hebrews under Moses has been connected with the peculiar behaviour of the tides in the Elamitic gulf, and

[1] *Lettres sur les études ecclésiastiques*, p. 119.

manna with a white truffle found in the Arabian desert or the sugary gum produced by certain acacias; but that does not alter the fact that in saving his people from massacre or hunger the Almighty was carrying out an intention, a plan that transcends any down-to-earth "scientific" explanation. Similarly it has been possible to make a list of the "ten plagues of Egypt" from documents found in the country itself and from observation of its geography, climate and fauna; but the simultaneous apparition of these phenomena, their extraordinarily widespread character, the enormous assistance they gave to the chosen people and the results they achieved obviously prove that they were willed by God.

The will of God is still more evident in the case of miracles which cannot be connected with any natural cause, especially those we see performed—forty-one times during the course of his life on earth—by Jesus, which impress themselves on our minds as the indubitable expression of the divine action by their sublime simplicity, their infinite charity and the lessons they teach. Confronted with incidents like the curing of the paralytic or the raising of Lazarus, vouched for as true by the Gospel, we must either recognize God's will at work or else reject the Gospel, the complete Christian revelation and religion as a whole. That is what St Thomas Aquinas meant when he laid much more emphasis on miracles as "signs of faith" than as proofs of faith.[1]

[1] In the *Summa Theologica*, II, II, Q. 178, art. 1, we find several passages in which this idea is formulated: St Thomas declared that "miracles are called signs because they are manifestations of a supernatural reality, an exceptional intervention by God".

Miracles are the *effect of faith*, whether it be the faith of him who performs them or the faith of those for whom they are performed. St Thomas quotes the words of St Matthew (13. 58): "Nor did he do many miracles there [i.e. Nazareth], because of their unbelief." Yet St Thomas says miracles serve to confirm faith, not as a proof of faith, but by causing the performance of the acts of faith which develop this virtue: "just as it is not sufficient to receive the grace of faith, but also necessary to have the grace to hear the teaching which instructs faith, so the performance of miracles is necessary for the confirmation of faith" (art. 5)

EVENTS AS ACTS OF GOD

But it is not by the miracles alone—far from it—that the
Bible makes God's action apparent. It would be stupid to let
oneself be in any way fascinated by these extraordinary incidents to the extent of being prevented from discerning something far vaster, God's actual plan, of which the miracles are
simply exceptional evidence; the sign would then be deflecting
us from the reality it denotes. We must recognize God's action
from one end of Scripture to the other; it is present in men's
minds as well as in events, gently leading humanity little by
little to greater enlightenment, making it follow, painfully no
doubt, but providentially, that ascending curve that we must
trace through the Bible if we wish to understand the sometimes
disconcerting succession of its heterogeneous books.

The Bible in its two parts, which are tightly bound together
and dependent on each other, is the account—an incomplete
one, no doubt, for there are gaps in it, but a perfectly coherent
one—of God's activity in the world, right from the start up to
the moment when, with the last of the Apostles about to disappear from the scene, the message of Revelation was entrusted to the Church of Christ; it is also, from the Creation
described in Genesis to the Last Judgement symbolically presented in the Apocalypse, the complete history of humanity in
the hand of God.

This history has a meaning, it obeys an intention; a meaning
and intention discerned by Christians and identified in their
eyes with the mystery of the Incarnation. There is Pascal's well-
known aphorism: "Jesus Christ, whom both Testaments look
to, the Old as its hope, the New as its model, both as their
centre" (*Pensées*, 740). The aphorism has a double meaning;
Christ is "the centre of the Scriptures" or, if you prefer, their
attained goal, because his teaching crowns the whole teaching
of the Bible; but, historically speaking, he is the secret thread
which binds together all the events. We do not understand a
word of the Bible if we are not conscious the whole time of the
double fact, primary in its importance, of the Incarnation of

the Word and the Redemption by the Cross. Christ is foretold not only by the Prophets and all the inspired passages in which his coming can be traced, but also by the very facts of history, the first clear signs of the divine purpose, from which was deduced, by the light of the Holy Spirit, the divine truth. Abraham's call, the crossing of the Red Sea, the creation of the Davidic kingdom, the deportation to Babylon, the revolt of the Machabees; all these events and many others can only be understood by reference to the coming of Christ. Symbolically they foretell it, historically they prepare the political, psychological, social and above all religious climate which was to enable the second Person of the Trinity to bring his message to humanity, and Christianity to triumph because it fulfilled a long-felt hope.

THE MYSTERY OF ISRAEL

It is impossible to consider God's purpose made manifest in events without coming upon a historical mystery, the mystery of Israel. As human author of the Bible, the Hebrew people asserts that it is in receipt of spiritual assistance, inspiration; as an actor in biblical events, it declares that it enjoys God's special protection, the Covenant. To what extent does a historical view of the facts corroborate these two assertions?

From the purely literary point of view, there is a problem which is insoluble if we rule out divine intervention; how was this people without arts, philosophy and any particular natural endowments able to produce this incomparable masterpiece, while people infinitely more advanced intellectually have left books full of gross moral and religious errors?

From the strictly historical point of view, how was this tiny people—in the time of Solomon's splendour it never exceeded a million souls—able to exert such widespread influence? Persecuted, tortured, reduced in the dark days of the captivity "by the waters of Babylon" to less than a hundred thousand exiles, how was it able to survive right up to the present day, while the mighty empires all round it have left us only ruins, inscriptions and mummies? And why did the long trial which was its destiny lead it step by step, from suffering to suffering, ever upwards towards the Revelation?

This mystery of Israel is so closely bound up with the deep meaning of the Bible that we are brought up against it just when we discover, in the Incarnation, the final significance of all the events of Scripture. To the question why the chosen people, which had brought forth the Messias and long been big with hope of him, refused him when he came, there is no answer but a supernatural one. The human reasons that Israel had for rejecting Jesus, if they do not excuse the wickedness of Calvary, at any rate allow us to understand the drama. Was a people which had had to struggle for generations against neighbours and oppressors, in whom it recognized enemies of its faith, ready to hear the universalist message of Jesus? Could a people whose religious leaders had obstinately taught strict observance of the letter of the law hear without anger that "the letter kills and the spirit alone makes us free"? Could a people which for centuries had expected a glorious Messias, who would restore its power and sovereignty, recognize this ineffable figure in the child of a carpenter of Nazareth, in an artisan surrounded by Galilean fishermen? But if we think of what was to be the terribly logical consequence of this quite comprehensible attitude, if we believe that the sacrifice of Calvary was necessary to the work of salvation—*sine sanguine non fit remissio*—are we not brought face to face with a decisive mystery? Even in its refusal Israel remains the instrument of God.

THE POTTER'S WORK

There is another divine purpose which can be traced from one end of the Bible to the other, inseparably united to that revealed in the march of events; it is the work of the perfecting of man, and it is essential to understand it properly if we do not want to encounter a serious difficulty: the apparent difference between the religion of the Old Testament and that of the New. Only the idea of guided development, of progressive enlightenment with a full revelation at the end of it, enables us to resolve contradictions which would otherwise give scandal.

Very often the Bible compares God to a potter modelling human clay; "As clay in the hand of the potter", says Jeremias, "so are men in the hand of God" (Jer. 18. 6). Scripture is thus the story of this progressive refinement, of this patient work by the Creator on his creature to bring him to greater perfection. And just as a potter does not transform the lump of clay that he is modelling into a vase with skilful curves instantaneously, so God reveals himself at work throughout the Bible and seems to enjoy displaying his alterations, his momentary defeats, his regrets and his fresh starts.

That is perhaps the most exhilarating aspect of the Bible; it gives a constant sense of progress. "The historian receives an extraordinary impression from the Bible," writes Fr de Lubac.[1] "The contrast between the humbleness of Israel's beginnings and the power of the seeds—explosives would be a better term —it bears within itself; the concrete and at first somewhat veiled form taken by its highest beliefs; then the majestic progress, the confident if mysterious march towards something vast and unforeseeable; nowhere else do we find anything even remotely resembling all this."

The truth that brings perfection and salvation was certainly not revealed complete by God at one blow; the clay did not receive its final beauty from the potter right from the start. All through Israel's history we have to note an ascent towards the Light, a slow advance in knowledge of the unutterable. To be sure, it was an ascent and advance that was constantly compromised and threatened, for it was made by men like ourselves, a prey to temptation and sin; but the miseries on which the biblical writers never hesitate to cast a harsh light, far from harming the truth of the picture as a whole, only reinforce it, just as virtue always looks more admirable when it blossoms

---

[1] *Catholicisme, les aspects sociaux du dogme*, by Henri de Lubac, S.J. (4th revised edn., Paris, 1947), p. 131. English Trans.: *Catholicism, A study of Dogma in Relation to the Corporate Destiny of Mankind*, translated by Lancelot C. Sheppard (London, 1950), p. 81.

next to vice. The great principle dominating the composition of Scripture is that of the ascent towards total discovery. This ascent is divided into three stages: Abraham receives the revelation of the unity of God; Moses, on Sinai, writes, at the dictation of the Almighty, the religious and moral law which is to rule the life of the chosen people; and finally the prophets contribute to a transference of religion from the realm of sociology, where loyalty to the sacred precepts is confused with membership of the chosen people, to within the individual, where each one is responsible for his own acts alone, for all his acts, according to the voice of conscience and under the gaze of God.

We have only to read the Old Testament to feel an urgent demand arising in our minds. These three stages are still only a preparation. We expect something else: a religion in which the whole of nature will be consecrated, divinized, in which the human condition itself will be assumed by the light that is life. "Christ has superseded the law", says St Paul (Rom. 10. 4), and the Epistle to the Hebrews states exactly how: "In old days, God spoke to our fathers in many ways and by many means, through the prophets; now at last in these times he has spoken to us, with a Son to speak for him" (Heb. 1. 1–2). What astonishes and sometimes shocks us in the religion of the Old Testament is only preparation and tentative essay, but everything contributes to a fulfilment whose other name is Revelation. All the great doctrinal themes of the Bible necessarily end in the Gospel; all the truths it communicates to men only disclose their full meaning in the light shed by the latter; and it is given to us to know the accents, the living Incarnation of the Word which God progressively allowed men to hear. Jesus is the form willed by the potter.

CHAPTER VIII

THE OLD TESTAMENT, THE
BOOK OF PREPARATION

THE TRADITION OF THE CREATION

The Old Testament recounts the first part of this sacred history. In its forty-five books it groups together everything preceding the coming of Christ.

It begins with a series of mysterious writings, bearing the title of Genesis, about the origin of the world and of man. They are among the most famous parts of the whole Bible, the parts which can be alluded to in anyone's presence without fear of incomprehension. How God made heaven and earth, how he modelled the first man from the primeval mud, and how, from this first living flesh of the male man—such is perhaps the meaning of the Sumerian syllable *ti*, which is also translated by "rib"—he drew the female; all these episodes form such an integral part of elementary education that it is impossible to imagine our civilization being unaware of them. They are immemorial traditions, bequeathed to the Hebrews by peoples who lived long before them. In the black tent by Mambre,[1] then in the little white houses of the Delta, the bards would intone them in the evenings, long chants in the oriental style, tales heard a hundred times yet always new. So, later, in Mycenaean fortresses, other poets would tirelessly recite the story of their great elders who went off to Troy to win back Helen and had many an adventure on their homeward journey.

[1] Mam(b)re in Canaan could be seen from the field where Abraham buried Sara (Gen. 23.19). [*Trans.*]

In the first eleven chapters of Genesis the revealed truth which is their basis thus rubs shoulders with popular tradition and also the thunder and lightning of an apocalyptic proclamation. In many respects the pages depicting the archangel with a fiery sword barring man from Paradise and the wrath of the Lord submerging guilty humanity under a terrifying waste of waters correspond to those in the last book of Scripture which were to portray the end of the world; a mysterious and significant connection. But what is especially admirable in these eleven chapters is their psychological profundity and their religious truth. Christian morality sprang from them; the picture that thousands of human beings have formed and still form of their destiny, the explanation of our inward misery, the hope that buoys us up, all the most decisive elements in us are the product of these pages. Above all, there is the great certainty of faith, the truth which was to be passed on right through the Bible down to us: there is only one God and everything in the world obeys his Law. The exacting and uncompromising monotheism of these pages is enough to differentiate them radically from the other cosmogonies of neighbouring peoples, with which they have been expressly compared.

Right from the start this testimony is declared to have been given by one people—one family, one line of descent. The link is expressly indicated. The Book of Genesis does not end—far from it—with the story of the flood and the drama of the tower of Babel, a prelude to the great divisions of humanity; a genealogy follows immediately, one of those long lists of names which occur frequently in the Bible and were considered enormously important by the Hebrews, as they were by all the peoples of the East. From the first man to the first witness of the revelation—and right down past him to Jesus—the line is direct, precise and clearly traced. That means that between the message of salvation and those immemorial traditions there is a close link; the one depends on the other. Those sublime myths are already the truth and the life; they are already the revelation.

THE AGE OF THE PATRIARCHS

However, the revelation began formally on the day when a nomadic Semite in the neighbourhood of Ur of the Chaldees heard an ineffable call and obeyed the supernatural command. What call? The call of the one god, the true god, of God. He whom the human spirit discovers, but can only know darkly, selected Abraham, son of Terah, as the messenger of his Word and ordered him to break with the errors and abominations of polytheism. We are confronted here with an essentially mystical and inexplicable fact, as mysterious in its essence and as tangible in its results as the mission of Joan of Arc, perhaps, for France. How, why, in a world soaked in idolatry, did a small bedouin clan, led by its chief, opt for the truth? The answer is obviously to be found in the will of God, already at work.

From the moment the Voice resounded, men were therefore face to face with the truth and their duty was to serve it. In this sense—a sense often recalled by our medieval sculptors—the whole of humanity, when it is faithful to the truth, is the child of Abraham. But will it be faithful? This question, which always arises, arose right at the beginning of the story. Abraham went off with his clan, leaving the pagan city, marching into the desert. Did he know, at the bottom of his heart, that his unprecedented decision was opening a new chapter in history, that until the end of time it was going to pose to the human conscience "the one and only problem"? He himself, like all those who dare to take great spiritual risks, had his doubts. Would the God who had summoned him continue to support him? Would he appear before him again to help and guide him? Yes; and it was on an evening when he felt discouraged and, as an act of faith, offered a sacrifice that he received the reply. God was present. God spoke; he granted his Covenant to his servant and to all his descendants. A contract was drawn up; the people later to be called Israel, Abraham's posterity, was to enjoy the distinction of special protection, it was to be the chosen people, as long as it remained faithful, carried out the Lord's commands and was the depository of the great truth of the One God.

Henceforth everything was to fall into place with remorseless logic. Sarah, Abraham's wife, had no children. Would God fail to keep his word? What was the point of the Covenant if the contracting party had no issue? The miracle took place; the old woman brought forth a child and was so delighted that he was called Isaac, that is to say, "son of joy." Yet God seemed to remain silent, or rather his will was not clear. What did he really want? Abraham believed that he expected the hardest sacrifice, that of this first child. There was nothing for it but to obey, hard as it might be to do so. On the high place the sacrificial knife was about to pierce Isaac's throat when the Angel of the Lord held back the father's hand and pointed to the ram that was to be substituted for the human victim. "I prefer obedience to sacrifice", a prophet was to say later; the lesson had already been given on Mount Moriah.

Faithfulness, obedience; but what else exactly did God want? Slowly, gropingly as it were, Abraham's descendants sought the answer, through episodes rich in symbols. Isaac's marriage signified that the clan of Terah was to remain pure and not mix its blood with any other; Jacob, "wrestling with an angel" for a whole night by the River Jabbok, was obliged to come to grips with his human condition, and choose between the flesh and the spirit, personal interest and his vocation.

Soon the whole people was confronted by this problem. In Egypt, where famine led them and Joseph settled them, Abraham's descendants perhaps thought that surrounded by idols with animals' faces they would easily be able to preserve their faith. The answer they received was persecution, suffering and anguish. Obeying God is not easy. But the seal put on his people by the Lord genuinely protected it. How many centuries of slavery were there? Two or three at least; but there was enough loyalty and courage left in Israel's soul for faith to survive the test. The first stage ends with the book of Genesis, the stage in which this still elementary but solid faith is proclaimed; the second is about to begin.

GOD'S LAWGIVER

Moses is so important that the Bible devotes no less than four books to him. Exodus tells above all the story of the origin of his mission and of his work until he draws near to the land which God had promised his people; it also describes many rules and ordinances fixed by God's great lawgiver. Leviticus consists almost entirely of a code of laws and collection of rites. With Numbers the narrative is resumed and shows the chosen people on the march towards the spot assigned by Providence. Finally, Deuteronomy is in some sort a spiritual testament of the great leader; his last instructions are noted with burning devotion, and we can almost hear the lawgiver's actual voice begging his people never to betray the law he has revealed to it.

That is Moses' true mission, his supernatural rôle, the one assigned to him when, already advanced in age—he was to die forty years later aged 120—a shepherd on the slopes of Madian, he heard God's voice in the burning bush calling him to action. There is scarcely a difficulty that he did not encounter. His first task was to snatch his people from slavery, and for that nothing less was required than the miraculous intervention of God, who smote the persecutors with the "ten plagues" and drowned their army in the Red Sea's swift returning waters. Then he had to combat the lack of understanding, the selfishness, the low passions—in a word, the call of the flesh—which urged the chosen nation to revolt and, at their leader's first absence, hurled it back into idolatry. But no matter; by his iron will, by his genius and with God's help, Moses was to force on this "stiff-necked people" the truth received on Sinai. The Tables of the Law, the Ten Commandments; those were the bases of the morality given by God's witness to his people and, beyond it, to the whole of humanity. And if this people needed forty years to accept them, the desert was there to provide an appropriate background to the trial.

So forty years went by. All the adults died, and Moses himself, too; for once doubting God and his power he was not to see the crowning of his work. But out of that horde of fugitives he had made a nation; and he had given it a constitution founded on the Ten Commandments which was to last for centuries. The second stage in the spiritual pilgrimage was over. "The one and only God," said Abraham; "and the Law", added Moses.

THE JUDGES AND KINGS

Now we have emerged into history, a history, it is true, still close to the popular chronicle and at the same time full of meaning. Israel now stands before the land pointed out by God as the fore-ordained scene of the fulfilment of its destiny. This land has first to be occupied, then, after the conquest, settled and organized. That is, some kind of government has to be set up, for it is obvious that a settled, agricultural nation cannot be ruled in the same way as clans of pastoral nomads. But immediately a serious problem arises, the problem that arises for all men as soon as they have begun to own property, land and wealth. In the poverty and homelessness of the desert God was near and loyalty relatively easy; will it be so easy when money and commerce have exercised their pernicious influence on Israel's soul? Will not God then abandon his people?

That is the great debate that goes on through the six books, at first sight purely historical, known as Josue, Judges, Samuel (two books that really form one) and Kings (again two consecutive books). Josue, Moses' successor, assisted by the Almighty, leads the chosen people to the conquest of the Promised Land. It is not an easy conquest, in spite of favourable historical circumstances, but it is brought to a successful conclusion and the Israelite nation is henceforth mistress of its fate. When a threat arises on the twelve tribes' vague frontiers or in that inner domain which is religion, God raises up a herald to wear his sword and preach his word, the "Judge" who commands in battle or reigns in peace. Thus it is a broken piecemeal history, darting its attention from one corner of Palestine to the other, and leaving the impression of an unstable and precarious government.

After two centuries the people begins to feel keenly the worry of this instability and wonders why it cannot have a single leader like its cousins, a king to assure its unity. The national assembly votes for this solution and Saul, apparently singled out by God for the part, is about to be crowned. But at this point a problem is raised by Samuel, the old seer, the sage whose task it is to anoint with holy oil the forehead, shoulders and chest of the king-elect. He puts the people on its guard. Israel is adopting the customs of others, but Israel is not like other peoples. The monarchy will perhaps be its temporal salvation, but what of its spiritual salvation?

In the event Samuel's prediction comes true. From the temporal point of view, in spite of severe crises threatening the country's unity at the accession of King David, afterwards, during the reign of his son Solomon, the arrangement is a success. But oppression soon sets in; the most ostentatious sovereigns are also those that cost their subjects the most trouble. From the spiritual point of view the outlook is still worse. Even David, devoted to God and mystical psalmist though he was, seriously disobeyed the divine law; Solomon's thousand wives find it only too easy to sap his loyalty to God. It looks as though the price of Israel's glory and earthly success will be the loss of its ideal and whole reason for existence. The Baals and Astartes worshipped just outside the shining temple of the One God are bound to draw down the wrath of heaven on the sinning capital, Jerusalem.

The drama has begun. Rent asunder into two hostile parts, the kingdom of Solomon rushes headlong to destruction; the trial is to teach Israel Yahweh's lesson. Slowly and patiently the Justice that none escapes draws nigh; two hundred years pass before it overtakes the northern kingdom, the one whose capital is Samaria, and three hundred and fifty before it overtakes the southern kingdom, Judah and Jerusalem. The spiritual

treason becomes more blatant; the kings think only of negotiat-
ing fruitful alliances with the pagans; they adopt their gods
and abominable customs; and in the centre of Jerusalem children are sacrificed to Baal, as they are in Phoenicia. But only
patience is needed; God's wrath is at work. The Assyrians and,
after them, Nebuchodonosor's mercenaries are his instruments.
Mangled, tortured, deported, the descendants of Abraham and
the kings at last see their fault. "Out of the depths have I cried
unto thee, O Lord; Lord, hear my voice. O let thine ears consider well the voice of my supplication."

THE MESSAGE OF THE PROPHETS

God was not silent all through this drama. He still spoke to
his people through the voices of his prophets; and the Bible
brings us their words in four books, one for Isaias, one for
Jeremias, one for Ezechiel and one for the "twelve minor
prophets", so called not because their message is less important, but because it is reported in fewer words. These mouthpieces of the Almighty differ in social origin, style and
temperament, but taken as a whole they have the same
character. Commissioned by God with the superhuman task of
recalling the chosen people to obedience, they carry out their
mission to the end without fear or hesitation; their lives are less
important to them than the message they bear. It was they who
finally saved faith, principles and hope. "Springs of living water
in the middle of an arid desert," Mgr Ricciotti calls them, "men
of providence whose teaching enabled Israel's soul to climb to
the third stage in its spiritual ascent."

The first of them are in action in the time of the kings; Osee
and Amos fighting with all their strength against the abuses of
their time; Micheas, when Samaria fell, pointing out the consequences but already proclaiming the hope he sees in the future;
Nahum recognizing and acclaiming in the fall of Nineveh God's
sovereign action in the world; Abdias exalting his people's
vocation in terms of a narrow nationalism.

The book bearing the name of Isaias, the greatest genius in

this whole amazing band of seers, spans the years from the age of Achaz and Ezechias to that of the Babylonian exile, such a lengthy period that scholars have long wondered if there were not in fact two, or perhaps even three, writers involved. Yet, in spite of variations in the style, the book as a whole forms a unity because of the messianic idea which inspires it from start to finish and provides the prophet with his most moving words. The promise of salvation given by Isaias in time of peace is reiterated more fervently in days of suffering and exile. From his text, and especially from the second part (chapter 40 onwards), rises a picture of a regenerate Israel led to salvation by the Messias.

Jeremias is the sorrowful and pathetic witness of the fall of Jerusalem and the temporal collapse of Israel. This drama, which he describes step by step, has its counterpart in his mind, where superhuman hope clashes with human despair, and universal love vies with hatred of infidelity.

Ezechiel, the third of the three "major prophets", who was also a witness of the drama, devotes less time to moral warnings than to the expression of a supernatural hope, formulated in striking terms. Corpses will rise again and flesh once more cover dried bones! So Israel, recalled to life by the Word ... and so on. This apocalyptic style, dear to latter-day Jewish religious writers, is also the one employed by the book of Daniel. Written in a quite different tone and probably composed of heterogeneous parts, it proclaims this same hope, no longer a temporal one limited to the kingdom of Israel, but reserved for those who live a righteous life, the hope of the kingdom of God.

Thus the prophets play a double rôle: they bring tidings of God's wrath before it is unleashed, but tidings of hope when the wrath has arrived and the people is prostrate and repentant. Then, when the exile is over and Israel has been able to return to its land, the last of them fight the good fight in another way. Aggeus is the champion of the material restoration, the man who demands a temple for the Lord; Zacharias lays more emphasis on the social and political restoration; Joel,[1] concentrating on an eschatological future, exalts the spiritual restoration and sees in penitence the means of retaining God's friendship; Malachias, too, calls for inward reform and proclaims the demands of faith; and in the book of Jonas, inserted among the prophets because the man of this name is a seer belonging to the same intellectual family, although it is only a mere story full of wonders but devoid of oracular pronouncements, there can be heard, like the first echo of Christian universalism, the call to an Israel with a universal mission, summoning all the peoples of the earth to salvation.

THE POST-EXILIC BOOKS

For the exile is over, and the chosen people, thanks to Cyrus' generosity, has been able to settle in Palestine again. But things are not what they were in days gone by, and old men lament the change. The hard toil of the return, the difficulties of restoration, cries of sorrow from those who feel sad when they compare the present with the past; that is what we find to start with in the first of the books constituting the last and extremely heterogeneous part of the Old Testament, Esdras and Nehemias. It was all over; Israel had lost her political freedom for many long centuries. First the Greeks, in the shape of Alexander's heirs, and then the Romans kept the chosen people in varying degrees of subjection. When the tyranny became intolerable, the Machabees organized a national rising. The Bible reports their exploits in two books, the first strictly and movingly historical, the second, it must be admitted, somewhat too much given to edification.

But there was something else to do besides record these glorious but unimportant deeds. While empires, in their rise and fall, unconsciously prepared the world in which the Gospel was to spread and flourish, the little Jewish community, shut in on itself and busily occupied in meditating on the spiritual

[1] It is difficult to give Joel an exact date; the Dominican biblical scholars of Jerusalem make him a contemporary of Osee and Amos.

deposit which it knew very well to be the only reason for its existence, was itself preparing—even to the profound reasons for its refusal—the world in which providence was to make possible the double mystery of the Incarnation and Redemption.

That is the light in which we must look at these post-exilic books in order to understand them; they contain a spiritual message, even those apparently episodic in character. Tobias demonstrates—in rather down-to-earth terms, perhaps—the doctrine of the rewarding of merit by God; Judith is a tale set in cruel times exalting the triumph of faith over human power; Esther is an episode in the lives of the Jews who remained in Persia, proclaiming the same lesson in a different language; Ruth, an exquisite book, on the surface is just an idyll, but it is rich in symbols lovingly used again by Claudel. Ruth's verses seem to point to the messianic horizon; it is placed before the book of Samuel in our Bibles because it introduces us to King David's ancestors.

But these lofty spiritual lessons are given above all by the "sapiential" books, which enlarge and refine them from century to century until they are not far below the level of the Gospel. There is the book of Proverbs, a sort of epitome of ancestral experience, full of aphorisms that have nourished the "wisdom of the nations"; there is Ecclesiastes, with its strong and bitter taste (the famous verse about the vanity of vanities is known to everyone), pointing to virtue as the secret of happiness; there is that mystical masterpiece, the Song of Songs, which, in the classical images of conjugal happiness, tells Israel and, beyond Israel, the human spirit, of the splendour of union with God; there is the book of Job, another masterpiece, not this time of poetry alone, but of dialectic too, probing man's heart and leading him to the calm contemplation of God's plans and mercy; there is Ecclesiasticus, a complete manual of the religious life for anyone wishing to discover the meaning of faith. Last but not least there is the book of Wisdom, which finds the secret of true life in the accomplishment of the divine will and shows that will at work in history. All these books, or at least their final versions, took shape during the last centuries of Israel before Christ. Appearing at a time when the Bible is poor in events they assume the value of evidence; they remind us that true life is not at the mercy of any occupying power but is lived on a plane and aims at a freedom which earthly tyrants are powerless to touch. In this way they foreshadow and prepare us for the message of Christ.

There remains the book of Psalms, which appears in the Bible among the sapiential and poetic books, but occupies a unique position. When were these songs of praise and dedication finally committed to writing? From what more or less ancient sources do the five collections forming the anthology spring? In a way, the answer is of no importance. From David to the sages of the Jewish community after the Exile, what their authors express is so lovely, so pure that the spirit of man will always find refreshment in it. The liturgy of Israel used them; the Christian liturgy knows no finer prayers and lays them under contribution for the bulk of its daily office. Glittering with images and symbols and unfailingly inspired, they are at the same time the literary masterpiece of the whole Old Testament and its spiritual epitome. The spirit of Christ himself was nourished on them and many a time their verses rose to his lips. They are one of the most moving indications of the link between the Old and the New Covenant.

CHAPTER IX

THE NEW TESTAMENT, THE BOOK OF REVELATION

AN AMAZING STORY

What an admirable and indeed astonishing story it is that fills the chapters of the New Testament! A man appears in the heart of Israel, a distant descendant of King David, but belonging to a humble family, the son of poor people. Long an obscure carpenter in a small village in Galilee, on attaining the age of thirty he "arises", as many prophets have done in days gone by, and travelling right through the Holy Land he speaks, teaches the multitudes and starts a current of opinion. Now this man is much more than a prophet; he is the Messias promised by Scripture; this Son of man is the Son of God. He proves it not only by the miracles he performs, but also by the sublime quality of his teaching. In him are visibly fulfilled Israel's expectation and the hope of the world. An unsurpassable model is set before humanity.

The religious leaders of Israel, however, blinded by their literal interpretation of the old Revelation and perhaps also by extremely temporal considerations, refuse to welcome this new Revelation. Regarded as a false messias, accused of blasphemy and sacrilege, Jesus of Nazareth is arrested, condemned and put to the most shameful and painful of deaths. Is it to be the end of this pitiful story, strikingly like that of many another pseudo-messias thrown up by the age? No. For this man who was defeated—the evidence is plentiful and compels belief—

suddenly triumphs; on the third day after his crucifixion his tomb is found empty, and for close on six weeks in succession he who has risen from the dead appears to one or other of his disciples. By the time he finally quits the scene, in a supreme manifestation of power and glory, those who had followed him and fled like frightened rats at his apparent defeat have regained courage and confidence. Henceforth they will believe and tell the world that the victim of Calvary was in very truth the Messias and the Son of God.

So Christ's first disciples set to work, and their story, as it unfolds, is almost as amazing as their Master's. How was this tiny kernel going to become a tree? How was this sect of poor Jews and Galilean fishermen going, in less than three centuries, to impose itself on the world, penetrate the whole vast Roman empire and substitute its own conception of life for that of ancient paganism? This Revolution of the Cross is itself a mystery. The New Testament describes it, showing the Apostles at the work of proselytizing (they call it evangelization) which will enable the seed sown by Jesus to produce enormous harvests. A new society rises on the foundations laid by him who was crucified at Golgotha, a prefiguration of that city of justice foretold for the end of time by the last book in the Bible.

This sublime story is told in a series of small works which differ considerably in tone but are all extraordinarily rich in texture. The first of them are so pure, so crystalline, that Renan himself called them as a whole "the most beautiful book in the world". Another is a lively and gripping narrative, a sort of adventure story, the story of the early days in the conquest of the world by the cross. Others are doctrinal treatises, the products of particular circumstances, but all sparkling with new ideas which reach right into the dark corners of the soul and force it to aspire to the light. The last is an apocalypse, resembling in form the many conceived by Israel in her last few centuries, but completely Christian in significance. Gospels, Acts of the Apostles, Epistles and Apocalypse; those twenty-seven tiny books contain a message so fresh, so rich and so inexhaustible that in twenty centuries it has lost nothing of its sparkle or topicality.

THE GOSPEL, OR GOOD NEWS

Christ, the living God, is, then, the only subject and the real author of the whole New Testament. The various books only report his life, his message and the circumstances of his appearance for the benefit of his Church after his death. The first part consists of the Gospel, in Greek "the good news", which the herald ran to announce after a military victory. To evangelize was to proclaim this good news, an act which had a venerable and solemn meaning, a religious connotation. For men of Israel, what could this good news be? None other than the news for which they had been hoping for two thousand years: the Messias has come, the kingdom of God is at hand and humanity is going to live under its laws. That is substantially what the Gospel says: Jesus of Nazareth is indeed the expected Messias and the criminal error which put him to death cannot prevail against this certainty; all the rest is only the logical consequence of this affirmation. So the Gospel is at the same time an account of the life, death and resurrection of Jesus and the formulation of the message he brought to the world; the two are identical.

Christ is present in it, a unique model for mankind. It is asserted, and he asserts himself, that he is both man and God. True man, he takes upon himself all the realities of life on earth (evil, from which he is miraculously preserved, is not a positive reality, but an absence), and sanctifies them by the example of his sublime life and death. For the divine is perceptible throughout the Gospel as an ever-present transparent aura which does not affect the genuine, and just as perceptible, humanity of the man-God. United to all men, his brothers, Christ carries them with him up to the supernatural realm where, cleansed of his faults and redeemed, man is more than man; for, true God, he has done all in divine fashion, thus assuring the regeneration of that wretched human nature which he wished to assume for the express purpose of giving man's mortal state its final religious import.

All that in the Old Testament was still only sign, expectation and promise is here accomplished. The Gospel is the climax of the whole Revelation.

THE THREE "SYNOPTIC" GOSPELS

Basically there is only one Gospel. The Good News which Jesus himself is and has brought to the world is handed on in a perfect and definitive form, which may be differently expressed by different books but is substantially one. St Irenaeus aptly speaks of the tetramorphous Gospel, that is, one Gospel with four forms. As early as the end of the second century we find Clement of Alexandria and the Muratorian Canon talking —and it is the only right description—of the Gospel according to St Matthew, according to St Mark, according to St Luke, according to St John, so as to indicate clearly that it is a question of one single set of facts communicated to men with different shades of emphasis.

It might be asked why the Church, when she realized the importance of these writings, did not try to unify them in one narrative. Attempts of this sort were in fact made by several scholars, including the historian Eusebius and, above all, the Syrian Tatian, St Justin's pupil, who did his work very skilfully. They became very popular, but the Church did not set the seal of her approval on them. With her marvellous sense of realities, she probably knew that the tiny differences between the texts, for from prejudicing their credibility, really strengthened it. Above all, with her profound respect for tradition, she did not consider herself entitled to tamper with documents that emanated directly from eye-witnesses.

The resemblances between the first three evangelists, Matthew, Mark and Luke, are particularly striking; many passages in their texts, when placed side by side, look so similar that they are clearly all variants of one single view or, in Greek, *synopsis* of the incident concerned; hence the description of these gospels as synoptic.[1]

They have 350 verses in common, that is, a third of St Matthew (1070) or St. Luke (1151) and more than half St Mark (677). Yet if we compare them with one another we find omissions, additions and differences. Thus St Mark knows nothing of Christ's childhood and omits the Sermon on the Mount, and St Matthew does not report the Ascension; on the other hand, St Luke, in his description of the miraculous birth of Jesus and his early years, is the only one familiar with certain precious details unknown to St Matthew, another authority for the childhood of Christ. Most of the differences are purely formal, but sometimes they look quite serious; for example, in St Matthew and St Luke, when Jesus talks to the apostles before they go off on their mission, he tells them to take nothing with them, "no wallet for the journey, no second coat, no spare shoes *or staff*", whilst in St Mark he recommends them to take "a staff for their journey and nothing more". Such differences prove above all that the Evangelists did not merely copy one another. The resemblances are bound up with the conditions under which the "Synoptics" wrote their books; each of them used the same sources, sometimes studied the books already published by the others and finally made his own personal contribution.

Although they vary in intention and talent from plain popular chronicle to seriously written history, the three Synoptics give one and the same impression. In accordance with a plan which must have been that of the primitive catechism—preaching of St John the Baptist and baptism of Christ, ministry of Jesus in Galilee, journey into Judaea up to Jerusalem, passion, death and resurrection—they retrace the external events of our Lord's life; they report his words as they sounded to his listeners and reflect his attitude with striking exactness; and they are obviously not concerned with scholarly arrangement or theological commentary. They form a record of Christ in three harmonious yet dissimilar parts.

[1] For examples of these similarities, see the end of this book.

THE "JOHANNINE" GROUP

The fourth Gospel, written in his old age by St John, Christ's favourite disciple, the Benjamin of the band of twelve, is quite different. Its differences of form and content were noticed very early on. The author's aim is clearly indicated at the end of his book (20. 31); he wishes to show that Jesus was indeed the Christ, the Son of God, so that all who read may believe in him and thus win salvation. His purpose, then, is apologetic and theological. That does not mean, however, that he does not preserve a very close link between him whom he is the first to call "the Word incarnate" and the actual circumstances of Jesus' life on earth. On the contrary, writing at a time when the three synoptic gospels were already widely read, and assuming the information they impart to be familiar, he provides details forgotten by Matthew, Mark and Luke. It is thanks to him that we know the length of Jesus' public life, the exact date of his death and many circumstances of the Passion. But fundamentally it is not this work of documentation that interests him. The facts are important, but only because of their supernatural significance and the spiritual lessons to be drawn from them. "In the beginning was the Word, and the Word was with God, and the word was God. . . ." We have only to read the first chapter of this book, that sublime passage that Catholics hear, only too often absent-mindedly, at the end of every Mass, to feel that its inspired author was carried aloft as if on wings; the fourth Gospel is the witness of a mystic, the testament of a soul at home with God.

The New Testament canon includes four other books from the same pen as this primary text. There are three letters or Epistles, probably written after the Gospel, the first addressed to a group of Churches in Asia, the second to a "Sovereign Lady" (who was perhaps a Church) and the third to one of the faithful called Gaius. They are short but moving pieces of writing; from Ephesus, where he feels like an exile, the old Apostle speaks to his distant friends in the quiet, affectionate voice of a hoary-headed old man. He begs them in a touching tone of love and charity to live in union with Christ and in horror of sin. St John is thus the first theologian of "sanctifying grace", and perhaps the most moving in his simplicity.

As for the Apocalypse, which St John wrote somewhere about 92–96, when he was deported to Patmos during the persecution of the emperor Domitian, this mysterious book with its jingling words and alternating light and darkness does more than cry to heaven the protestations and hopes of threatened Christianity. Its flashing images depict the whole of human destiny and trace the curve of future history, a destiny and history whose ultimate goal is the end of time and the return of Christ in glory, in accordance with the invitation of the book's last words: "Come, Lord Jesus, come!" It bears witness to the burning conviction that buoyed up the early Christians, namely that the Son of Man would soon return, and also to the eternal Hope that animates the Christian soul in every age.

THE "PAULINE" GROUP

We now come to another figure, St Paul, who is very different from the beloved disciple, but equally fascinating. Far from being one of the Twelve like John or Matthew, as a pupil of the Pharisees he was at first an enemy of the Christians; the Lord himself had to summon him to his service, in a mysterious scene smacking of drama and ecstasy, on the road to Damascus, in the hard glare of the midday sun. But as soon as he had been vanquished by the Light, Saul, now transmuted into Paul, threw himself headlong into the service of the God who had laid him low. He made himself into an authentic apostle by the outstanding quality of his proselytizing, his indefatigable zeal and his martyrdom.

The New Testament introduces him to us in two ways. On the one hand, he occupies the foremost place in the Acts of the Apostles, the last of the Bible's historical books and one of the most exciting. Written by an extremely well-informed contemporary, none other than St Luke, that cultivated Greek doctor who was Paul's companion on his travels and also wrote the third Gospel, it is the account, half in chronicle-, half in diary-form, of the great adventure undertaken by the first Christians when, very few in numbers, they set about carrying to the pagan world the message entrusted to them. It is an extremely precious piece of evidence about the period, for Luke was interested in everything, an excellent observer and far from in-sensitive. But for him, what should we know of the spiritual reasons which determined the loyalty of the first witnesses to Christ crucified? What should we know of that community at Jerusalem which provided the first shelter and storage for the seed of Truth? What could we say about the problems that arose for this primitive Church? How could we write the biography of the Prince of Missionaries, the Apostle of the Gentiles, that St Paul whom so many chapters of the Acts show us at work? No doubt this work by a disciple who had not enjoyed direct contact with the Lord lacks the "gentle and terrible" impact of the Gospels; Christ himself is no longer present, living and speaking divine words; all the same, this picturesque and gripping book is inspired all the way through by admirable faith. Christians have too long neglected it and are returning to it now, at a time when, as in those far-off days it depicts, everything can be summarized in the need for loyalty.

The New Testament also brings us fourteen letters or Epistles by the Paul portrayed at work in the Acts, and they are perhaps the profoundest pieces of writing in the whole Bible. The Apostle wrote them during his extensive travels, when he was in Galatia or Palestine, in Greece or at Rome, at liberty or in prison. He addressed some to Churches or groups of Churches, which explains why they read like encyclicals, and others to private persons who were Christians and friends. From all of them wells up teaching that enlightens the spirit; not academic theology, unfeeling and tedious as it was so often to be, but the science of God transformed into the science of life and death, a theory of knowledge and a supreme revelation. There is scarcely a question that has aroused the interest of the Church in any age that does not find an answer in these fourteen letters, or at any rate the basis for an answer. And what a style! Spontaneous and vivid, it abounds in unforgettable phrases. "Where then, death, is thy victory; where, death, is thy sting? It is sin that gives death its sting..." (1 Cor. 15. 55). Whoever has understood the meaning of these words and many others is far advanced in the supreme study. A giant who changed the face of the world, a genius who drew out of Christ's teaching all that was implicit in it, Paul appears as the man of destiny who enabled Christianity to become the doctrine that was to conquer the world. And from the epistle to the Romans and the two to the Corinthians, Christians of all ages have drawn instruction so rich and ever fresh that twenty centuries have not exhausted its treasures.

THE "CATHOLIC" EPISTLES. THE CHURCH AS GUARDIAN OF THE DEPOSIT

Still other disciples had written letters worthy of attention on account of their spiritual content or the doctrinal authority recognizable in them. Very early, as with Paul's epistles, the custom was established of handing on these precious documents from community to community. The Church has retained some of them in the canon of the New Testament; they are called "catholic Epistles". One of them is by St James—perhaps James the son of Zebedee, the brother of St John, or James the son of Alphaeus, who were both counted in the Twelve; or else James "the brother of the Lord", that is, his cousin, who was the first bishop of Jerusalem[1]—a short, crisp and picturesque piece of writing, reminiscent of the sapiential books of the Old Testament, reminding every believer of the duty of putting his religion into practice, of joining works to faith. Two others bear an illustrious signature, that of St Peter, the Prince of the Apostles; they are powerful, vehement and equally concise and sober. They give the impression of being full of apostolic majesty. One of them is particularly addressed to

[1] Who, according to a very precise tradition, is in any case the same as James the son of Alphaeus, commonly known as St James the Less.

those of the faithful who have had, or will have, to pass through the fire of trial; the other is a moving exhortation to practise the virtues which enable a man to face death without fear, in the certainty of finding mercy. As for the short epistle of St Jude, probably written by Jude "the brother of the Lord", who is mentioned in St Mark's Gospel (Mark 6. 3) but is not necessarily the Jude known as Thaddaeus who was one of the Twelve, it is an indictment, not unlike St Peter's second Epistle, of those Christians who live badly, "changing the grace of God into debauchery", and thus delay the victory of the faith. Behind these writings we can sense the life of the Church, with problems, difficulties and crises not very different from those familiar to us.

With the last lines of the Epistles and the last appealing cries of the Apocalypse the Book comes to an end; the message has been delivered in full and the Revelation is complete. But it is significant and certainly intentional that all the second part of the New Testament should have depicted, either expressly in fact or analogically in symbols, the Society born of Christ properly organized and legitimately entrusted with the protection of the sacred deposit. Guarantor of the truth of the holy text, alone authorized to explain it in accordance with the supernatural illumination bestowed by the Holy Spirit on her first leaders at Pentecost, the Church prolongs the mystery of Scripture in the mystery of her own being. Fundamentally that is what she means by Tradition.

CHAPTER X

THE "MYSTIC MILL" AND THE SENSES OF THE BIBLE

FROM THE OLD TO THE NEW TESTAMENT

The problem that arises for anyone who picks up this compact, complex book with its often surprising vocabulary and mysterious undertones, in whose words the most simple-minded reader senses a supernatural purpose, is that of understanding it. We are all more or less in the position of the high official of the queen of Ethiopia who appears in the eighth chapter of the Acts of the Apostles. When the deacon Philip asked him if he understood what he was reading, he replied modestly, "How could I without someone to guide me?" Tradition answers this expectation and enables the Church to provide replies to the innumerable questions that occur to anyone who takes up the sacred text.

For Christians who read the Bible, the first question is that of the connection between the New Testament, the basis of their faith, and the Old, which at first sight, it must be confessed, looks somewhat disconcerting. What connection is there between the Mosaic precept, "an eye for an eye, a tooth for a tooth", and Jesus' sublime command, "If a man strikes thee on thy right cheek, turn the other cheek also towards him ... do good to those who hate you, pray for those who persecute and insult you"? It seems as if there is an irreconcilable opposition between the Jewish Bible—especially the ancient parts—and the Bible of Christ.

The problem can only be resolved by reference to the conception, already alluded to several times, of a divine plan, a progressive revelation, a slow but sure ascent of Israel's soul towards the light. It is perfectly true that the two Testaments are conceived on different planes. Jesus himself emphasized this difference when he said at the Last Supper: "This is my blood, of the new testament", implying that the Old was superseded. And St Paul writing to his friends at Corinth (2 Cor. 3. 14) similarly contrasts the Old Testament with the full truth of the New.

However, it would be a mistake to imagine that the two parts of the Bible are simply juxtaposed and quite unrelated; the Church turns its back on this conception by including the books of the Old Testament in the canon of Holy Scripture. On the contrary she asserts that there is a definite and necessary connection between the two parts. In many medieval works of art —in a stained-glass window at Chartres, for example—the four major prophets may be seen carrying the four evangelists on their shoulders. It is a perfect piece of imagery; the New Testament is based on the Old.

First of all, there are resemblances of form. The general style of the Gospels, Epistles and Apocalypse is not so very different from what we are accustomed to in the Jewish Bible. The same intricate arrangement of rhythms, repetitions and alliterations has been traced as in the old texts; it comes from the "oral style". The balanced phrases of the Sermon on the Mount have their parallels in Genesis and the Prophets; the parables so often on Jesus' lips belong to the same family as the *midrashim* of Israel.

Besides, we only have to read the Gospels to see that Scripture plays an important part in the life and thought of Jesus. He was nourished from his youth on this sacred treasury of his people; it was in the Law and the Prophets that he learnt to read. To be sure, he found much more than the spirit of his race in them, he found his Father's work; but it is important to note that he was brought up on these books and continually quotes and refers to them. And that is true of others besides Christ. For example, it has been shown that the sublime phrases of the *Magnificat* which welled up from Mary's pious heart consist from beginning to end of biblical allusions and references.

And what about St Paul? Never did the former pupil of the Pharisaic scholars forget the inspired books of ancient Israel to which he had devoted so many hours of study; his thought and style are soaked in them.

In the actual domain of religious revelation, the New Testament appears as the continuation of the Old. After all, Jesus said that he came "not to abolish the Law", the venerated Torah, "but to fulfil it". His teaching is directly linked to the oldest tradition of his people, for whom the first commandment was "to love God above all else". The second commandment, which the Gospel describes as "equal to the first"—"to love one's neighbour as oneself"—was by no means strange to the Hebrews, for Leviticus (19. 17–18) had already taught it to them; all that Jesus did was to give its real meaning and universal import to a principle that too many Jews restricted to within the narrow limits of their nationalism. The messianic hopes of the chosen people, and their expectation of a Saviour, were taken up by Jesus, who stripped these, too, of their nationalistic and temporal characteristics in order to give them their supernatural significance. If Christians were more familiar with the Old Testament, they would know that the God to be found in it is the same as the one they worship; a God who so loves men that the demands of this love are frightening, who wants us to win salvation "in fear and trembling"—as St Paul (Phil. 2. 12) as well as the book of Tobias (13. 6) says—but is also, in the Old as well as the New Testament, the Good Shepherd (Gen. 48. 15; 49. 24; Isaias 58. 11–14; Micheas 7. 14–15 and many other passages) the attentive and merciful Father.

FROM ANNOUNCEMENT TO REALIZATION

However, even if there is no break or gap between the Old and New Testaments, it is essential to understand clearly how the transition from one to the other takes place. As we said above, Christ himself indicated that an important stage had been reached, the stage of accomplishment and realization. "If the New Testament is contained in the Old," said St Augustine, "it is now the New that gives the Old its full meaning." *Quod*

Moyses velat, Christi doctrina revelat, wrote Suger, Abbot of Saint-Denis, wise minister of Louis VI and Louis VII of France. The formula is to be seen in almost identical form on a statue of St Paul in the church of St Trophimus at Arles: "The Law of Moses hides what Paul's teaching reveals; the grains of corn handed over on Sinai have been turned by the Apostle's efforts into flour." That is the "mystic mill" that Romanesque and Gothic sculptors loved to depict; it can be seen, for example, on the capital of a column at Vézelay.

So between the two parts of the Bible there is more than a difference of climate; that is quite obvious and proceeds from the spirit of love enveloping all Jesus' teaching and radiating from his person, a spirit of love in strong contrast to the Jewish spirit; there is the certainty of an accomplishment, a realization. Israel's revelation, though great, was incomplete and Christ's puts the finishing touch to it; but we cannot understand the Bible if we forget that this ultimate achievement existed in promise and presentiment in the inspired soul of a people that issued from Abraham, and that, in the sacred texts, we can and must discover it.

If it is legitimate and necessary to use the Old Testament to interpret the New, it is much more so to consider the old Covenant in reference to the New; and that is how Christians must read the Bible if they are to grasp all it contains. In this way everything is illuminated and confirmed. The Old and New Testaments, in their double rôle, then form one by the evidence, the progressive completion and the moral support they provide for each other, up to the perfect conclusion and the regeneration of man in God through Christ. That is what made Pascal say: "To understand Scripture, we need a sense which reconciles all the contradictory passages. . . . The real sense is not the Jewish one; but in Jesus Christ all contradictions are reconciled." Similarly Claudel said: "The Old Testament, lyrical or devotional poetry that it is, is incomprehensible without that invisible, approaching presence which arranges and guides it all, down to its shades of emphasis and softest undertones, and creates round it a sort of magnetic field of prophecy. The Old

Testament is incomprehensible without the New." Once again we are reminded of St Paul's words: *Finis enim legis, Christus.*

It is this "magnetic field of prophecy" that we have to discover if we wish to understand the Bible as a unity. The progress of events and instruction right through the book is, as it were, subtended by a supernatural force transcending time and explaining history in advance: the *spirit* of *prophecy*. It envelops the whole of the Old Testament and gives it its true significance. Not only the inspired men known as prophets are endowed with it; all the heroes of sacred history, in so far as God made use of them, enjoyed the privilege: Abraham, conscious of himself as "father of the human multitude", Jacob blessing his posterity before dying, King David, in a splendid psalm, dimly foreseeing his distant descendant, are all authentically endowed with the spirit of prophecy. Everything happens as if, in the divine plan, the Bible were a huge book already in existence before the events it was to describe, to which inspired men had access.

This spirit of prophecy does more than animate the heroes chosen by God—patriarchs, kings and prophets—who have the concrete privilege of foretelling the future. We have already seen, in tracing the curve of Israel's destiny, that before taking shape in the heroes' consciousness, the prophetic intention and significance are revealed in the facts of history; the chosen people is itself, as a whole, a prophetic figure. And again, in so far as the spirit of prophecy colours the whole sacred book, this book itself must be understood as revelation of the future which it contains in germ. In what the Bible reports, in the very terms it uses to report it, we are entitled to try to discern the secret which it has to impart to us.

Especially the one in which all the others are epitomized: that of the Christ, the Messias who brings salvation. The great moral and spiritual ideas which the teaching of Jesus was to formulate definitively had not remained, as we know, in the enlightened consciousness of the chosen people, in the state of pure abstractions; they had literally been clothed in flesh; they had come to life in a being whose shape was projected into the future. This being, the Messias, man's archetype, messenger of the divine will, supernatural agent of Revelation and Salvation, was conceived and carried within herself by Israel and that is her imperishable glory. The duty of Christians, when they read the Bible, is therefore to recognize behind the words and symbols this figure on whom their salvation depends.

The expected Messias—for us, Christ—is foretold all over the Jewish Bible. He is mentioned as early as the third chapter of Genesis—that proto-gospel—and in the blessing of Sem (Gen. 9. 26-7). It is he whom Abraham and Isaac and Jacob glimpsed in the mists of the distant future. It is his glory that is prefigured by the glory of the kings. It is he who is foretold in such precise terms by Samuel's mother (1 Sam. 2. 1-10). Needless to say, it is he who is described by the Prophets properly so called, by Osee, Micheas, Isaias, Jeremias and Ezechiel, and in all his aspects, for in decisive verses Isaias foretells the man of sorrow and his redemptive sacrifice. It is he of whom the Psalms sing, in his victory (2, 78, 110) and in his passion (22, 31, 49). And how many events in the Old Testament only take on their true meaning when viewed in this perspective! The Paschal Lamb that spares the faithful the blows of the angel of death, the brazen serpent the mere sight of which cures the sick, the manna that feeds the wanderers in the desert; all these episodes and many others have a prophetic meaning. In themselves these events may seem to smack of the mere anecdote, even of vaguely animistic or totemistic customs; but interpreted in the sense of the prophecy and the figure, what a mysterious, inexhaustible significance they acquire!

THE THREE SENSES OF THE BIBLE

Understanding the Bible, then, means going further than the literal sense. A sentence of Holy Writ always means more than the actual words of which it is composed; over and above its concrete, literal meaning it awakens echoes, hints at secret truths and reveals figuratively what human language cannot express. That is one of the main premises of the Church's teaching, and the same conviction lies behind various aspects of the liturgy. Jesus himself surely legitimized the procedure when he spoke of the "miracle of Jonas", who was in the belly of the sea monster for three days and then escaped, to signify his own death, his stay in the earth and his resurrection on the third day. The Church is adopting exactly the same point of view when she exalts Mary, the Mother of God made man, in the actual words that the Bible applies to Wisdom, "created from the beginning of the world and before all the centuries". It is possible to carry this interpretation still further, as the early Fathers of the Church did with great enthusiasm, and to identify symbolically the destiny of man with the actual events unfolded in the Old Testament: we are exiled on earth, as Israel was in Egypt; we are restored to life by going through the waters of baptism as Moses' people were restored to their destiny by going through the waters of the Red Sea. The art of medieval cathedrals is quite incomprehensible except by reference to this interpretation of the Bible by symbol and significant image. And it is to this spiritual knowledge of the sacred text that we are invited to aspire by some of the most imperious phrases in the encyclical *Divino afflante Spiritu*.

It is customary to say that the Bible has three senses: a *literal* sense, an *allegorical* or *spiritual* sense and an *accommodated* sense. People sometimes speak of typical, moral, anagogical, mystical, figurative and various other senses, but they can all be reduced to these three. Some writers, by means of a questionable extension of the accommodated sense, limit themselves to distinguishing between the literal sense and the spiritual sense. The debate or even dispute between those who emphasize the literal sense and the champions of the spiritual sense has been going on for centuries. Just as the literalist school of Antioch opposed the allegorical conceptions of the Alexandrian school, so Claudel stood out vehemently against the literalist views of Fr Lagrange and his pupils at the Ecole Biblique. It is really a futile dispute; a few moments' thought will convince us that the spiritual sense cannot conflict with the literal sense which, objectively, contains it; and the most "spiritual" exegesis can have no other aim, if it is valid and not mere improvisation and fantasy, than to elicit the inner meaning of a text already sifted by literal exegesis.[1]

An example will make clear what is to be understood by the three senses of the Bible. Let us look at a passage in Numbers (21. 9): "Moses made a brazen serpent and set it up on a post, and if anyone was bitten he looked at the serpent and was saved." In the *literal* sense, that means that the events really happened historically as the words relate. When St John gives us to understand (3. 14–15) that the serpent represented Christ raised up on the cross, we are dealing with a spiritual or allegorical sense. Finally, when Philo of Alexandria writes that the serpent—Eve's serpent—represents pleasure, and that the soul, bitten by it, must turn its eyes to the serpent of Moses to recover health and life, he is using an accommodation.[2]

For the Christian, especially the Catholic reminded of it by papal teaching, his first duty is to know and thoroughly understand the literal sense. In opposition to the over-enthusiastic, even when they were men of genius like Origen, who were ready to throw overboard the literal sense and to retain only the allegory, the Church has given preference to the opinion that Holy Scripture always has a literal sense and that we are never entitled to say that such and such a passage has only a spiritual significance. "Let interpreters bear in mind", says the encyclical *Divino afflante Spiritu*, "that their foremost and greatest endeavour should be to discern and define clearly that sense of the biblical words which is called literal."

But it is also clear that to rest content with this sense is to condemn oneself to stripping the Bible of its richest harmonies, and Claudel is right to castigate the excesses of a too "scientific" exegesis. Away with the "watery breasts of the literal

---

[1] The "spiritual" or "allegorical" sense (the terms are of no importance) is therefore a sense added to the literal sense to foretell or adumbrate a mystery or event in the life of Christ or the Church. Such a sense must be attested by the N.T. or by the virtually unanimous consent of the Fathers and tradition.

[2] For a more detailed discussion of the three senses of Scripture, see *A Catholic Commentary on Holy Scripture* (London, 1953; New York, 1957, Nelson), pp. 53–60. [*Trans.*]

sense"; the spiritual interpretation furnishes richer milk. At this point it must be repeated that to study the Bible as one does the Iliad or the Aeneid, to narrate sacred history in the same way as that of the Hittites or Cretans, is to make a radical mistake, at any rate if one claims to do anything more than provide an introduction to a profound knowledge of the text. We must look beyond the immediate contents of Scripture to the divine plan as a whole and try to understand the economy of revelation. Once again, that is just what we are wisely called upon to do by Pius XII's illuminating encyclical: "Wherefore the exegete, just as he must search out and expound the literal meaning of the words, intended and expressed by the sacred writer, so also must he do likewise for the spiritual sense, *provided it is clearly intended by God. For God alone could have known this spiritual meaning and have revealed it to us.*"

These last words, which we have italicized, seem to be aimed at the excesses of certain "*accommodating*" exegetes, very popular in the East, whose adventurous hypotheses, or rather acrobatics, have long interfered with the really profitable reading of the Bible. To see in the stone which young David projected at Goliath with his sling the "corner-stone" on which Christ's enemies will stumble, or in the staff which he held a prefiguration of the cross carried by Jesus; to see in the scarlet ribbon hung out by Rahab on the walls of Jericho at the time of Josue's attack a symbol of the blood shed by Christ on Calvary: these are bold ideas whose usefulness has not always been very clearly demonstrated. Accommodation may have provided mystical spirits with assistance in their meditations, and some of the greatest saints—St Bernard, for example—have made it yield highly spiritualized results; it is none the less true that it deals in purely human additions to the sense and should be employed with caution. *Divino afflante* recognizes that this approach can render good services in the day-to-day business of preaching, but advises having recourse to it "with moderation and restraint".

CHAPTER XI

THE BOOK OF MAN, TOO

"LOINS AND HEARTS"

Trying to understand both the literal and the spiritual sense of the Bible means, then, seeking to see into God's plan; it also involves coming to know man. Mgr Weber's penetrating description of the Bible as "the book of man and the book of God" cannot be bettered. It should be read and pondered with this double character in mind. A divine book, which did not "fall ready made from Heaven" but was written, in the supernatural light of the Holy Spirit, by men; for that very reason the Bible is a profoundly human book, which awakens all kinds of echoes in the mind of those approaching it with a little intelligence and good will; prisoners in their gaols, invalids in their suffering, travellers and missionaries buried in the depths of hostile countries have times out of number found interest and consolation nowhere but in its pages. It is a never-failing spring at which humanity is constantly slaking its thirst.

The clarity of the Bible is admirable. It sparkles with epigrams, devastating argumentation and analyses unsurpassed in acuteness by any psychologist. He of whom it has been said that "he sounds loins and hearts", when he inspired the authors of the Bible as they wrote the pages, also granted them a share in that total knowledge of the creature, man, which is the privilege of the Creator alone.

It is not only Christ's great definitive precepts that reach straight down to those regions of the mind where there is no further escape from the truth that is justice, where everything to do with man is revealed in all its nakedness: "Let the dead bury their dead!"; "Let him who is without sin cast the first stone!" St Paul's thrilling phrases are almost as striking and penetrating: "a sting of my flesh", "the man of sin" or "this mortal must put on immortality". The books of the Old Testament, too, display this inside knowledge of human nature, which is rich in all kinds of lessons. From it, as much as, or perhaps even more than, from the Greek philosophers with all their mastery of the "Know thyself" technique, flows western psychological literature. It is not for nothing that the wisdom of the nations, nourished on the book of Proverbs, has made real proverbs out of aphorisms like "the fear of God is the beginning of wisdom" or "ill-gotten gains bring no profit". But if we read the whole Bible more closely, we find it full of far-sighted observations. The moving questions of Job face to face with the mysteries of the human condition are our questions, too. "Where does wisdom come from, and where is the place of understanding?" "Why do the wicked live? Why do they grow old, and why are they powerful?" "If a man dies, will he live again?" These questions and many others which perpetually torment us are the ones which the holy man of God puts to himself. And the splendid cries of pain and hope uttered by David, the repentant sinner, are our own cries when the distress of living and despair at being men rise in our throats and choke us. "Lord, I stumble, I am reduced to extreme dejection.... I drag myself miserably through the day.... However I confess my sin with a sincere heart, for I know that the cause of my anguish is my iniquity.... Do not abandon me, O my God, do not remove thy presence from me; help me, Lord, for thou art my salvation!"

A profound knowledge of the human heart, but also the sense of sin, which gives any psychological analysis its real depth, a sense of faith and trial; that is what we find in the Bible, the most human of human books.

THE BEAUTY OF THE BIBLE

The Bible is also human in another way: by its literary qualities and moving beauty. We have already mentioned its variety which, within the framework of a fundamental unity, puts different kinds of writing side by side and thus keeps the reader's interest fresh. The great historical frescoes like Exodus, Kings, Machabees or the Acts of the Apostles, which, broadly speaking, are just as objective as the chroniclers and historians of Greece and Rome, will still grip anyone discovering them for himself and taking the trouble to read them right through, instead of resting content with the fragments that appear in the liturgy or the miserable summaries given by only too many books of "sacred history". The shorter narratives, in which the stories have a moral purpose, *midrashim* like Judith, Jonas, Esther or Tobias, carry the reader along in such lively fashion that modern writers have only needed to transpose and develop them to make them yield subjects for literary works.

As for formal beauty, it strikes the eye on innumerable occasions and in innumerable ways. No purely human poetry has ever been able to rival the sublime inspiration of the Psalms, of whose verses Lamartine said, calling to mind the time when his mother read them aloud on winter evenings: "I realized that that must be how you spoke to God". The delicate freshness of phraseology, so well suited to the violence of the emotions, which forms the charm of the Song of Songs, has never been surpassed by a purely human love song—precisely because it is not simply a human love song. It would be impossible to describe the wonder we feel before the created world better than these words about the return of spring in Palestine do: "Winter is over now; the rain has passed by. At home, the flowers have begun to blossom; pruning-time has come; we can hear the turtle-dove cooing already, there at home. There is green fruit on the fig trees; the vines in flower are all fragrance" (Song of Songs 2. 12). This marvellous, transparent simplicity cannot be surpassed. In a different key, it is also impossible to find greater tragic poetry, expressing man's deepest anguish, than certain passages in Isaias, Ezechiel and Jeremias. And it is doubtful whether the greatest visionaries—men like Dante, Blake, Poe, Hölderlin and Novalis—have ever equalled in intensity of vision the pages of the Apocalypse, but for which, in any case, their work would probably not exist.

For, from this point of view, too, the Bible has endowed humanity with irreplaceable formative material and it cannot be too much deplored that in the educational systems of most of the great civilized countries Scripture does not play as important a part as the literatures of Greece and Rome. In fact, nowadays it is generally granted only a derisory place, confined as it is to brief and quickly forgotten lessons of elementary religious instruction. Classical literature has a valuable contribution to make, but the study of the Bible would add unique and irreplaceable elements to our intellectual training; and since we find in Scripture works containing a synthesis of the Greek spirit and the Hebrew tradition, St Paul's synthesis, the Epistles of the great Apostle of the Gentiles seem particularly suited to act as instruments of that training.

Yet what the literary study of the Bible reveals goes, in a sense, beyond literature. The beauty of a literary work proceeds either from the perfect adaptation of the form to the expression of the thought and feeling—as with western masterpieces—or else from an upsurge of lyric emotion translated into a stream of images that sweeps the form along and expands it, as with the masterpieces of the East. But in the Bible a third factor appears; the beauty does not arise simply from the perfect harmony of form and content or from the subordination of one to the other; all through its pages we detect a reflection, an "aura", an inspiration or, in short, a presence. It is the Word, which was in the beginning as it will be at the end, shining through the text it has dictated, the Word which was made man and took a body, a brain and a voice like ours. Even the beauty of the Bible bears witness to the incarnation.

"FOR OUR INSTRUCTION"

In the Bible, then, man meets himself and marvels; he does more, for from Scripture he receives a constantly renewed lesson. Everything in the Scriptures, says St Paul, was put down "for our instruction" (Rom. 15. 4). Still, it will be just as well to define what we are to understand by that and what kind of instruction is meant.

We must know what it is permissible to ask the Bible and what it is absurd and pointless to ask it. "Does God take care for oxen?" says St Paul (1 Cor. 9. 9), which is to be understood in this way: to know God and love him, it is not necessary to know in which class of animals the bovine family should be placed. Science, in all its forms, operates on a different plane from the Bible; Scripture does not set out to give scientific instruction, but religious instruction. Any intellectual effort aiming at the pursuit of knowledge of creation for its own sake has no connection with what the Bible has to teach us; the real domain of holy writ is not the material world and its method is not that of logic. The two spheres are quite different.

That is why all efforts to "explain" or "justify" the text of the Bible scientifically, or to "harmonize" it with the principles of science—which are transitory, in any case—are merely ridiculous. "The Holy Ghost", says the Encyclical *Divino afflante Spiritu*, "who spoke through the mouths of the sacred writers, did not intend to teach men truths concerning the essential nature of visible things, because such truths were in no way profitable to salvation." Time and time again we have seen the collapse of systems claiming to invalidate or confirm the text by means of astronomy, geology, Durkheim's[1] sociology or, more recently, the study of prehistory. Some of these attempts have left their effects on people's minds; for example, some good Christians still imagine they are defending the truth of the Bible by asserting that the "six days" of the Creation correspond to the periods of Darwinian evolution, to the division of time geologically into the primitive, primary, secondary, tertiary and quaternary ages. Nearer our own time, efforts, just as doomed to failure, have been made to relate the ancient traditions reported by the Bible about the origin of man to the discovery of the fossilized remains of early human races. The

[1] French sociologist (1858–1917) who held the view that "social data exist independently of individual facts". [*Trans.*]

best reply to such attempts is the reminder that it will be difficult to explain how it is that Genesis makes the first smith a
grandson of Cain, whilst the iron age begins about the time of
Josue. . . . As Dom Charlier put it so well: "No conflict and no
accord are possible between the concrete imagery of a faith and
the abstract observations of a technique."

That does not mean that no lessons of a scientific character
can be drawn from the Bible. Scripture asserts that the Creation
did not take place "ex nihilo" or at random; it is at variance
with any philosophy maintaining that reality does not exist,
that the world is a sort of dream, like the shadows on the wall
of the Platonic cave; it implies as a matter of faith the orginal
unity of humanity and is consequently opposed to the hypothesis of "polygenesis", that is the simultaneous appearance of
several human couples at different points on the globe. That is
the subject which at the moment forms the centre of most discussions on the problem of "the Bible and science"; it is by no
means impossible that the solution to this particular problem,
as to many others, will appear of its own accord with the evolution of science and the widening of knowledge.

The radical difference in plane and perspective is no less
striking in the case of the Bible and philosophy. By philosophy
we mean a special discipline, aiming at a different form of
knowledge from scientific knowledge, but equally strange in
itself to the religious impulse, a discipline which moreover is
based on rational principles entirely different from those held
by the inspired writers. So it is absurd to interpret the Bible
according to the intellectual systems constructed by philosophy;
a Hegelian interpretation of Holy Writ is just as pointless—
but not more so—as a Platonic or Bergsonian interpretation.
Of course, in its ultimate purpose, philosophy meets revealed
Scripture again, for all absolute knowledge ends in God; that
is why, from the early Greek Fathers to St Thomas, the thinkers
of the Church worked so hard to put philosophy at the service
of religion. But this harmony between philosophy and religion
arises, not on the level of methods, but on that of faith and

wisdom; and although philosophy claims to pursue wisdom, in the last analysis wisdom proceeds from Revelation.

And that is even true in a sense of theology itself. In so far as theology, too, is a technique it lies outside the province of the Bible; it is quite obvious that the inspired authors of the latter lived in an intellectual climate innocent of the methods and classifications of St Thomas Aquinas. That does not mean that the two are incompatible or contradictory; Scripture offers in the crude state, as it were, what theologians have subsequently classified, thought out and elaborated; but Scripture is much more than any system, for if theology is the "science of God", knowledge of the Bible initiates the reader into a science which is a way of life; it demands more of him than intellectual consent; it demands a commitment, an act of faith.

If Scripture has been given to us "for our instruction", then, it is education of a very particular kind: supernatural, religious and nothing else. And this is just as true of our moral education as of our intellectual or scientific education. Taken as a whole on its face value, the Bible can scarcely be regarded as a handbook of practical ethics; the New Testament contains nothing that conflicts with the principles of ethics, but the same can hardly be said of the Old. If one modelled oneself on some of the kings and important characters in the Bible one would go far; and, even when account has been taken of the punishments that almost always follow the crimes, it would scarcely be advisable to follow certain biblical customs to the letter. In this connection, too, it is essential to look at Scripture as a whole, with the two parts complementing each other, and against the background of a divine plan in course of realization, if we wish to understand the grand sweep of its moral teaching. Many a sentence in Holy Writ, many a lesson to be drawn from the experience and destiny of the chosen people, reminds us that the whole of morality is based on the Bible; there is not a principle, however resolutely secular it would like to be, that did not originate, and often receive its final formulation, too, in Scripture. A society that departs from biblical principles is slipping into the abyss and is near destruction. Social morality, sexual morality, commercial morality, and others, are all there. Ecclesiasticus was long the manual of morality handed to young Christians. "If I had to form a man from childhood as I thought best", said Bossuet, "I should like to make him choose a few good passages of Scripture and to make him read them often until he knew them by heart." And Mgr Dupanloup, who spent a great deal of time on the sacred text, drew this conclusion from his studies: "One closes it armed from top to toe."

The truth is that to anyone reading the Bible, human book that it is, everything that interests man seems to be both definitively formulated and at the same time sublimated, spiritualized and carried up on the wings of inspiration towards a reality transcending the accidents of life and our mortal limitations. The spirit finds in it a climate that encourages expansion and elation. What gives unity, as we have seen, to these heterogeneous books is also what gives its true meaning to the teaching they contain: the presence of the Holy Ghost, the aspiration towards God.

CHAPTER XII

"THIS HUNGER TO HEAR

THE WORD OF GOD"

UNDERSTANDING THE BIBLE WITH THE HEART

The fundamental attitude of mind in Scripture—aspiration towards God, love reaching out to him, the ardent desire one day to possess him—is the only thing which can enable us to penetrate its mystery. To understand the Bible, it is not enough to have studied, more or less superficially, a few manuals of sacred history or introductory matter, or to have some knowledge of the higher criticism and Palestinian archaeology. "God did not grant the sacred books to men", says the Encyclical again, "in order to satisfy their curiosity or provide subjects for study and research." There is a spiritual climate which alone makes the reading of the Bible possible, let alone fruitful, if one understands by reading anything more than grasping the superficial meaning of the words. To read it as history or as a treatise is to prevent oneself absorbing the full sense of the history and doctrine it contains. This has been admirably expressed by Maurice Zundel[1]: "You can only understand Scripture on your knees."

So we must approach the Bible and always read it in a spirit of reverence and love. To take reverence first, on opening its pages everyone should repeat to himself the words of the Lord to Moses, "This is holy ground" (Exod. 3. 5), that is, put aside

[1] *Poème de la Sainte Liturgie* (2nd ed., St Maurice, 1934). Eng. trans. *The Splendour of the Liturgy* (London, 1939; and New York, Sheed & Ward).

any empty curiosity and still more—it is hardly necessary to say this—the cheap humour sometimes derived particularly from episodes in the Old Testament. But more important still is love. It is necessary to love the Bible in order to understand it and to experience before it what was described by Claudel, who for the last twenty years of his life lived on terms of daily familiarity with the text, as "a constantly growing sense of wonder". There is a general law, formulated by a medieval French mystic, Hugh of St Victor, in these perfect terms: "Love is superior to knowledge; it is greater than intelligence: we love more than we understand. Love can approach and enter where knowledge remains outside." Nowhere can this rule be more strictly applied than in the case of Holy Scripture. What remains obscure or seems absurd to the scholar is mysteriously illuminated for a humble Curé d'Ars or a little Carmelite of Lisieux. "If you want to profit from Scripture", says the *Imitation of Christ*, "read it with humility, simplicity and faith." More than in any other sphere, the supreme power of comprehension and consent in biblical study is the one Pascal denoted by his admirable private term, "the heart".

This power of consent and comprehension must be total and totalitarian; it must control the whole mind. To enter into the spirit of the Bible it is not sufficient to superimpose on dry analyses a few pious commentaries; the spiritual attitude of its heroes and writers, its fundamental intention must be completely adopted. We must listen receptively to the great themes of the book: the theme of the love of God, the theme of the call that goes out by preference to those who suffer and are despised by the world, the theme of the invitation to ally oneself with God and to live at one with him, the theme of God's infinite mercy and the theme of invincible hope. We must also experience in ourselves the great spiritual emotions that inspire the text from one end to the other: the urge to loyalty, anger against the world's injustices, joy even in suffering and time of trial. Above all, we must completely adopt that attitude of confident humility and private exaltation defined in the Psalmist's cry: "Let our raised hands be like the evening sacrifice". The Bible can only be properly understood in the posture of prayer.

PRAYING WITH THE BIBLE

The inspired singer's prayer must be repeated when we read the Bible if it is to awaken all its echoes in our hearts. In the deepest sense of the term, and in many different ways, it is a *book of prayer*. To start with, since Scripture can only be understood by faith and there is no living faith without prayer, the reader is obviously called upon to pray. After all, what is praying but making oneself, in Claudel's words, "accessible to the divine whisper", attentive to the orders and intentions of a transcendent will and mind? And nowhere is it asserted more clearly and more frequently than in the Bible that this will and mind direct the world, and that man's only merit lies in humble submission to them.

The Bible is a book of prayer in other ways, too. If the Church in her capacity of teacher advises the faithful to approach in large numbers and on frequent occasions "this table of celestial doctrine which our Lord has set up for Christian people through the ministry of his prophets, apostles and doctors", it is because she knows that this table is laid with the richest of foods. The comparison with a table—it comes from *Spiritus Paraclitus*, the encyclical of Benedict XV—is already used in a book that cannot be suspected of not aiming at the spiritual nourishment of souls, the *Imitation of Christ*, which speaks of the two tables put within reach of the faithful by the divine Master, namely, the table of the altar and that of Scripture.

Yet it does happen that some devout Christians experience a certain disappointment when they open the Bible. They expect to find uplifting and heart-warming phrases and are faced instead with dry lists of ritual observances, the fierce imprecations of some of the prophets and the enigmatic sentences of the Apocalypse—if not the matrimonial adventures of the kings. It must be admitted that the Bible in no way resembles a manual of devotion; apart from the Gospels and sapiential books, it has little to offer the believer nourished on the *Imitation* or even the *Spiritual Exercises* of St Ignatius of Loyola. The Bible is much more a book of prayer than a book of prayers—a plural which often has an adverse effect on the singular!

However, even from this point of view, it still has a great deal to offer us. First of all, taken as a whole, it forms a method of learning how to pray; it teaches us how to live a religious life. To limit ourselves to the Old Testament only—it is true *a fortiori* of the New—the Bible teaches us that prayer does not simply consist in a ritual (Gen. 4. 7; or Sam. 15. 22; or again Isaias 63. 3–12) but in a state of mind and, still more, in a way of living; that it is not simply a series of well-turned phrases— "let your words be few in number", says Ecclesiastes (5. 1)— but should be, as Jesus proclaims, "Worship in spirit and truth" (John 4. 23). In contradistinction to the superficiality and affectation of only too many devotions, the Bible's prayer is strong, straightforward, sober and virile; the sublimest of prayers, that of Christ, the Lord's Prayer, epitomizes it perfectly.

Strictly speaking, the Bible does contain numerous admirable prayers capable of furnishing the faithful soul with the words of many a devout ejaculation. The Christian's cry of adoration, the *Sanctus*, his cry of repentance, the *Miserere*, his cry of anguish, the *De profundis*, his cry of gratitude, the *Magnificat*, are all taken from the Bible. It is not only on the lips of Jesus, Mary, the Apostles or other leading figures in the Gospel—old Simeon, for example, with his *Nunc dimittis*, or the Centurion of Capharnaum, with his *Domine non sum dignus*—that we find lovely, simple formulas, wonderfully adapted to the aspirations of the soul; the Psalms are full of them, and many are famous. Less familiar are Abraham's prayer of intercession (Gen. 18. 17–33), Moses' supplication after the incident of the golden calf. (Exod. 32. 11–34), David's humble thanks in reply to the promises of the prophet Nathan (2 Kings 7. 18–19), Solomon's glorious and faithful thanks at the dedication of the Temple (3 Kings 8. 22–53), those of Ezechias, Baruch, Esdras and

Daniel, and finally the "Proverb" (30. 7–9) in which the faithful soul simply asks God to let it live in sincerity, simplicity and justice. Prayers of praise and prayers of petition, prayers of repentance and prayers of gratitude, they are all in the Bible; all that is necessary is to go and look for them.

Yet more important than all these separate prayers, beautiful as they are, is the fundamental attitude of prayer revealed and taught by the Bible, the attitude of the man continually striving to realize the highest side of his nature, the man for whom the whole of life is prayer and sanctification. Just as the whole story told by Scripture is subordinate to God and his plan, so all the life-giving nourishment to be obtained from it by man only exists in so far as it is fertilized by God. But that can only be understood by someone who has read and fathomed Scripture as a whole in all its fullness. "Examine the Scriptures", said Christ, and that means not only "understand the meaning of the words", but also "listen to the profound lessons they contain". We must pray with the Bible as a whole.

THE BIBLE, THE CHURCH'S PRAYER

The relationship established between God and the believer by means of the Bible is an extremely personal one: each word has been addressed to me personally; it was I who was summoned to the Covenant with the One God, it was to me that Yahweh spoke on the top of Sinai, it was to me that the prophets promised a "living redeemer" and Christ the resurrection of the body. Nevertheless this relationship also has another character: it is kept alive through the medium of a people, a tradition and a line of descent; it is guaranteed by the authority of a community of which I am a member; it is literally as communal as it could be.

The effort now going on to give back to the Mass its character of communal prayer—a character asserted in so many formulas like the collect and the commemorations of the living and the dead but long neglected—has its logical counterpart in the revival of liturgical prayer, which is essentially biblical.

Liturgical revival and biblical revival go hand in hand. The word of God takes on its full resonance when it is proclaimed during the course of a liturgical ceremony, for it is the communal prayer *par excellence* of the Christian congregation, the prayer of the universal Church looking up to God.

It is obviously not an accident that the choral office consists, by and large, in the weekly recitation of the psalter and that the breviary aims at effecting, during the space of a year, a *lectio continua*, that is to say, a complete reading of the Bible.[1] It is not by accident, either, that the four great Christian festivals—Christmas, Epiphany, Easter and Whitsun—are accompanied in the liturgy by a selection of passages from the most widely separated parts of the Bible, as though to bring home the unity of the divine message. On the other hand, if the liturgy owes much to the Bible, the Bible also owes a great deal to the liturgy: above all, that minimum knowledge of its text possessed by too many Christians who only read it in their missal, but also a sort of permanent topicality, a sort of contact with our hopes and fears, our moods of confidence and anguish. The Church has borrowed many of her prayers from the Bible because she wished to demonstrate the continuity of revelation and her faithfulness to the spirit of God. At the same time she makes her children feel that the spirit that filled the Patriarchs and the Prophets is the same as the one that agitated the air on the day of Pentecost, and that the revelation entrusted to her is simply an endless prolongation of the one received some four thousand years ago in Ur of the Chaldees by a young Semite called Abraham.

Liturgical prayer is the reply to those Christians who are separated from the Catholic community and believe that the Bible, as a direct, personal message from God, makes it permissible to dispense with the Church established by Christ, as if the message had not been delivered to a people collectively organized by the will of God. The early Fathers already knew that much; for them faith in Scripture and faith in the Church were the same thing, not only because the truthfulness of the

[1] Complete symbolically, at any rate.

text was guaranteed by canonical decision, but also because for them tradition was the living Bible, the Bible prolonged by the Church. At a time when this Church, by the voice of her infallible Head, redoubles her injunctions to read and study the Bible, one feels more convinced than ever that it is in the Church and through her that Scripture assumes its fullest import. Her sacraments are to the life of the soul what the sacred text is to the life of the mind: the bread and wine of a more real existence than this one here on earth.

BIBLICAL MAN IS GOD'S FAVOURITE

Such is the Bible, "the book of man and the book of God", the document that preserves the sacred deposit. We said at the beginning of these pages that it formed the foundation of all true humanism and that without it our conception of the world and of man would not be what it is. Now that we have come to the end of this rapid survey of its contents and implications, we can see still more clearly that it is indeed man in all his potentialities who is delineated in it, the real man, he who is not just an animal or a machine, he whose destiny is neither absurd nor hopeless, man fully conscious of his vocation and his significance.

We find in the Bible a conception of man which it is quite easy to define: it is a man who "stands before God" (3 Kings 18. 15; often in St Paul); a man who does not regard himself as the toy of blind fate or obscure and demoniacal forces, but as a factor in the divine plan; a man who knows that he is called by the divine will to a destiny that is unique and not determined by some mathematical law of probability or series; a man who prays, and knows as he prays that he is collaborating in God's work; a man who thinks that the world will improve in proportion to the improvements he makes in himself; a man, in short, who, as he stands before God, is also supported by God, and looks upon this state of dependence as his greatest pride and his greatest hope

Admittedly this biblical man is radically different from the man of Péguy's "modern world", the man who thinks he is free and says so, but finds before him nothing but the void or a countenance with empty eye-sockets speaking the language of the dead. Modern man does not wish to believe, refuses to pray, admits only social and utilitarian laws, thinks the only way of collaborating with nature is by means of vast engineering projects and scientific discoveries and is irritated at the mere idea of being "supported" by an invisible power. But when we see what results this philosophy leads to, what annihilation the process of refusal and negation which we are witnessing is bound to bring with it, the old biblical conception gains by the contrast: it looks exceptionally full of certainty and hope. The Bible is the book of the living God; we know now what it costs to be a man in the age, predicted by a prophet of darkness, when "God is dead".

That is the background against which we must consider the renewed topicality of the Bible; the phenomenon amounts to a protest. It corresponds to an anguish, an expectation. This, too, was predicted in the Bible. "A time is coming, says the Lord God, when there shall be great lack in the land, yet neither dearth nor drought. Hunger? Ay, they shall hunger for some message from the Lord" (Amos 8. 11). And that time of great hunger has come.

TRESSERVE, SUMMER 1955.

TABLE OF CONCORDANT PASSAGES IN THE GOSPELS

1. The healing of the paralytic at Capharnaum

Matt. 9. 1–8	Mark 2. 1–12	Luke 5. 17–26
So he took ship across the sea, and came to his own city. And now they brought before him a man who was palsied and bedridden; whereupon Jesus, seeing their faith, said to the palsied man, Son, take courage, thy sins are forgiven. And at this, some of the scribes said to themselves, He is talking blasphemously. Jesus read their minds, and said, Why do you cherish wicked thoughts in your hearts? Tell me, which command is more lightly given, to say to a man, Thy sins are forgiven, or to say, Rise up, and walk? And now, to convince you that the Son of Man has authority to forgive sins while he is on earth (here he spoke to the palsied man), Rise up, take thy bed with thee, and go home. And he rose up, and went back to his house, so that the multitudes were filled with awe at seeing it, and praised	Then, after some days, he went into Capharnaum again. And as soon as word went round that he was in a house there, such a crowd gathered that there was no room left even in front of the door; and he preached the word to them. And now they came to bring a palsied man to him, four of them carrying him at once; and found they could not bring him close to, because of the multitude. So they stripped the tiles from the roof over the place where Jesus was, and made an opening; then they let down the bed on which the palsied man lay. And Jesus, seeing their faith, said to the palsied man, Son, thy sins are forgiven. But there were some of the scribes sitting there, who reasoned in their minds, Why does he speak so? He is talking blasphemously. Who can forgive sins but God, and God only? Jesus knew at once, in	It chanced one day that he was teaching, and that some Pharisees and teachers of the law were sitting by, who had come from every village in Galilee, and Judaea, and Jerusalem; and the power of the Lord was there, to grant healing. Just then, some men brought there on a bed one who was palsied, whom they tried to carry in and set down in Jesus' presence. But, finding no way of carrying him in, because of the multitude, they went up on to the housetop, and let him down between the tiles, bed and all, into the clear space in front of Jesus. And he, seeing their faith, said, Man, thy sins are forgiven thee. Whereupon the Pharisees and scribes fell to reasoning thus, Who can this be, that he talks so blasphemously? Who can forgive sins but God and God only? Jesus knew of these secret thoughts of theirs, and said to

God for giving such powers to men.

St Matthew cuts the story short; St Mark, followed to a large extent by St Luke, is much more vivid and circumstantial.

his spirit, of these secret thoughts of theirs, and said to them, Why do you reason thus in your minds? Which command is more lightly given, to say to the palsied man, Thy sins are forgiven, or to say, Rise up, take thy bed with thee, and walk? And now, to convince you that the Son of Man has authority to forgive sins while he is on earth (here he spoke to the palsied man): I tell thee, rise up, take thy bed with thee, and go home. And he rose up at once, and took his bed, and went out in full sight of them, so that all were astonished and gave praise to God; they said, We never saw the like.

them openly, Why do you reason thus in your hearts? Which command is more lightly given, to say, Thy sins are forgiven thee, or to say, Rise up and walk? And now, to convince you that the Son of Man has power to forgive sins while he is on earth (here he spoke to the palsied man), I tell thee, rise up, take thy bed with thee and go home. And he rose up at once in full sight of them, took up his bedding, and went home, giving praise to God. Astonishment came over them all, and they praised God, full of awe; We have seen strange things, they said, to-day.

2. The healing of the woman with an issue of blood and the raising of Jairus' daughter

Matt. 9. 18–26	Mark 5. 21–43	Luke 8. 40–56
While he thus spoke to them, it chanced that one of the rulers came and knelt before him, and said, Lord, my daughter is this moment dead; come now and lay thy hand on her, and she will live. So Jesus rose up and went after him, and so did his disciples. And now a woman who for twelve years had been troubled with an issue of blood, came up be-	So Jesus went back by boat across the sea, and a great multitude gathered about him; and while he was still by the sea, one of the rulers of the synagogue came up, Jairus by name, and fell down at his feet when he saw him, pleading for his aid. My daughter, he said, is at the point of death; come and lay thy hand on her, that so she may recover, and	When Jesus returned, he found the multitude there to greet him; they had all been awaiting him. And now a man named Jairus, who was a ruler of the synagogue, came and fell at Jesus' feet, imploring him to come to his house, for he had an only daughter about twelve years old, who was dying. It happened that, as he went, the multitude pressed about him closely. And

hind him and touched the hem of his cloak; she said to herself, If I can even touch the hem of his cloak, I shall be healed. Jesus turned and caught sight of her; and he said, Have no fear, my daughter, thy faith has brought thee healing. And the woman recovered her health from that hour. So Jesus came into the ruler's house, where he found mourners playing the flute, and the multitude thronging noisily; and he said, Make room there; the child is not dead, she is asleep; and they laughed aloud at him. But when the multitude had been turned away, he went in and took the girl by the hand, and she rose up. And the story of these doings spread abroad through all the country round.

Three accounts very characteristic of the evangelists' styles: Matthew dry and colourless; Mark extraordinarily concrete, lifelike and moving; Luke more delicate and sober.

live. So he turned aside with him, and a great multitude followed him, and pressed close upon him. And now a woman who for twelve years had had an issue of blood, and had undergone much from many physicians, spending all she had on them, and no better for it, but rather grown worse, came up behind Jesus in the crowd (for she had been told of him), and touched his cloak; If I can even touch his cloak, she said to herself, I shall be healed. And immediately the source of the bleeding dried up, and she felt in her body that she had been cured of her affliction. Jesus thereupon, inwardly aware of the power that had proceeded from him, turned back towards the multitude and asked, Who touched my garments? His disciples said to him, Canst thou see the multitude pressing so close about thee, and ask, Who touched me? But he looked round him to catch sight of the woman who had done this. And now the woman, trembling with fear, since she recognized what had befallen her, came and fell at his feet, and told him the whole truth. Whereupon Jesus said to her,

a woman who for twelve years had had an issue of blood, and had spent all her money on doctors without finding one who could cure her, came up behind and touched the hem of his cloak; and suddenly her issue of blood was stanched. Then Jesus said, Who touched me? All disclaimed it; Master, said Peter and his companions, the multitudes are hemming thee in and crowding upon thee, and canst thou ask, Who touched me? But Jesus said, Somebody touched me; I can tell that power has gone out from me. And the woman, finding that there was no concealment, came forward trembling and fell at his feet, and so told him before all the people of her reason for touching him, and of her sudden cure. And he said to her, My daughter, thy faith has brought thee recovery; go in peace.

While he was yet speaking, a messenger came to the ruler of the synagogue, to say, Thy daughter is dead; do not trouble the Master. Jesus heard it, and said to him openly, Do not be afraid; thou hast only to believe, and she will recover. When he reached the house, he would not let anyone come in with him,

My daughter, thy faith has brought thee recovery; go in peace, and be rid of thy affliction.

While he was yet speaking messengers came from the ruler's house to say, Thy daughter is dead; why does thou trouble the Master any longer? Jesus heard the word said, and told the ruler of the synagogue, No need to fear; thou hast only to believe. And now he would not let anyone follow him, except Peter and James and James' brother John; and so they came to the ruler's house, where he found a great stir, and much weeping and lamentation. The child is not dead, she is asleep. They laughed aloud at him; but he sent them all out, and, taking the child's father and mother and his own companions with him went in to where the child lay. Then he took hold of the child's hand, and said to her, Talitha, cumi, which means, Maiden, I say to thee, rise up. And the girl stood up immediately, and began to walk; she was twelve years old. And they were beside themselves with wonder. Then he laid a strict charge on them to let (*continued in column 3*)

except Peter and James and John, and the child's father and mother. All were weeping and bewailing her, There is no need to weep, he told them; she is not dead, she is asleep. And they laughed aloud at him, well knowing that she was dead. But he took her by the hand, and called aloud, Rise up, maiden, and she rose up there and then with life restored to her. He ordered that she be given something to eat, and warned her parents, who were beside themselves with wonder, to let no one hear of what had befallen.

nobody hear of this, and ordered that she should be given something to eat.

3. The blind men of Jericho

Matt. 20. 29–34

When they were leaving Jericho, there was a great multitude that followed him. And there, by the road side, sat two blind folk, who heard of Jesus' passing by, and cried aloud, Lord, son of David, have pity on us. The multitude rebuked them, bidding them be silent; but they cried out all the more, Son of David, Lord, have pity on us. Then Jesus stopped, and called them to him; What would you have me do for you? He asked. Lord, they said to him, we would have our eyes opened. And Jesus, moved with compassion, touched their eyes, and immediately they recovered their sight, and followed after him.

Same comments as for the preceding account. It will be noticed, moreover, that the three accounts do not agree in small details: entering or leaving Jericho; one or two blind men (it is true that St Matthew's plural is perhaps purely literary). It is one of those cases in which the traditions followed by the evangelists preserve only the approximate facts.

Mark 10. 46–52

And now they reached Jericho. As he was leaving Jericho, with his disciples and with a great multitude, Bartimaeus, the blind man, Timaeus' son, was sitting there by the way side, begging. And hearing that this was Jesus of Nazareth, he fell to crying out, Jesus, son of David, have pity on me. Many of them rebuked him and told him to be silent, but he cried out all the more, Son of David, have pity on me. Jesus stopped, and bade them summon him; so they summoned the blind man; Take heart, they said, and rise up; he is summoning thee. Whereupon he threw away his cloak and leapt to his feet, and so came to Jesus. Then Jesus answered him, What wouldst thou have me do for thee? And the blind man said to him, Lord, give me back my sight. Jesus said to him, Away home with thee; thy faith has brought thee recovery. And all at once he recovered his sight, and followed Jesus on his way.

Luke 18. 35–42

When he came near Jericho, there was a blind man sitting there by the way side begging. And he, hearing a multitude passing by, asked what it meant; so they told him, that Jesus of Nazareth was going past. Whereupon he cried out, Jesus, son of David, have pity on me. Those who were in front rebuked him, and told him to be silent, but he cried out all the more, Son of David, have pity on me. Then Jesus stopped, and gave orders that the man should be brought to him; and when he came close, he asked him, What wouldst thou have me do for thee? Lord, he said, give me back my sight. Jesus said to him, Receive thy sight; thy faith has brought thee recovery. And at once the man recovered his sight, and followed him, glorifying God; all the people, too, gave praise to God at seeing it.

4. Quadruple synopsis (examples of this are rare except in the story of the Passion)

First multiplication of bread

Matt. 14. 13–21	Mark 6. 30–44	Luke 9. 10–17	John 6. 1–15
Jesus, when he had heard it, took ship from the place where he was, and withdrew into desert country, to be alone; but the multitudes from the towns heard of it, and followed him there by land. So, when he disembarked, he found a great multitude there, and he took pity on them, and healed those who were sick. And now it was evening, and his disciples came to him and said, This is a lonely place, and it is past the accustomed hour; give the multitudes leave to go into the villages and buy themselves food there. But Jesus told them, There is no need for them to go away; it is for you to give them food to eat. They answered, We have nothing with us, except	And now the apostles came together again in the presence of Jesus, and told him of all they had done, and all the teaching they had given. And he said to them, Come away into a quiet place by yourselves, and rest a little. For there were many coming and going, and they scarcely had leisure even to eat. So they took ship, and went to a lonely place by themselves. But many saw them going, or came to know of it; gathering from all the cities, they hurried to the place by land, and were there before them. So, when he disembarked, Jesus saw a great multitude there, and took pity on them, since they were like sheep that had no shepherd, and began to give them long instruction. And	And now the apostles came back and told Jesus of all they had done. And he retired, taking them with him, to a desert place in the Bethsaida country, where they could be alone. But the multitudes heard of it, and followed him; so he gave them welcome, and spoke to them of the kingdom of God, and cured those who were in need of healing. And now the day began to wear on; and the twelve came and said to him, Give the multitudes leave to go to the villages and farms round about, so that they can find lodging and food; we are in desert country here. But he told them, It is for you to give them food to eat. We have no more, they said, than five loaves and two fishes, unless	After this, Jesus retired across the sea of Galilee, or Tiberias, and there was a great multitude following him; they had seen the miracles he performed over the sick. So Jesus went up on to the hill-side, and there sat down with his disciples. It was nearly the time of the Jews' great feast, the paschal feast. And now, lifting up his eyes and seeing that a great multitude had gathered round him, Jesus said to Philip, Whence are we to buy bread for these folk to eat? In saying this, he was putting him to the test; he himself knew well enough what he meant to do. Philip answered him, Two hundred silver pieces would not buy enough bread for them, even to give each a little. One of his disciples (it

five loaves and two fishes. Bring them to me here, he said; then he told the multitudes to sit down on the grass, and when the five loaves and the two fishes were brought to him he looked up to heaven, blessed and broke the loaves, and gave them to his disciples; and the disciples gave them to the multitude. All ate and had enough, and when they picked up what was left of the broken pieces they filled twelve baskets with them; about five thousand men had eaten, not reckoning women and children.

when it was already late, his disciples came to him and said, This is a lonely place, and it is late already; give them leave to go to the farms and villages round about, and buy themselves food there; they have nothing to eat. But he answered them, It is for you to give them food to eat. Why then, they said to him, we must go and spend two hundred silver pieces buying bread to feed them. He asked, How many loaves have you? Go and see. When they had found out, they told him, Five, and two fishes. Then he told them all to sit down in companies on the green grass; and they took their places in rows, by hundreds and fifties. And he took the five loaves and two fishes, and looked up to heaven, and blessed and broke the loaves, and gave these to his disciples to set before them,

thou wouldst have us go ourselves and buy food for all this assembly. About five thousand men were gathered there. So he said to his disciples, Make them sit down by companies of fifty; and they did this, bidding all of them sit down. Then he took the five loaves and the two fishes, and looked up to heaven, and blessed them, and broke, and gave them to his disciples, to set before the multitudes. All ate and had their fill, and when what they left over was picked up, it filled twelve baskets.

was Andrew, Simon Peter's brother) said to him, There is a boy here, who has five barley loaves and two fishes; but what is that among so many? Then Jesus said, Make the men sit down. There was no lack of grass where they were; so the men sat down, about five thousand in number. And Jesus took the loaves, and gave thanks, and distributed them to the company, and a share of the fishes too, as much as they had a mind for. Then, when they had all had enough, he told his disciples, Gather up the broken pieces that are left over, so that nothing may be wasted. And when they gathered them up, they filled twelve baskets with the broken pieces left over by those who had eaten. When they saw the miracle Jesus had done, these men began to say, Beyond doubt, this is the dividing the fishes, too, among them all. All ate and had enough: and when they took up the broken pieces, and what was left of the fishes, they filled twelve baskets with them. The loaves had fed five thousand men.

prophet who is to come into the world.

St John is never content to reproduce the accounts of the synoptics; he adds details omitted by them which are always full of interest.

SELECT BIBLIOGRAPHY

See also other volumes in this part of the series. Works by non-Catholic writers are marked with an asterisk

1. *English Translations of the Bible.*

   Rheims-Douay Version. There are many editions of this standard translation.

   KNOX, R. A.: *A New Translation From the Latin Vulgate,* Burns Oates, London, Sheed and Ward, New York, 1956.

   Westminster Version (ed. C. Lattey, S.J.). A translation from the original tongues which began in 1913. The N.T. was completed in 1935; the O.T. is still appearing. The N.T. and Psalms are embodied in *The Catholic Bible in the St. Peters' Edition,* published by Hawthorn Books, New York, 1958.

   New Testament. Translation by James A. Kleist and Joseph L. Lilly. (Bruce, Milwaukee, Wis., 1954).

   Confraternity Version. An American translation. The New Testament published in 1941 is an extensive revision of Challoner's edition of the Rheims version. The Old Testament is a translation from the original tongues which began with Genesis in 1948 and is not yet complete (St Anthony Guild Press, Paterson, N. J.).

2. *Introductions to the Bible.*

   A. General

   ROBERT, A., and TRICOT, A.: *Guide to the Bible. An Introduction to the Study of Holy Scripture,* trans. from the French, two volumes (Newman, Westminster, Md, 1955).

   STEINMUELLER, J. E.: *A Companion to Scripture Studies,* three volumes (Wagner, New York, 1941, 1942).

   POELMAN, R.: *How to Read the Bible* trans. from the French (Kenedy, New York, 1953).

   B. Old Testament

   JONES, A.: *Unless Some Man Show Me* (Burns Oates, London and Sheed and Ward, New York, 1951).

   McKENZIE, J. L., S.J.: The Two-Edged Sword (Bruce, 1956).

   C. New Testament

   LAGRANGE, M. J.: *The Gospel of Jesus Christ* trans. from the French (Newman, Westminster, Md, 1943).

WARD, M.: *They Saw His Glory. An Introduction to the Gospels and Acts* (Sheed and Ward, London and New York, 1956).

3. *Commentaries.*

A Catholic Commentary on Holy Scripture. Contains a commentary on every book of the Bible, thirty-four introductory articles on every aspect of biblical studies and extensive bibliographies. (Nelson, London, and New York, 1953).

KNOX, R. A.: *A New Testamentary Commentary for English Readers,* three volumes (Burns Oates, London and Sheed and Ward, New York, 1953–6).

VAWTER, BRUCE: *A Path Through Genesis* (Sheed and Ward, 1956).

4. *Encyclicals and other official Church documents.*

Providentissimus Deus, 1893.

Spiritus Paraclitus, 1920.

Divino afflante Spiritu, 1943. Published as a pamphlet by the Catholic Truth Society, London, which also publishes a number of other pamphlets on biblical subjects. All the encyclicals on biblical subjects are printed in Vol. I of Steinmuller's *Companion to Scripture Studies.*

Enchiridion Biblicum. Documenta Ecclesiastica Sacram Scripturam spectantia. Auct. Pont. Comm. de re Biblica, Rome, 1954.

5. *Manuscripts of the Bible.*

*KENYON, SIR F.: *The Story of the Bible* (John Murray, London, 1936, Dutton, New York).

*KENYON, SIR F.: *Our Bible and the Ancient Manuscripts* (Eyre and Spottiswoode, London, 1958).

*KENYON, SIR F.: *The Bible and Modern Scholarship* (John Murray, London, 1948).

6. *Historical Background.*

*ALBRIGHT, W. F.: *The Archaeology of Palestine* (Penguin Books, London and Baltimore, 1949).

DANIEL-ROPS: *Israel and the Ancient World,* trans. from the French (Longmans, London and New York, 1949).

DANIEL-ROPS: *Jesus in his Time,* trans. from the French (Burns Oates, London, 1955, Dutton, New York).

7. *Geographical Background.*

GROLLENBERG, L. H.: *Atlas of the Bible,* trans. and ed. by H. H. Rowley and Joyce M. H. Reid (Nelson, London and New York, 1956).

*MORTON, H. V.: *In the Steps of the Master* (Methuen, London, 1934, Dodd, New York).

*MORTON, H. V.: *In the Steps of St Paul* (Methuen, London, 1936, Dodd, New York).

8. *Concordances and Harmonies.*

THOMPSON, N., and STOCK, R.: *Complete Concordance to the Bible in the Douay Version* (Herder, St. Louis, 1942).

LAGRANGE, M. J., adapted by J. M. T. Barton: *A Catholic Harmony of the Gospels* (Burns Oates, London, 1930).

9. *The Synoptic Problem.*

BUTLER, B. C.: *The Originality of St Matthew. A Critique of the Two-Document Hypothesis* (Cambridge Univ. Press, Cambridge and New York, 1951).

10. *Dead Sea Scrolls.* There is already a vast literature on this subject, much of it based on unsound scholarship or coloured by anti-Christian prejudice. The books listed here provide a balanced introduction.

MURPHY, ROLAND E.: *The Dead Sea Scrolls and the Bible* (Newman, Westminster, Md., 1957).

*ROWLEY, H. H.: *The Dead Sea Scrolls and their Significance.* A small booklet giving an account of the finds and a brief review of the various interpretations of their significance up to Nov. 1954.

(Independent Press, London, Allenson, New York, 1955).

*ROWLEY, H. H.: *The Dead Sea Scrolls and the New Testament* (S.P.C.K., London, 1957).

GRAYSTONE, G.: *The Dead Sea Scrolls and the Originality of Christ* (Sheed and Ward, London and New York, 1956).

See also the volume on the subject of the Dead Sea Scrolls appearing in this series.

WHAT IS CANON LAW?

IS VOLUME

80

OF THE

Twentieth Century Encyclopedia of Catholicism

UNDER SECTION

VIII

THE ORGANIZATION OF THE CHURCH

IT IS ALSO THE

34TH

VOLUME IN ORDER OF PUBLICATION

Edited by *HENRI DANIEL-ROPS of the Académie Française*

WHAT IS CANON LAW?

By RENÉ METZ

Translated from the French by MICHAEL DERRICK

HAWTHORN BOOKS · PUBLISHERS · New York

First Edition, January, 1960
Second Printing, February, 1962

NIHIL OBSTAT

Andreas Moore, L.C.L.

   Censor Deputatus

IMPRIMATUR

E. Morrogh Bernard

   Vicarius Generalis

Westmonasterii, die XXIV OCTOBRIS MCMLIX

CONTENTS

INTRODUCTION

Most people are badly or not at all informed about the legislation of the Church, and the clergy for their part are inclined
to be uncommunicative if the conversation turns to canon
law, a subject which gives the appearance of being enveloped
in mystery. It is sometimes said that canon law conjures up
in some minds the idea of the Inquisition. It is difficult to say
why this should be so, for there is no sort of justification for
such an association; on the contrary, the purpose of canon
law is to protect particular interests against any arbitrary
action on the part of superior interests; it is not an instrument
of subjection but a guarantee of individual liberty.

It is our intention in this book to provide a general outline
of the law of the Church as it is today. Fully to understand
the present-day law it would be necessary to go back to the
earliest centuries and to glance in turn at the successive landmarks in the history of ecclesiastical law and institutions.
That is the only way of making it clear that that law is a living
reality, for there is almost always a dramatic tale to tell about
the origins of juridical decision. All the law does is to record
in formal terms the solution which brought a dispute to an
end after years of uncertainty; clear and straightforward, it
shows at first sight not the least trace of the conflict which
brought it about. A recent illustration is provided by the
priest-workers of France, whose position gave rise to so much
discussion. The Holy See has now definitely ended the experi-
ment and instructed the French bishops to seek new means to
the same missionary end. In considering the terms of this
ruling it is unlikely that many will remember the dramas and
conflicts of conscience that led up to it. So it is also with all

juridical institutions; they come to life if one takes the trouble
to trace them to their sources. Any complete account of the
law of the Church demands an excursion into history, to
bring to life the drama which lies at the origins of its various
provisions.

It would likewise be necessary to introduce the reader to
the archives and libraries of the abbeys, bishoprics and universities of the Middle Ages, to show him certain ancient
collections of the laws of the Church compiled at Rome and
in Italy from the fifth century onwards, and then in Spain
and in the lands of the Franks: The Dionysiana, the Hispana,
the Hadriana, the False Decretals, the Decree of Burchard of
Worms, the Gregorian collections and those of Chartres. After
the first decades of the twelfth century we should have to
pause to look attentively at the collections which later on
were to constitute the *Corpus juris canonici*: the *Decretum* of
Gratian (about 1130–40), the Decretals of Gregory IX (1234),
the *Liber Sextus* of Boniface VIII (1298), the *Clementinae*
(1317), the *Extravagantes* of John XXII and the *Extravagantes communes*.

Such a programme of study is very attractive, but we have
had to forgo it for the simple reason that it could not be
satisfactorily carried out within the limitations of space imposed upon us. The size of the book left a choice between
two alternatives, it being our task to introduce the reader to
the present-day law of the Church. We could devote the first
part of the book to the history of canon law and the second
to that law as it is today; or alternatively we could sacrifice
the history and deal only with the law as it is today. We have
chosen the second course, not because it is any easier, and
not from preference, but because we judged that this was the
only way of giving the reader a general survey, incomplete
though it may be, of the legal system of the Church. If we
had chosen the first plan we should not have been able to do
more than give the barest bones both of the history of canon
law and of the present legislative system. We have preferred

to treat only one aspect, the contemporary law, to avoid having to reduce what we say to a too superficial level, which is the risk that we should have incurred in deciding for the former solution.

In a brief introductory chapter we raise the delicate problem that the law of the Church presents. The account which follows is divided into two parts. The first part deals with theoretical questions concerning canon law, since the very title of the book emphasizes that it is about the law. The second part is devoted to the subjects of ecclesiastical legislation; in this we make a comprehensive survey of the law and juridical institutions of the Church. By way of a conclusion we shall show what interest in the canon law there is in the twentieth century.

It seems useful to define some of the terms of which we shall make use in the course of this study and which are possibly not familiar to all readers: ordinary, residential bishop, titular bishop, abbot and prelate *nullius*, vicar and prefect apostolic, major superior.

The term ordinary refers in general to all those who enjoy the power of government (jurisdiction) *in foro externo*—that is, in the field of public behaviour as opposed to *in foro interno*, the field of conscience. These are the pope in the whole Church; in the diocese the residential bishop and the vicar general; in missionary countries the vicar or prefect apostolic and the vicar general who has the title of pro-vicar or pro-prefect; in abbacies and prelatures *nullius* the abbot or prelate *nullius* and the vicar general. In the exempt religious institutes of priests—exempt, that is to say, from episcopal jurisdiction; religious institutes dependent upon the Holy See —the ordinary is the religious who bears the title of major superior. The term ordinary without qualification refers to all in this list. The expression "ordinary of the place" refers to the same persons, with the exception of the religious superiors, who do not possess territorial jurisdiction but only personal jurisdiction. In the following pages we have so far as possible avoided the term ordinary and have used instead the word bishop, which is easier to recognize and understand, even though in some cases it may be less precise; we imagine the specialists will not judge us too severely for this.

The residential bishop is the prelate at the head of a fully active diocese; the titular bishop is a prelate appointed by the pope to one of the ancient episcopal sees that survive as honorary titles, where the people were once Catholic but where the territory passed long ago to unbelievers, so that they are now sees *in partibus infidelium*. Coadjutor and auxiliary bishops are "titulars" of these ancient sees.

Prelates *nullius* and abbots *nullius* are priests—sometimes bishops—who govern a small piece of autonomous territory, not dependent upon any diocese; whence the word *nullius*, the word *dioecesis* being understood. There has been a prelature *nullius* in France since 1954: that of Pontigny (with one parish), which is entrusted to the *Mission de France*. In Switzerland, to give another example, there is the abbey *nullius* of Einsiedeln. There are no prelatures *nullius* in Britain or the United States, but there are many in Latin America, especially in Brazil.

Vicars and prefects apostolic govern missionary territories. As a general rule a vicar apostolic receives episcopal consecration and a titular see but a prefect apostolic does not.

A major superior, in centralized religious institutes, is the religious who is responsible for a number of religious houses: provincials and superiors general have the right to the title of major superior, together with their deputies. In the monastic orders, in which the monasteries have kept some degree of autonomy, the various abbots have likewise the right to the title of major superior. But the status of an ordinary is reserved to the major superiors of the religious institutes which are exempt from the jurisdiction of the bishop and in which most of the religious are priests: the Benedictines, the Franciscans, the Redemptorists, the Jesuits and so on. The major superiors of religious institutes in which most of the religious are not priests do not have the right to the title of ordinary:

this is the case, for example, with the provincials and the superior general of the Brothers of the Christian Schools. It is the case also with the major superiors of the religious institutes which are not exempt from episcopal jurisdiction, even if all their religious are ordained priests; but these institutes are very few.

CHAPTER I

THE JUSTIFICATION AND ORIGINALITY OF THE LAW OF THE CHURCH

The Catholic Church has her legal provisions: she has her law. She has a well-arranged, complete and up-to-date juridical system.

Is this a sign of strength, or, on the contrary, a sign of weakness? Of greatness or of poverty? Are Catholics proud of the juridical institutions of the Church, or, on the contrary, are they inclined to be embarrassed, to have a sort of complex about them?

This is so serious a question that it must be faced at the very outset of an account of the laws of the Church. No Catholic can be indifferent to the issues in this debate. It distresses many Catholics who are deeply attached to the Church; they have not found the opportunity or the courage to get to grips with this infidelity. The problem concerns the very structure of the Catholic Church; it is fundamental. This is one more reason for opening the discussion without reservations; the truth shall set us free.

THE REASON FOR CANON LAW

The Church is accused of being a juridical institution and not a saving institution. More specifically, it is said that from a community of faith, such as she may originally have been, she has become a juridical community. The reproach is directed against her by our contemporaries, but it is by no means peculiar to our times. As early as the fifteenth century she was afflicted by it; and there is no reason to think that the Catholic Church will be treated with less severity in the centuries to come.

With her law, it is said, the Church traffics in the work of salvation. She makes a business out of the supernatural. Her legalism leads infallibly to formalism.

We must begin by acknowledging that the attitude and the actions of certain members of the Church, in the past as in the present, all too often justify these accusations. The chronicles of the Middle Ages provide disedifying examples enough of the traffic in relics and indulgences; men dared to translate years in purgatory into financial terms. And how many Catholics are there at the present time who regard their religious obligations as purely material observances in which the soul has no part? Assistance at Sunday Mass and the Easter confession and communion have become altogether external acts which they perform because the laws of the Church oblige them to do so. They observe the requirements of a code, that of the Church, so that their account in the next world may be on the credit side; thus do certain Catholics regard the work of salvation.

We should blame not the institution but the men. The institution cannot be perfect. It has had its imperfections in all periods, and it will have them until the end of time: quite simply, because we are at the meeting-place of the finite and the infinite, the created and the uncreated, the human and the divine.

Christ entrusted the work of salvation to the Church—that is, to men. Because of this, he gave the Church roots in history and made her subject to all temporal contingencies. It is in the Church and through the Church that men must in principle attain their supernatural destiny. To speak of the Church is to speak of a society. And a society requires at least some organization. Unless it is made up of angels—and what should we know about it then?—no society can survive without rules. There must be a certain order if we are not to have disorder, or even anarchy. But man is often too much of an individualist to accept without any reservation arrangements imposed upon him by his fellow-men, even if they have received their mandate from God. He will always tend to follow his own fancies. A means of defence against individual whims will be necessary. Moreover, a society cannot do without resources; it must be able to meet its expenses, it must provide for the subsistence of its ministers. But the danger of trafficking immediately lies in wait for it; strict control will be necessary, supported when need be by sanctions. Finally, the activities of a society necessitate a certain exterior display; it needs buildings, assembly places. Hence a society becomes involved in all the complex machinery of public administration, and sooner or later it will be assailed by the temptations of power. Only through an unrelaxing vigilance can undue harm be avoided.

When he entrusted the work of salvation to a society composed of mortal men Christ accepted all these risks in advance. In practice, he obliged his Church to organize herself, to control the orthodoxy of her members, to protect herself against factions; he obliged her, in short, to furnish herself with a code of laws, with all the humiliating consequences that that entails. This was to associate a juridical organization with the community of faith, but it was not to reduce the community of faith to a legal institution. The distinction is an important one.

The Founder of the Church in fact indicated some elements of such an order. He preached the good news to his contemporaries, but he did not leave to the arbitrary will of those who heard him the task of communicating his message to future generations. He gave that task to a band of men, chosen with much prudence and wisdom. The Twelve were very clearly aware of their responsibility, and after the Master had left them they acted with authority, and took the decisions which were necessary when it was a question, for example, of deciding the conditions of admission to the Church. From apostolic times the beginnings of the law of the Church became apparent; St Paul played the leading part in working it out. The Christian community increased in numbers, its members being found in all the Mediterranean countries. The first organization was soon not enough and had to be extended. The hierarchy was developed, and new states of life came into existence as, together with the simple faithful and the ministers of the young Church, men and women responded to Christ's appeal which commended perfect chastity to them. It became necessary to define their place in the community.

This organization was still clearly only in its beginnings. It was very primitive. Some have declined to recognize the characteristics of law in it, saying that the Church of the first centuries was guided only by grace and the charismata. A German university professor of the last century, Rudolf Sohm, devoted all his undoubtedly considerable talent to the service of this cause, striving, with logic of some force, to show that in its beginnings the Church knew nothing of any law. According to him it was very much later that she burdened herself with a code of laws. He even placed as late as the twelfth century the birth of what he called the juridical Church, which was no longer in accordance with the intentions of her Founder.

Sohm started from an *a priori* conclusion and brought out its implications with implacable logic, and he is therefore not easy to refute if one accepts his starting-point. But therein lies the whole problem. That is why Sohm's reasoning has not been followed even by his Protestant colleagues. The fallacy lies in the way law is conceived. It goes without saying that the Church of the first centuries had no precisely defined juridical system, still less any technique or science of law. But all the elements of a true juridical system were present. The authorities made rules and demanded their strict application. Councils did not spare those who made trouble and did not hesitate to impose very severe sanctions on those who were not amenable to discipline.

In the fourth century the Council of Nicaea (325) calls canons the disciplinary measures of the Church; the term canon, κανών, means, in Greek, a rule. There is therefore a very early distinction between the rules enacted by the Church (*canones*; κανόνες) and the legislative measures taken by the State, called νόμοι, *leges*. Hence came the practice in the western Church of speaking of the law of the Church as the *jus canonum* or *jus canonicum*. The expression has been in general use since the high Middle Ages. Canon law means the legislation of the Church. Writers some centuries later use another expression again: *jus ecclesiasticum*, ecclesiastical law. The two terms, canon law and ecclesiastical law, were then interchangeable until the twentieth century, and so they remain at the present time, although a distinction is beginning to be made. Among informed writers canon law refers now to the whole corpus of legislative texts enacted by the Church and ecclesiastical law to all legislative texts concerning the Church promulgated by civil authorities.

The emerging law of the earliest times developed in proportion as the needs of the ecclesiastical society grew. Since the twelfth century there has existed a wise juridical system which amid all the good and bad periods in the history of the Church has constantly adapted itself to the circumstances of the time, up to this present day. The code of laws of which the Church disposes in no way detracts from the dignity of the Church. It is certainly a sign of weakness, but of a weakness for which the Church is not responsible; its explanation is to be sought in the fallen state of men. If we were pure spirits the community of faith could live without rules. Since salvation is for all men born of human flesh, the Church has not been at fault in her mission; she has remained faithful in principle to the intentions of her Founder in supporting the community of faith with juridical institutions.

Finally, it must not be forgotten that the Church is not to be identified with her legislative texts. The Church indeed has laws, but she has very much else besides. The Church has within her riches of another order and another value than her canons. She has her theology, her mysticism, her liturgy, her morality. And it is important not to confuse the Gospel and the Code, theology and legislation, morality and jurisprudence. They are on different levels. To seek to identify them would be to commit a kind of sacrilege. The legislation is at the service of the Church, at the service of the work of salvation; its function is to guide man in the pursuit of his destiny, and to make its achievement easier for him. Its part is a very modest one in fact, despite misleading appearances. The juridical machinery is only one aspect of the Church, and above all it does not represent the essence of the Church. The Church is the Mystical Body of Christ, but her historical character necessarily brought forth a juridical system and juridical institutions.

Law has its purpose in the Church. It is justified, as we have just shown. But this is a law of a special character, the original nature of which we must now emphasize.

THE ORIGINALITY OF CANON LAW

Canon law differs from secular law because it serves a society which is not like other societies. It is the special character of the Church which gives it its originality.

Conceived and instituted by Christ, the Church is concerned with the next world. She guides men to their salvation, to eternal life. Canon law is called upon to lend its assistance in this work, which is work of an exceptional order. It therefore shares to some extent in the exalted credentials of the Church, and is distinguished from all other systems of law by its purpose, its origin and its scale.

Canon law is essentially concerned with the individual man. The basic object of its attention is the human person, who, according to Christian teaching, is of inestimable worth. Man has been redeemed by the blood of God. Canon law does not

2—W.C.L.

provide the means for raising him up to the divine level which is his destiny; that is the business of the Church as such. But it is for canon law to help man in finding, using and retaining the means of salvation which the Church provides for him.

Modest though this part is, it confers a special dignity on canon law, placing it on a level which helps to emphasize its originality. The specific purpose assigned to the law of the Church is the source of special characteristics not found in other systems of law; we refer especially to the conception of the relations between public law and private law, the distinction between the "internal forum" and the "external forum", sin and crime, the power of order and the power of jurisdiction. A rapid analysis of these various elements will show how this is so.

The Church is a society, is composed of members. What is more important to her, individuals or the community? There is no question but that everything is centred upon the human person. The Church as a society also has duties towards God which must be fulfilled, but in what we may term a secondary manner only; the essential part of her task is to lead each individual man to his supernatural end. Hence the distinction between public law and private law is more difficult to make in canon law than in the legal system of civil societies. In theory, of course, there is no obstacle to the division of canonical institutions into two parts, the public and the private, but when one looks more closely into the matter the division is seen to be not easy; the theory cannot be easily disassociated from the reality. The Church, her constitution, all her administrative structure are at the service of the individual, not the other way round. This does not mean that the Church must meet the interests of one or some of her members to the prejudice of the community as a whole; she does not have to protect individual whims or fancies, but the good of all. Her law is at the service of what is called the common good, provided that that phrase is understood in its specific sense—for its true meaning has often enough been distorted by political regimes during recent decades. It may happen

that the common good conflicts with the particular and immediate interests of a member of the Church. In that event the
individual must yield to the general order, especially if it is a
question of interpreting the divine law, positive or natural.
It is enough to think of marriage; the law of indissolubility
often gives rise to painful situations from which there is no
escape. For many years, generally until the death of the partner in the first marriage, a second union cannot be ratified by
the Church, and the partners to any such second union live
outside the full life of the Catholic community. There are
some to whom this condition is the cause of great suffering;
the Church suffers with them, but cannot do what they want,
because to do so would be to compromise for the sake of two
people the good of the great mass of the members of the
Church. It is still, therefore, for the sake of the good of each
of the members of whom the Church is composed that she is
stern in certain individual cases. The good of the society as
such is a secondary consideration; each member regarded
individually is the object of her constant care, for it is the
salvation of each one that she must ensure.

The assistance which it is for canon law to give the Church
in this task is very delicate. The work of salvation essentially
concerns the soul, and the soul is outside the direct reach of
the legislator. The proper field of law is the exterior field,
called in canonical language the external forum. The field of
the soul or the realm of conscience—in canonical language
the internal forum—is not directly affected by canon law;
at least, not the sacramental "internal forum". The law certainly desires an interior acceptance, as we have said; it is
precisely when acceptance by the soul is incomplete that we
get formalism. But the legislator has enough respect for the
value and the greatness of the human soul to know that it
would be unworthy to intrude in this enclosed field that is
reserved to God and to the confessor to whom God has given
this special commission. It would be almost profane for the
legislator to interfere in the field in which the direct relations
between God and the soul are conducted. Here he denies

himself access. It is the field of morality and not of law, of the confessor and not of the canonist.

So canon law knows nothing of sin. It is concerned with infractions of the law; not with sin but with crime; for that is the word which canonists use for transgressions of canon law. It is not for canon law to judge directly an offence committed against God; there are so many intimate considerations to be taken into account in understanding sin properly so called, which only the confessor has the right to know. But if canon law is not concerned with sin, that is by no means because it gives only a strictly penal character to its laws. On the contrary, it is because it has so great a respect for the intimacy of the relations between the soul and God that it deems it wrong to attempt to force them into the patterns of a juridical system. This is a field in which juridical institutions are not concerned; it is the province of morality. A priest is aware of it only as a confessor, and not as the administrator of a parish. The distinction between the two fields is not always easy to make, the difficulty coming from the fact that in practice the two rôles must often be assumed by the same person: a parish priest is almost always a confessor as well. The work of a confessor brings him into the province of the relations between the soul and God; he is the judge of the offence against the Lord, the judge of sin. The work of a parish priest as such is confined to the external forum, and, at the most, to the non-sacramental internal forum.

We have stressed the need for a clear distinction between law and morality, and the reasons for it, but in doing this it has been very far from our intention to maintain that canon law has only a penal character. The overlapping between the two fields is obvious in everyday life. Canon law does not in practice know any law which does not to some extent appeal to the conscience. It may be said that a purely penal law does not exist in the juridical system of the Church. That is why canon law is not ineffective even if it is not enforced by punishment properly so-called. In the background there are always God's sanctions, there is always sin, even though, in our opinion, the legislator should not have had to avail himself of those sanctions. He would be guilty of an abuse if he made a direct appeal to the sanctions of morality—that is, to sin—in order to give greater weight to his law; that would amount to a sort of supernatural blackmail, opening the way to the worst injustices. A superior may be tempted to appeal to the will of God in order to exact obedience from a subordinate when he ought from the first to take his stand by canonical procedure, thinking that he can in that way spare himself the trouble of invoking the law, which in fact exists for no other purpose than to guarantee the liberties of the subordinate. The appeal to conscience here becomes the easy way out; the superior ought only to take it in the full knowledge of what he is doing, if he does not want to risk weakening and discrediting this supreme argument.

In short, the grandeur of the part played by canon law calls for scrupulous care on the part of the legislator and the authorities responsible for applying the laws. Everything here is a question of nuances—relations between the individual and the community, private law and public law, the internal forum and the external forum, crime and sin.

It is for canon law to help man to attain his supernatural destiny: for his end lies in the next world. It should not be concluded from this that canon law is not concerned with man's temporal well-being. A human being has a body as well as an immortal soul, and the two are intimately related. The old saying is still apposite, about the *mens sana in corpore sano*. That is why the Church, through her law, has always had a regard for the "human good" of her members, while always knowing and recognizing that that duty belongs essentially to the civil power; it is only in a secondary manner that canon law intervenes to promote the material good of man. But it does not neglect that good; history provides the proof of this, and during the past sixty or seventy years the popes have insisted strongly upon it. In the encyclical *Ad Apostolorum Principis* of June 29th, 1958, on the position of the Church in China, Pius XII "recalls once again that it is precisely the doctrine of the Church which exhorts and urges Catholics to cherish a sincere and profound love of their country here on earth, to respect the public authorities, the natural and positive law of God being safeguarded, and to give their generous and fruitful support to every undertaking capable of leading to a true progress, peaceful and orderly, as well as to the true good of the community".

Canon law owes its special character to the special purposes of the Church which it serves. It owes it, in the second place, to its origin. It is based upon divine authority; its assizes are in the next world, not in this. All power in the Church comes from above; the ecclesiastical society is not a democracy. The leaders of the Church, her ministers, do not derive from the people the power with which they are invested; their mandate is from God. Christ entrusted his power to the apostles, who transmitted it to their successors. The Twelve received power in its plenitude from the Master; their disciples inherited it in the same way. In principle nothing has changed through the centuries; the pope and the bishops today, like the apostles, possess in their respective spheres the plenitude of government, which we call the power of jurisdiction: the pope in the universal Church and the bishops in their dioceses. So the division between the legislative power, the executive power and the judicial power, rightly so important in true democracies, is difficult to imagine in the Church. In theory the distinction gives no trouble; it is made in all the treatises and text-books of canon law. But in practice confusion is inevitable; the three powers are combined in the same person. In his diocese a bishop is at once legislator and judge, and is charged with the application of the law and its sanctions. It is true that in most cases the bishop does not exercise his mandate to judge, but entrusts it to one of his subordinates. But this is because he chooses to do so; there is in principle nothing to stop him from taking over the function of his *officialis*. And what is true of the bishop in his diocese is even more true of the pope in the universal Church.

The lack of a sharp distinction between the powers is not the only special characteristic of which canon law must take account: the Church knows, in addition to the power of jurisdiction, another power which has no counterpart in civil societies—the power of Order. Charged to guide men to their salvation, the Church must provide them with the means of salvation, which are the supernatural graces. The power of Order gives the capacity to transmit to others the means of salvation which the Church dispenses. The two powers are distinct: one who has the power of Order does not necessarily have the power of jurisdiction as well, and *vice versa*. A titular bishop possesses the plenitude of the power of Order, but he has no power of jurisdiction. A residential bishop, on the other hand, has both the power of Order and the power of jurisdiction. A parish priest participates in the power of Order and to some degree in the power of jurisdiction. A confessor cannot exercise his functions unless he is endowed with the power of Order, but his power of jurisdiction is restricted to the internal forum.

The third feature which gives canon law its unique character is its geographical extension. Whereas the various systems of secular law are confined to limited areas, the competence of canon law extends to all territories where the Church has her members; practically, therefore, it extends through the whole world. It knows neither frontiers nor differences of race or colour. All men are equal before God, and therefore in the Church, so long as they have not been invested with a particular power of Order or jurisdiction.

Canon law is universal; it is concerned with a vast polyglot multitude representing all the nations and all the races of the globe. But this universality, which is a source of unity, must be offset by a certain diversity. The legislator has an obligation to take account of variations in local conditions, in temperament, in customs. There are some laws that cannot be the same in detail for the Japanese and the French, the Indo-Chinese and the English, the South Africans and the Finns: slight variations are required, which it is easy to introduce in all laws which do not directly interpret the natural or positive divine law. That is why canon law must in principle be very adaptable; and if it is not so then the law must provide the means of making it adaptable in case of need. These opportunities in fact exist; the most usual means is the dispensation, which makes it possible to waive the obligation which the law imposes, whenever for one reason or another it would involve grave disadvantages.

Dispensations figure largely in the law of the Church; civil law is not unfamiliar with them, but they are much more frequently used in the ecclesiastical society. This has indeed been made a reproach against the Church, which has been accused of opportunism. The reproach is unjustified; the universal character of canon law compels frequent recourse to dispensation. We should on the contrary admire that harmony between unity and diversity which canon law achieves.

To the marks of originality in canon law to which we have been drawing attention another characteristic must be added: its enduring quality. The Church has not in principle been affected by the vicissitudes which affect other societies; she is destined to survive even to the end of time. Canon law as such is identified with whatever happens to the Church; its continuance, therefore, can know no other limit in time than that of the human race itself. This does not mean that the laws of the Church are unchangeable; in so far as they do not reflect the divine law, natural or positive, they follow the movement of terrestrial things.

Such are the special characteristics of canon law. It enjoys a privileged state. Its end, its origin, its field of application and its permanence place it above the systems of law of secular societies and give it a dignity all its own. So it was only an apparent difficulty which we raised at the outset in asking whether canon law is a sign of weakness or of greatness in the Church. There is no opposition; the dilemma is resolved in unity.

The Church's need of juridical institutions is the ransom of the human condition. The presence of law in the Church is evidence of the frailty of men; it is a sign of weakness. But that law which temporal contingencies have made necessary is not a system of law like others; it shares in the high dignity of the society of which it is the modest servant. Canon law, in some of its features, reflects both the weakness of mankind and the greatness of God, the one by its origin, and the other by its vocation; two things which accord at the deepest level with the message of Christianity itself.

PART I

THE ORIGIN AND NATURE OF THE LAWS OF THE CHURCH

We have shown that the existence of laws and juridical institutions in the Church is fully justified, and that this system of law has features which distinguish it from all others and which give it its originality. Problems of a more practical interest can have our attention now.

The Church has laws: that is a fact. It is important in the first place to know their origin. It goes without saying that the Church shows the greatest respect for the divine law, natural and positive, which represents the primary source of canon law. The Church is the interpreter of the will of God to the faithful in setting before them in concise form the laws which are contained in Scripture and those which are implicit in human nature. One cannot say that the Church is the author of these laws; she does no more than incorporate them in her legislation and when necessary provide penalties for those who transgress against them. She cannot dispense from these laws, which are outside her power of jurisdiction and which moreover form only a small part of her legislation. They are, therefore, only of secondary interest in this study.

When we raise the problem of the origins of canon law what we have in mind are those numerous prescriptions of which the Church really is the author and which, by that very fact, have the character of human dispositions. The Church that has made them can also unmake them, can dispose of them in whatever way circumstances may seem to make appropriate; she can modify them, suppress them, give dispensations from them in particular cases. She decides the conditions of application, determining the time when they come into force and who are subject to them.

Such, then, are the laws properly to be called the laws of the Church, which will be the object of our study. We shall examine the manner in which they are instituted and applied and eventually modified or abrogated. After this analysis, which will remain somewhat theoretical, we shall assess the legislative work of the Church in modern times. In this we are particularly favoured; for after centuries of hesitation the Church has all at once made an astonishing effort in the legislative field. Within the space of a few decades the law of the Latin Church and of the Eastern Churches has been codified. Since 1917 diocesan synods have been meeting regularly every ten years; assemblies which give the bishops an opportunity to bring forward their diocesan legislation. It is true that particular legislations are of no great interest in this time of great centralization, but they nevertheless deserve to be mentioned, be it only for the sake of completeness.

We shall therefore study in turn the genesis of the canonical laws, their characteristics, and the official collections in which the laws of the Church are contained at the present day.

CHAPTER II

THE GENESIS OF THE LAWS

The Church has laws which are properly of ecclesiastical origin; she is the author of them. We have to determine who in fact enacts these laws; in other words, which are the persons and bodies which hold legislative power in the Church. Then we shall show how these laws are established, that is, made binding and brought to the public knowledge: the manner of their promulgation. Finally, we shall define the part played by custom in contemporary canon law, since that also is a source of laws.

THE HOLDERS OF LEGISLATIVE POWER IN THE CHURCH

It need hardly be said that competence is not the same if it is a question of laws affecting the whole Church or only of laws applicable to a limited area. Hence we must consider separately the authors of universal laws and the authors of particular laws. It is true that the former have authority to intervene within limited areas; they can establish laws peculiar to a given territory. The reverse is not true; persons and bodies whose jurisdiction is limited to one part of Christendom have no power to make laws binding all the members of the Church.

Universal laws

The establishment of universal laws derives in the first place from the authority of the Sovereign Pontiff. The Church is not conceived on democratic lines; her constitution is on the monarchical pattern. Authority is combined in one single person, who reserves power in all its forms to himself—legislative power, judicial power and "executive" or coercive power. The pope enjoys supreme and entire jurisdiction in the universal Church and, contrary to what was affirmed by certain canonists of the seventeenth and eighteenth centuries, in each local Church as well. He is able to make laws binding the whole of Christendom, but he can also make them for a single diocese. The bishop, who is in principle master in his own territory by virtue of the apostolic succession, has no right to resist such a direct intervention in his affairs on the part of the Sovereign Pontiff. Such an intervention is rare, but it is not impossible.

The Sovereign Pontiff receives his plenary powers immediately upon his election. It is in virtue of the newly received office that he enjoys his power; the assembly of cardinals which chooses him does not confer it upon him. As soon as he is elected the pope is in possession of sovereign jurisdiction in the Church, and he retains it for the rest of his life, provided at least that he does not abdicate. He does not depend upon any superior authority, so that it is not within the competence of any body to limit his jurisdiction, still less to deprive him of it or, if such a situation should arise, to receive it from him if he should renounce it.

The field of the pope's legislative power has no other limit than that of the spiritual good of Christendom, and, secondarily, its temporal good if faith or morals are affected, so that alongside the strictly ecclesiastical sphere there is a common ground in which the pope's legislative power has to be exercised in certain circumstances. Marriage is the institution *par excellence* in which spiritual and temporal interests are intertwined.

All universal laws are enacted by the Sovereign Pontiff, either in person or, in his name or with his ratification, by one of the bodies which assist in the government of the Church. Legislative prescriptions emanating directly from the pope personally are known nowadays as apostolic constitutions or decrees *motu proprio*; one speaks briefly of a *motu proprio*. The form of an apostolic constitution is used, as a general rule, for documents of special importance; the form of a *motu proprio* in principle implies a document of a less solemn character. In describing a document as a *motu proprio* the pope shows, as the words indicate, that he has taken on his own initiative the decision which is conveyed; he has not been prompted by a petition, or at any rate he desires to assume full responsibility for it. But too much importance should not be attached to this distinction, for the documents which these two terms, apostolic constitution and *motu proprio*, describe have the same significance from a legislative point of view.

Two bodies, under the authority of the Sovereign Pontiff, hold supreme legislative power in the Church: these are the ecumenical council and the Roman congregations. The dispositions which they enact have the same value as those which come from the pope; they affect all Christendom.

The ecumenical council is an assembly which brings together the representatives of the whole Church. Its purpose is to give its attention to the general interests of Christendom, to debate them, and to take measures to promote the good of the Church throughout the world. It includes participants of two kinds: participants by right, who have to be summoned, and participants who attend not by right but by special invitation on the occasion of each council. The former have a deliberative vote in the meetings—*ius habent suffragii deliberatavi*: these are the cardinals, the residential bishops, the abbots and prelates *nullius*, the abbots general of the monastic congregations and the superiors general of the exempt institutes of priests. To these are added, as a general rule, a certain number of theologians and canonists as participants not of right, who come by invitation and on a consultative basis only.

So as to give the necessary authority to its decisions, the council is endowed with sovereign legislative power in the universal Church. To be legitimate, however, and so to be able to exercise its jurisdiction, it must satisfy various requirements which safeguard the absolute superiority of the pope.

It is for the Sovereign Pontiff to summon the ecumenical council, to preside over it either in person or through a delegate, and to decide what it shall discuss and in what order; if occasion should arise he may transfer, adjourn or dissolve it. If the pope dies the council is at once adjourned and is only able to resume its sessions at the bidding of the new pope. Finally, the decrees of the council only obtain their full and definitive validity when they have been confirmed by the pope; their promulgation is only legitimate when he has explicitly ordered it. These various provisions leave no room for the least doubt about the superiority of the pope over the council. There can, therefore, be no question of appealing from a papal decision to the ecumenical council; the appeal would be without effect. It nevertheless remains true that, within defined limits, the ecumenical council possesses sovereign power over the Universal Church.

As everyone knows, these assemblies are rare, although one is now being convened. There has only been a score in the whole history of the Church. That summoned by John XXIII is in fact the twenty-first ecumenical council in the history of the Church. The twentieth was convened at the Vatican in 1869 and was brought to a premature close by the events of 1870; and that was the first ecumenical council since the sixteenth century, when the Council of Trent was in session from 1545 to 1563. It is easy to understand why these assemblies only meet so seldom. An ecumenical council is a cumbersome affair, not at all easy to arrange; its very convocation presents many difficulties; the debates are not easy, and often not very fruitful. That is why in modern times the papacy has recourse only exceptionally to the great institution of the ecumenical council. To assist in the government of the Church the modern papacy prefers to avail itself of the permanent organizations at its disposal: the Roman congregations.

These congregations, whose origin goes back to the sixteenth century, correspond, broadly speaking, to the ministries of a modern state. They are gathered about the pope, and each specializes in one of the numerous fields with which the pontifical administration has to concern itself—the sacraments, the faith, the discipline of the clergy and the laity, the organization of ecclesiastical territories, religious, the missions, studies, the liturgy, the ceremonial of the pontifical court, the Eastern Church, relations with temporal States. The Roman Curia includes altogether eleven congregations properly so-called.

All these bodies act in the name of the pope, in virtue of the mandate which he has given them, but no important and exceptional step can be taken by them without his being previously informed. In this respect again, therefore, the sovereign province of the Roman Pontiff is assured. But within these limits each congregation in its own sphere possesses jurisdiction over the whole Church. The competence of each is restricted to its particular rôle; it is exclusive, and not cumulative. In the legislative field their activity is shown especially in the Instructions in which each congregation interprets and defines the existing laws in its own field, and in regulations providing for their better application. When circumstances lead them to want to publish new laws, modifying the law of the Code, they must obtain the special authorization of the pope and the agreement of the Commission for the Interpretation of the Code of Canon Law which Benedict XV established on September 15th, 1917: precautions which practical considerations and the necessity of coordination require.

Such are the bodies which, with the Sovereign Pontiff, hold supreme legislative power in the Church, and which can therefore enact universal or general laws. All other persons or institutions which possess legislative power in the Church are restricted in their activity to a defined area or to a group of individuals; they are only entitled to make particular laws, imposing obligations that are limited to the territory of the persons under their jurisdiction.

Special laws

Legislative power limited to special laws belongs to the plenary council, the provincial council, the residential bishops and similar prelates, and to the general chapters of exempt institutes of priests.

A plenary council brings together the representatives of several ecclesiastical provinces. It is not an institution which holds its sessions at regular intervals. Its meeting has an occasional and exceptional character, but it is governed by provisions that are careful to safeguard the sovereign authority of the pope even in this limited field.

The Sovereign Pontiff reserves to himself the right of authorizing the meetings of plenary councils, of deciding or approving the delimitation of the territories whose metropolitans and bishops have made the proposal to meet together in order to take measures in common. More, the pope appoints a legate to whom he gives the commission to convene and preside over the council. Finally, the decrees cannot be promulgated until they have been examined by the Holy See—by the Congregation of the Council—and have received its approval. But, meeting under valid conditions, the assembly has legislative power for the whole of the territory which it represents; the measures which it enacts have the force of law throughout the area. The ordinaries of places within that area can only dispense from them in special cases; they have no power to dispense from them throughout their territories since they are not individually the authors of these laws: it is the council as such which has legislative power and which acts as legislator.

The members of a plenary council by right, in addition to the papal legate, are the metropolitans, residential bishops, diocesan administrators, abbots and prelates *nullius*, vicars and prefects apostolic and vicars capitular of the region; in short, all those prelates who at the time of the council are responsible for autonomous ecclesiastical divisions. The members by right, whose presence is obligatory, have a deliberative vote at the meetings. Others can be summoned—titular bishops residing within the area, canonists, theologians, religious superiors. Titular bishops, if they are summoned, have the right to vote unless the contrary has expressly been decided; the other clergy have only a consultative vote, *suffragio non gaudent nisi consultivo*.

As a general rule, plenary councils are regional assemblies. It is rarely that they bring together all the episcopate of one country and so take on the character of national councils, although there are some examples of national councils to be pointed out in the last century and in the early years of the present century: three councils for the United States of America, at Baltimore in 1852, 1866 and 1884; three for Australia, at Sydney in 1885, 1895 and 1905; one for Canada at Quebec in 1911. Today national councils are not in favour with the Holy See, which remembers unfortunate experiences in the past with certain assemblies of this kind. Yet some plenary councils of a national character met between the two world wars, in China (1924), Portugal (1926), Indochina (1934), Poland (1936) and Brazil (1939).

National plenary councils must not be confused with the regular meetings of the bishops which take place in some countries. These meetings have properly speaking no jurisdiction; they have no legislative power. They are concerned simply with discussing certain questions, issuing directives and making recommendations which do not have the character of legislative measures in the proper sense of the term. They are not what is meant by a plenary council.

The provincial council is a regular and obligatory institution which must meet at least once every twenty years. It brings together the representatives of an ecclesiastical province. It is convened and presided over by the metropolitan archbishop and, if he is prevented or the see is vacant, by the senior suffragan bishop in the order of elevation to the episcopate. It meets preferably at the metropolitan church, but any other place in the territory of the province may be chosen for sufficient reasons. Archbishops, bishops and abbots and prelates *nullius* who do not belong to any metropolitan province are not for that reason exempted from participation in a provincial council. They are attached to the council of a province which they have chosen for this purpose with the approval of the Holy See and by a decision which they cannot subsequently vary. They are not free in their choice, since in principle they must opt for the metropolitan province most closely adjacent to their territory. In France, for example, there are three ordinaries in this position: the Archbishop of Marseilles and the Bishops of Strasbourg and Metz. Marseilles has opted for Aix-en-Provence, and Strasbourg and Metz both for Besançon.

The members by right of the provincial council are in the first place the prelates who at the time of the meeting are governing autonomous territories within the province (residential bishops and abbots and prelates *nullius*, and perhaps vicars capitular and diocesan administrators apostolic) together with those governing territories which do not belong to a metropolitan province and are therefore attached to the council; all these members have a deliberative vote. A second category of members by right is composed of two representatives of each cathedral chapter or, where there is no chapter, of the college of diocesan consultors; of the major superiors of the exempt religious institutes of priests; and of the superiors of the monastic congregations. These members are not allowed to vote. Other members of the secular or regular clergy may be invited to attend, but likewise only with a consultative status. On the other hand, titular bishops residing in the province are in principle allowed to vote if they are summoned to the council.

The provincial council is concerned to promote good morals, to correct abuses, to resolve certain controversies and to maintain or restore discipline. It has the same authority as the plenary council in the territory of its jurisdiction; it can, therefore, introduce measures which will have the force of law throughout the province and in the territories of prelates attached to the council. The ordinaries of the places have no authority to give general dispensations from laws enacted in the council; they are able only to dispense from them in particular cases; they are not the direct authors of these laws, but the conciliar assembly, inasmuch as it possesses legislative power. But the decrees of provincial councils must be submitted to the Holy See for examination and approval before they are promulgated, in the same way as the decrees of plenary councils.

The provincial council as an institution has not yet proved itself in modern times. The text which lays it down that provincial councils must meet every twenty years dates only from 1917. Formerly the intervals were much briefer; the Council of Trent had required that provincial councils should take place every three years, but the practice had fallen into disuse. We are still too near the innovations of 1917 to be able to estimate the value of what was then decided. The initial twenty-year period came to an end just before the war of 1939–45, and it was impossible to convene provincial councils during the war years. What will happen in the future we cannot tell. Provincial councils are similarly envisaged for the missionary countries, but the law leaves it to those responsible for convening them in these territories to decide when they shall meet, not prescribing any particular interval between them.

In addition to the council, canon law prescribes a five-yearly meeting of the bishops of each ecclesiastical province, but this episcopal assembly has no legislative power in the province. The bishops discuss problems of common interest, and it is left to each to take in his own territory whatever measures he deems opportune.

Legislative power in the diocese and similar territories (prelatures and abbacies *nullius*, vicariates and prefectures apostolic) belongs to the holder of supreme jurisdiction in each territory. In the diocese this is the bishop, in the prelature *nullius* the prelate, in the abbacy *nullius* the abbot, in the vicariate and prefecture apostolic the vicar and the prefect apostolic respectively. If the diocese is governed by an admini-

strator apostolic legislative power is entrusted to the administrator. If the see is vacant the cathedral chapter, or, where
there is no chapter, the college of diocesan consultors provisionally exercises legislative power until, within eight days,
a vicar capitular has been elected by the chapter or the
college; so it is also with the prelatures and abbacies *nullius*.
In the event of the bishop, prelate or abbot *nullius* being
prevented from exercising his functions by imprisonment,
banishment, exile or personal disability, in such a way as to
be unable even to communicate by letter with his people,
legislative power passes to the vicar general, or to the vicars
general if there are several of them, or to another ecclesiastic
nominated by the bishop, prelate or abbot *nullius*. In vicariates and prefectures apostolic, legislative power is provisionally exercised, in the event of vacancy or impediment, by the
pro-vicar or pro-prefect whom each vicar or prefect must
appoint as soon as he comes to his office. As a result of these
provisions, no ecclesiastical territory ought at any time to be
deprived of the necessary authority to take legislative
measures which circumstances may make necessary.

A bishop makes laws, generally speaking, in order that
universal laws may be more expeditiously applied in his
territory. To this end he takes measures to make the provisions of the general law more specific, when need be providing
penalties for those who offend against them or, within the
limits fixed by the law, increasing the penalties already provided for by the supreme authority. In practice his legislating
activity is exercised only within the framework of the general
law, or in connection with problems, few indeed, for which
the supreme legislator has not provided. Despite the authority
which he possesses in his diocese, the bishop cannot make
provisions which would go directly against the law made by
higher authorities, in permitting for example what the general
or provincial law forbids or in forbidding what is expressly
authorized by the general or provincial law. The same rules
apply to other prelates who, like the bishop, enjoy legislative
power in their respective territories.

It is for the bishop to decide how he will exercise his legislative power. He makes laws in almost complete freedom; in
some fields he is obliged to seek the views of his chapter and,
very occasionally, its consent. From time to time the bishop
must consult the representatives of the clergy, assembled in a
synod to take measures for the good of the diocese.

The diocesan synod is an assembly of members of the clergy
which, like the provincial council, must meet at regular intervals; the law says that it should take place at least every ten
years. It is convened and presided over by the bishop. In
principle the synod is held in the cathedral church. It does not
discuss the general interests of the Church; its purpose is to
examine with the bishop the special difficulties and needs of
the clergy and faithful of the diocese. The members by right
are the vicars general, the canons of the cathedral chapter or,
if there is no chapter, the diocesan consultors; the superior of
the major seminary, the deans, the parish priests of the town
or city in which the synod takes place, one parish priest from
each deanery chosen by his fellow parish priests, a delegate
from each collegiate church, the abbots of monasteries and a
superior from every religious institute of priests established
in the territory of the diocese. If he so decides the bishop may
also summon other members of the clergy, secular or regular.
But, unlike the plenary council and the provincial council,
the diocesan synod has no legislative power. The bishop alone
is the legislator; the members by right, like others who are
invited, are only his advisers, and all have only a consultative
vote. They can make proposals. The bishop invites them to
discuss the measures which he is thinking of taking for the
good of the diocese, but he remains free to accept or reject
their views. He is not bound by the agreement of the majority,
except in seeking approval for his nominations of the synodal
examiners, the parish priests who serve as consultors and the
synodal judges; but the selection of these persons does not
constitute a legislative measure. It is the bishop, and not the
assembly, who gives legal value to the decrees brought forward during the synod, which are known as synodal statutes;

he alone signs them, which clearly shows the purely consultative rôle of the assembly. Moreover, the legislative provisions published by the bishop in the course of the synod or outside the synod are not submitted to preliminary examination and endorsement by the Holy See, contrary to what we have seen to be the case with the decrees of plenary and provincial councils.

In the vicariates apostolic also the law provides for the meeting of a synod to advise the vicar apostolic, but no fixed interval is laid down for the convocation of the vicarial synod. Prefects apostolic, on the other hand, are not bound to convene a synod. Prelatures and abbacies *nullius*, being so small, have no synodal assemblies.

Other authorities exercise legislative power not within the boundaries of a given territory but with regard to the individuals who come under their jurisdiction. These are notably the chapters general of the exempt religious institutes of priests, which may enact laws for the members of their congregation or order. The chapters of other institutes have only a governing power, and not legislative power properly so called; they are able to publish ordinances, but not laws.

Finally, the faithful also participate in the legislative power of the Church to some degree, through the force of custom. It will be well to explain with some care the part that belongs to the people, to avoid any misunderstanding.

THE PART PLAYED BY CUSTOM

In the past custom was an important source of law; in our own time it is much less so. Its part is increasingly obscured in the contemporary civil societies of the modern world; it is now more marked in the Church, and more in the Eastern Churches than in the Latin Church.

In accordance with the general constitution of the Church, custom must be sanctioned by authority before it can become a source of law; it is not the people who confer the force of law by the constant performance of the same acts. The faithful provide the material element, which is clearly necessary; the assent of the superior adds the formal element. The special assent of authority is not required; a general or legal assent suffices. The legislator establishes once and for all the conditions that a custom must observe if it is to acquire the force of law; every usage which complies with these conditions automatically has the approval of the authority and by that very fact acquires the value of a true legal disposition.

At the present time the Sovereign Pontiff gives his assent in advance to every custom which is reasonable and can show that it has existed legitimately for forty successive and complete years. A usage would not be reasonable if it were contrary to the natural or positive divine law or if it were explicitly censured by the law. Thus the legislator has expressly censured every usage which may seek to place two parish priests at the head of the same parish. Such a custom, being explicitly censured, is deemed not reasonable; it cannot, therefore, acquire the force of law, however long it may endure. On the other hand, if the law should contain a simple clause forbidding every contrary custom but without explicitly censuring it, it would not be impossible to prescribe against such a law; but to become legitimate the custom contrary to such a law must be shown to have been in existence for time immemorial.

Such are the authorities which hold legislative power in the Latin Church. The list of them which we have given is limiting, in the sense that no authority lower than the bishop, similar prelates or those who may on occasion replace them is qualified to enact laws. Legislative power is denied to vicars general, and *a fortiori* to deans and parish priests. No intermediate authority between the Holy See and the bishop save the plenary council and the provincial council has the right to make laws. The metropolitan archbishop has no jurisdiction of a legislative order within the province; his power is strictly confined to the territory of his own diocese. In the Eastern Churches the patriarchs occupy a special position to which we have nothing to correspond in the Latin Church.

They form an intermediate stage between the Holy See and the bishops. But this position is peculiar to those Churches.

All the authorities which we have mentioned are able to make laws within the limits of their competence. But the establishment of laws is not an arbitrary action; it is subject to certain rules, of which the chief is that of promulgation, of which we shall now briefly treat.

THE PROMULGATION OF ECCLESIASTICAL LAWS

Legislative measures taken by the competent authorities must be brought to the knowledge of the public so that they may acquire the force of law. This is what is called promulgation: by this act the superior makes known the decision that he has reached to those subject to him and manifests to them his intention of binding them to the observance of the new provision. Promulgation is an absolute condition for the effectiveness of a law; those concerned must know what obligation it is that is being placed upon them. Once it has been promulgated the law has its legal existence for all those to whom it is addressed; when that time has come all must submit to it, even if in practice they have not received individual knowledge of it; for no one is deemed to be unaware of the law. In certain cases, however, ignorance can excuse from its observance.

The method of promulgation varies according to the laws. In the past the legislative texts of the Holy See were affixed to the basilicas of the Vatican and the Lateran, to the palace of the Apostolic Chancery and in the Campo dei Fiori. Posted up in the city (*Urbi*), a law was deemed to be promulgated to the whole world (*Orbi*). In our own time the promulgation of pontifical laws is effected by their publication in the official *Acta Apostolicae Sedis*, which is published about once a fortnight; this method of promulgation was introduced by Pius X in the constitution *Promulgandi* of September 29th, 1908, and confirmed by the Code of Canon Law in 1917. The pope reserves to himself the right to make use of other procedures for promulgation if he judges it opportune in certain circumstances; but that is exceptional; publication in the *Acta* constitutes the regular and normal method of promulgating pontifical laws.

Decrees of the ecumenical council are promulgated in whatever way the council may itself decide. So also with the decrees of plenary and provincial councils; there is no fixed rule. It is for each assembly to determine by what means it proposes to bring its laws to the knowledge of those concerned. Bishops and other prelates enjoy the same freedom; the law does not impose a defined method of promulgation upon them. As a general rule they promulgate to the synod itself the legislative measures which they take during a synod; those which they take at other times are usually published in the official organ of the diocese. Insertion in the diocesan bulletin is the most usual means of promulgating episcopal laws.

In principle a law becomes binding from the moment of its promulgation. But in certain circumstances there may be reasons for not making certain laws immediately binding, when time must be left for those whom they affect to become informed about them. For this reason the legislator often provides for a delay between the promulgation of a law and its entry into force; this delay, known as the *vacatio*, varies according to the nature of the law in question.

The *vacatio* is three months for pontifical laws, beginning from the date of the issue of the *Acta Apostolicae Sedis* in which the law has been published. A text appearing in the issue of the *Acta* for January 15th comes into force immediately after midnight in the night between April 14th and 15th, for the date is deemed to occur immediately the hour of midnight is past. There are exceptions to this rule. In special cases the Holy See may extend or shorten the *vacatio*; if this is done notice is given in the text of the law. The last book of the Code of Canon Law for the Eastern Church, containing the law of persons, was promulgated on June 2nd, 1957, and came into force on March 25th, 1958. Sometimes the law is of immediate application, with the *vacatio* altogether suppressed. This is notably the case with all prescriptions which concern faith or morals; there is no delay in the application of a decree condemning a clearly pernicious book.

There is no law specifying the delay before the entry into force of the decrees of plenary and provincial councils. The legislator leaves it to the members of these assemblies to determine what time shall elapse before the obligation is imposed.

Episcopal laws come into force with their promulgation, for the territory which a bishop governs is not so great that there is need of much time to make sure that the laws become known. These laws, therefore, have no *vacatio* before their application; their entry into force is immediate. But there is nothing to prevent a bishop from granting in certain circumstances a *vacatio* of which he will decide the duration. This is generally done with synodal statutes. The Bishop of Strasbourg, for example, promulgated the statutes of the synod of 1948 on November 7th, 1948, and fixed their entry into force for January 1st, 1949. Almost all bishops do the same; their synodal statutes only become binding when a given time has elapsed since the promulgation.

CHAPTER III

THE CHARACTERISTICS OF

THE LAWS

We have decided which authorities possess legislative power in the Church, and we know how their prescriptions acquire the force of law. It remains to discover who is subject to canon law, what are its essential properties, and in what ways it permits dispensation.

THOSE SUBJECT TO CANON LAW

Three considerations arise in deciding who is subject to canon law; baptism, age and the use of reason. Only those who fulfil these three conditions, specified by the law, are bound to observe the laws of the Church.

The reception of baptism is the primary condition. Christ subjected those who are baptized, all those who are baptized, but only those who are baptized, to the jurisdiction of the Church. It is by baptism that a human being becomes a subject of the visible Church, and by baptism alone. The Church has no immediate jurisdiction over those who are not baptized; she cannot, therefore, impose her laws upon them. At the most she can reach them indirectly by enacting laws for her subjects which have consequences for others; such is the case with the laws she makes to regulate marriages contracted between her subjects and non-baptized partners.

In principle the Catholic Church claims jurisdiction over all those who are baptized, whoever they may be, even over those who have been baptized outside the Church or who, baptized in the Church, have since left her. Hence all are in theory the subjects of her laws, at any rate unless she has expressly exempted them from them; she does this, for example, for the form of marriage and for the impediment of disparity of cult. Baptized persons who have never belonged to the Catholic Church are dispensed from the canonical form of marriage if they marry among themselves or with non-baptized partners; their marriage is valid in the eyes of canon law, in whatever manner they may make their marriage promises. These same persons are not bound by the impediment of disparity of cult; their marriage with a non-baptized person is perfectly valid, as is not the case with the marriage of a Catholic to a non-baptized person when, unless there is a dispensation, the union is null. These express exemptions aside, the laws of the Church in principle bind all those who are baptized. But the question is a purely theoretical one for baptized persons who have never belonged to the Catholic Church, save for laws the breach of which involves the nullity of the act (*leges irritantes*; invalidating laws) or the juridical incapacity of the persons (*leges inhabilitantes*; incapacitating laws); ignorance exempts them from the observance of others.

Besides baptism, the use of reason is clearly required; the insane or feeble-minded and small children are not held to the observance of the law. Lastly, the law requires the minimum age of seven full years. Younger children, even if their faculties are fully developed, are exempt from canonical laws unless a special provision has been made to the contrary. Thus children must comply with the law of annual confession and Easter communion as soon as they attain the use of reason, as they often have before the seventh year. On the other hand the penalties known as *latae sententiae*, which are automatically incurred when an offence is committed, cannot be incurred until the age of puberty, which is fixed for this purpose at fourteen years for boys and girls alike. The obligation of fasting does not begin until the majority is attained, at twenty-one completed years, and ceases at the beginning of the sixtieth year.

Such are the principles which in general govern submission to the laws of the Church. We shall see the details of their application regarding universal laws and particular laws in treating the properties of law. In practice, of course, this only concerns purely ecclesiastical laws; those which interpret the divine law, positive or natural, bind all men without exception and admit of no exemption. Canonical laws, on the other hand, are human dispositions and so admit of dispensation. More than in any other legislation is it necessary in particular cases to relax the obligation inherent in the law; the general laws of the Church are made for all Christians, whose conditions of life often vary very much. In certain circumstances the observance of the law may involve grave hardship; the remedy is found, as we have said, by means of dispensation, about which we must now say a little more.

DISPENSATIONS

Dispensation is the act by which, in a special case, the competent authority suspends the obligation of the law for one or more persons subject to it. The law itself is not suppressed; it remains intact, and continues to bind all others subject to it. It is solely the obligation which is suspended in favour of particular persons by the intervention of the competent authority. Nor can there be any confusion between dispensation and excuse. In the latter case also the obligation of the law ceases for one or more subjects, but without the intervention of authority. The person concerned cannot in conscience find himself held to the observance of the law because he can bring forward grounds for exemption; for example, physical or moral inability to fulfil the obligations imposed, or uncertainty arising from the existence of the law. Ignorance is another frequent cause for excuse, if it is not culpable, or not gravely culpable, at least when laws which invalidate acts or render persons unfit to perform them are not concerned; ignorance can never excuse from the observance of invalidating or incapacitating laws: the marriage of two persons related within the third degree is null even if those concerned are unaware of the degree of kinship between them. After the discovery of the impediment they can separate, or else they must validate their union by seeking dispensation from the impediment from the competent authority. Dispensation, then, is the sole means of obtaining freedom from the obligation imposed by invalidating or incapacitating laws; and it also makes it possible to suspend the obligation of the law in a case where no ground for excuse properly speaking exists. The authority intervenes at the demand of the subject for whom the observance of the law involves hardships.

The power of dispensing lies with the author of the law, with his successor or with his superior, and with those persons to whom they have delegated this right. The pope, therefore, can dispense from all the laws of the Church, from general laws introduced by himself, his predecessors or general councils; he can also dispense from particular laws enacted by lower authorities—plenary and provincial councils, bishops and similar prelates. As a general rule the Sovereign Pontiff delegates his powers to the various Roman congregations which are charged with granting dispensations in matters within the sphere of their competence.

Residential bishops and other local ordinaries (vicars and prefects apostolic, abbots and prelates *nullius*, their vicars general and their deputies) dispense from laws peculiar to their territory of which they themselves or their predecessors have been the authors and, in special cases, from laws of the plenary council and the provincial council. Moreover, these same persons, together with the major superiors of the exempt religious institutes of priests, have very wide delegated powers. Thus they are allowed to dispense from all the general laws of the Church whenever the three following conditions are simultaneously fulfilled: that recourse to Rome is outstandingly difficult, that delay in the granting of the dispensation may lead to grave hardships for those concerned, and that the question concerns a law from which the Holy See is accustomed to dispense. Thanks to this provision, the lower authorities are in a position to deal with the most delicate situations.

Parish priests, confessors and simple priests also have the power, conceded to them by right, to dispense from certain general laws. Parish priests are able to dispense from fasting and abstinence, as well as from the obligations arising on Sundays and other holidays of obligation: assistance at Mass and abstention from manual work. When there is danger of death and in other urgent circumstances they can grant dispensations from impediments to marriage. In certain cases confessors and simple priests can also dispense from these impediments.

Every dispensation must in principle be based upon a just and reasonable cause. This is a condition required for the concession to be licit, and even for its validity if the dispensation is granted by an authority lower than the author of the law. If a bishop should dispense from diocesan laws without a reason the dispensation would be valid but not licit. If in virtue of the power delegated to him by the Holy See he should dispense from a pontifical law without reasonable cause the dispensation would be not only illicit but invalid as well.

THE PROPERTIES OF CANON LAW

An ecclesiastical law is a general and permanent provision which concerns the future and of which the range of application is in principle restricted to the territory of the legislator. In saying this we have defined its properties, which are universality, perpetuity, non-retrospective effect and territorial limitation. These elements are of course not as such peculiar to ecclesiastical law; they characterize practically all laws of every kind at the present time. They nevertheless deserve our attention, since an analysis of them sheds light on some specific features of the laws of the Church.

A canonical law has a general character. It is not addressed to an individual as such, or to a number of individuals taken in isolation or united only by private interests. It concerns a true collectivity. Its purpose is not to provide for a special case; the purpose of the law is to resolve situations affecting everybody and of a recurring nature. The collectivity to which it is directed is of varying importance; it may be the universal Church, or it may be a greater or smaller part of Christendom. But not all the various groups within the society of the Church are qualified to receive special laws; to be the subject of legislation of their own they must fulfil certain conditions which it is not easy to define. The opinions of canonists do not agree in this matter. The diocese itself presents no problem; it constitutes without any doubt a collectivity capable of receiving laws. About the parish, however, opinions vary. Some canonists say that a parish cannot receive laws, while others think, and it seems rightly, that a parish fulfils the necessary conditions and therefore can be the special subject of laws.

If the law properly speaking is not directed at individual cases, the Church is not on that account unequipped to deal with particular situations affecting only one or a few persons. She has an institution, the precept, which is peculiar to her. Contrary to the law, the precept is a provision of special character addressed to individuals or communities which are not capable of receiving laws. It consists of an order notified to an inferior by the competent superior; a bishop gives a precept if he forbids one of his priests to return to the parish in which he has served as a curate. A precept, in the true sense, can only be given by a person who has the power of jurisdiction *in foro externo* (which does not necessarily include legislative power): the bishop, the vicar general, the major superior of a religious institute. The parish priest is not entitled to communicate precepts in the true sense to his parishioners; the governing or fatherly authority with which he is invested permits him to give orders to his parishioners,

4—W.C.L.

but such orders do not have the character of jurisdictional precepts.

The law provides two ways in which a precept may be given: the private form and the solemn form. In the first case the superior conveys the order verbally and in the absence of witnesses; in the second case he uses a written instrument formally drawn up to attest its authenticity, or else informs the person concerned of the order in the presence of two witnesses. Given in solemn form the precept is not limited to the terms of office of its author; its duration is undefined, unless the contrary is stated. If it is not observed it can become the subject of judicial proceedings in the ecclesiastical court. The precept given in private form comes to an end with the jurisdiction of its author, and if it is not observed there can be no punishment involving canonical penalties in the stricter sense. But whatever its form the precept has a personal and not territorial character; it accompanies the person concerned wherever he goes, even if he leaves the territory of its author's jurisdiction.

The second characteristic of a canonical law is its perpetuity. The law is intended to subsist for an indefinite time; it must give the society of the Church the element of stability that is essential to good order and the common good. This does not mean that in fact a law will have an unlimited life, for perpetual does not mean the same as eternal. On the contrary, every ecclesiastical law which is not based on the divine law, positive or natural, must be adapted to the varying circumstances of each successive period; if it became fossilized in an obsolete form it would no longer fulfil its purpose, which is to promote the good of the members of the ecclesiastical society. Hence, when circumstances so require, it must be possible to revise laws which have become unsuited to their time and place.

Responsibility for revising laws is reserved in principle to the legislator himself, to his successor or to his superior; to the Sovereign Pontiff for universal laws and for the particular laws of which he is the author; to the plenary council and the provincial council for laws enacted in those assemblies; to the bishop for diocesan laws. Various courses of action are open to the legislator with regard to laws which have become obsolete. He can simply suppress a law, without replacing it with another; this is *abrogation*. He can also enact a new provision which is flatly opposed to the law in force. The new measure supersedes the old law, and there is no need expressly to decree its suppression; this is *obrogation*. Lastly, the legislator may make provisions which introduce certain modifications into the existing law; this is *derogation*.

Within the limits fixed by the law, those subject to laws may likewise play their part in suppressing them by constantly following a contrary usage: legitimate and reasonable custom of forty years' duration can abrogate or derogate a law. Lastly, it is admitted that a law ceases to exist when the reason for its existence has been lost, if the reason has disappeared conclusively and in regard to all. It is thus that we must understand the character of perpetuity in canon law: it ensures endurance and stability without tending to fossilization.

Canon law is characterized in the third place by its effect in time. In principle it governs human actions of the future and not those of the past. In juridical language we say that it has no retroactive effect. It therefore guarantees acquired rights.

Two reasons are leading all contemporary legal systems to adopt the traditional principle that laws are not retroactive— a principle found in Roman law as well as in the classical canon law. The first reason concerns the very purpose of law, and especially of ecclesiastical law, which must essentially guide man in the pursuit of his destiny. It is not the actions of the past which interest the legislator, but the actions of the future which man is called upon to face. The other reason is that society would be lacking in the stability and balance which are essential to it if actions done in the past remained always liable to be challenged by the law.

But strictly speaking this rule concerns only the judge who enforces the law, and not the legislator. In other words, the legislator, if he deems it appropriate in certain circumstances, is himself authorized to make provisions of which the effect is retroactive, going back into the past: canon 10 of the Code of 1917 is explicit on this point. However, this intention is never presumed; if the legislator intends to give his law retroactive effect he will expressly say so in its text. Clearly, for reasons of which we are aware, these cases must be exceptional, and laws with retroactive effect are therefore rare. The classic example is that of the constitution *Provida* of January 18th, 1906, concerning mixed marriages concluded before a non-Catholic minister by Germans within the frontiers of the German Empire. The law not only concerned future unions, but had a retroactive effect: by this same constitution, the pope had ratified all the earlier mixed marriages which, because of the absence of a Catholic minister, had not been validly contracted. As we know, the provisions of the constitution *Provida* remained in force until 1918.

The Code of 1917 gives retroactive effect to penal laws in the two cases envisaged in the second and third paragraphs of Canon 2226; but it happens that the provision is in favour of the offender, in lightening or even suppressing the penalty, so that there is no ground for accusing the legislator of having infringed the principle that laws are not retroactive.

The first of these two texts concerns the case of an offender on whom the penalty provided for has not at once been inflicted after the perpetration of the offence. Meanwhile a new law has been promulgated which modifies the penalty by making it less severe; in place of a suspension, for instance, which the old law demanded, it provides only for a simple penal remedy, an admonition. The judge must observe the new law, more favourable to the accused, even though the offence was committed under the old law which in theory ought to be applied. The new law has, in this case, a retro-active effect.

The second text refers to an offender upon whom a vindi-cative punishment has been imposed.[1] A new law is brought in which modifies the old one by suppressing the punishment that was attached to it: the offender will at once be released from his punishment, for the new law has retroactive effect.

Finally, canon law is territorial and not personal; the range of its application is in principle restricted to the limits of the jurisdiction of the legislator. Territoriality represents the fourth property of the laws of the Church.

At the time when the Code now in force was drawn up there had been some division of opinion among canonists about the range of application to be attributed to the laws of the Church. Some held that their application should be personal; they believed that the laws must have a personal character and must in consequence bind those subject to them wherever they might go, even if they should leave the territory for which the laws had been enacted. Mgr Eugenio Pacelli, the future Pius XII, had at that time been a strong supporter of this view; he published an important study of the subject in 1912, which ran into several new editions after he had be-come pope; it was entitled *La personalità e la territorialità delle leggi specialmente nel diritto canonico*. Others inclined towards the territorial system, maintaining that laws ought only to have binding force within the boundaries of the terri-tory for which they are promulgated, and only over those persons who have their domicile or quasi-domicile there[1]; visitors passing through on their travels would not be subject to them, nor would those for whom they were made if they should be absent from the territory.

The conception of territoriality prevailed, but not com-pletely. In principle, laws have a territorial character; yet canon law does not exclude laws of a personal character. Territorial application is presumed; personal application is

[1] These terms are explained on later pages.

not. If in a special case a legislator wishes to give his law a personal effect he must make his intention clear. Personal laws are exceptions to the rule; a legislator would be guilty of an abuse if he enacted only personal laws, unless his jurisdiction should itself be of a personal and not territorial order, as is the case with the jurisdiction of the superiors of religious institutes, which is why the legislation of religious as a general rule bears a personal character, binding the religious everywhere.

There would be nothing to prevent the enactment of a law of both personal and territorial application, in a particular case and for sufficient reason; all would be bound to observe it, passing travellers and the subjects of the legislator even if they should be absent from the territory. But this would be something exceptional; under canon law as it is at present laws are in principle territorial.

It is easy to apply this principle to the various categories of law. Take episcopal laws, as an example of the particular laws. According to the principle of territoriality diocesan laws bind only the bishop's own subjects; that is to say, the persons who have a domicile or quasi-domicile in the diocese and are in fact residing there. As soon as they leave the diocese these same persons are no longer held to the observance of their bishop's laws, apart from those very few laws of which the violation would involve undesirable consequences in their diocese of origin: if a bishop forbids his parish priests to be absent from their parishes for more than a week during the paschal season, then a parish priest absent from the diocese does not have the right to invoke the territorial character of the law to exempt himself from it.

Strangers are not bound by the particular laws of the diocese in which they are staying, apart from certain exceptions for which the law provides. These include, in the first place, laws which concern the formal drawing up of such juridical acts as wills, contracts and legal procedures; strangers must conform to the practices of the country for all these acts, according to an old legal maxim: *locus regit actum*. They are likewise obliged to observe local laws which concern public order and of which the violation would cause scandal, as for example laws forbidding attendance at certain theatres or cinemas. The provisions of the law would favour "vagabonds", or *vagi*—that is to say, persons who have nowhere any domicile or even quasi-domicile—who would hardly be bound by any particular law. Hence the Code lays it down that vagabonds will be held to the observance of all the particular laws of the territories in which they are for the moment staying.

Pontifical laws of a universal character bind all Catholics, since the territory of the Church extends throughout the terrestrial globe. However, if a particular territory has been dispensed from the observance of a general law, travellers passing through it are likewise exempted; on the other hand, if a subject of this territory enters an area which is not dispensed from the general law he is bound to observe it. The feast of St Joseph is a holiday of obligation according to the general legislation of the Church, but French Catholics are dispensed from abstaining from manual work on that day by virtue of an indult of Cardinal Caprara, granted after the conclusion of the concordat of 1801. An Italian staying in France can take advantage of the dispensation, but a Frenchman who is in Italy on March 19th must conform to the observance of the law, since this is a question of a general law and not of a law peculiar to the country; he will be bound to assist at Mass and to abstain from work.

We have now seen how the Church establishes her laws, and which persons are bound by their provisions; and their properties have likewise been discussed. We must next examine the result of the legislative activity of the Church, for it is important to know whether the Church uses the legislative power with which she is invested, and to what extent. We shall confine ourselves to the legislative work of the contemporary period, taking stock of what has been done in the last fifty years.

CHAPTER IV

THE LEGISLATIVE WORK

OF THE CHURCH

If we are to survey the legislative work of the Church in the contemporary period it is well to make a clear distinction between what is general or universal and what is particular or local. The legislative activity of the Roman authority has been particularly intense since the beginning of the century, and that of the lower authorities has been more modest. This unequal division springs from the growing importance of the central power which, from a desire for uniformity, makes laws in fields which in the past were left to local legislators.

At the level of the universal Church, the great event of our time was the promulgation in 1917 of the Code of Canon Law, *Codex juris canonici*. That is one of the great dates in the history of the Latin Church; the year 1917 is one of the most important landmarks in the history of canonical collections in the west. Some years later the Eastern Churches also were in their turn to have the advantage of a new Code.

THE CODE OF CANON LAW

For very many years—to be precise, since 1317—no official collection of the laws of the Latin Church had been promulgated, so that by the nineteenth century the legislation of the Church had become exceedingly complicated. To clarify a point of law it was necessary to consult a mass of different works: the immense *Corpus juris canonici*, the collections of papal bulls, the acts of the councils, the records of the decrees of the Roman congregations. Canonical science became the preserve of a few specialists. The great mass of the clergy had no interest in it; it was far too difficult for them. Moreover, many laws had fallen into disuse, and a great number were no longer appropriate to the conditions of the times.

The appeals for a codification of the whole of canon law made at the Council of Trent had led to no result. From that time onwards complaints flowed ceaselessly to Rome; and they became particularly pressing when it was announced that an ecumenical council would meet at the Vatican in 1869. "We were divided on many points", said one who took part in the Vatican Council, "but one point on which we were all in agreement was the necessity of reconstituting canon law." With the declaration of war in 1870 the deliberations of the council suffered a grievous blow; hardly had the debates been seriously begun than they had to be interrupted and the discussion of numerous questions had to be indefinitely postponed. The council suspended its sessions on October 20th, 1870; it had not had time even to touch upon the plans for the codification of canon law.

Neither Pius IX nor Leo XIII was bold enough to undertake this work; they contented themselves with making partial reforms of special urgency. It must be admitted that the task was not easy; it presented quite exceptional difficulties. It was Pius X who had the courage, the audacity to embark upon the adventure—for that is what it was at that time; shrewd canonists such as Mgr Boudinhon and Mgr Many, to say nothing of Friedberg, did not conceal their apprehension.

Six months after his elevation to the pontifical throne, on March 19th, 1904, Pius X announced his intention of codifying the law of the Church. At the same time he entrusted responsibility for the codification to a commission of cardinals, and charged them to add to their number, for the practical work involved, a number of consultors chosen from among the most distinguished specialists in canon law and theology.

The very important position of secretary to this commission of cardinals and president of the council of consultors was given to the former professor of canon law at the Institut Catholique in Paris, Mgr Pietro Gasparri, who was at that time secretary of the congregation for extraordinary affairs. Gasparri, who was made a cardinal in 1907, became the moving spirit of the great undertaking, its linch-pin, so to say. The distinguished Protestant historian of canon law, Ulrich Stutz, compares him to Raymund of Peñafort, who compiled the fine collection of legislative texts promulgated in 1234 which is known as the Decretals of Gregory IX: "another Raymund of Peñafort", he writes, "but much more active and more effective".

By a letter of March 25th all the bishops of the Latin Church were invited to take part in this great work by making their views on the codification known within four months. Although unable to convene an ecumenical council, Pius X wanted the work to reflect the opinion of the entire Church. The consultors set to work without delay under the direction of Mgr Gasparri. The subject-matter was shared out between the various specialists who had to produce the draft texts coming within their competence. Two commissions, one sitting on Thursdays and the other on Sundays, examined the various drafts proposed, making their observations and returning them for reconsideration; the Vatican's printing shop was at Gasparri's disposal night and day for printing the texts of the various drafts. A version judged finally acceptable was submitted to the commission of cardinals, who had to examine it in at least two of their sessions before giving it their final approval.

It was in this way that, thanks to arduous and exciting work, carried out, as an essential condition of success, in the most complete secrecy, it was possible to bring the work of codification to a conclusion in a very short time for an undertaking of such magnitude. As early as 1912 the Holy See communicated a provisional version of the first two books of the new Code to the residential bishops and similar prelates, and to the major superiors of religious institutes, requesting them to make their comments. A provisional version of two further books was circulated in 1913, and of a fifth in the following year. By the end of 1914 the codification had been practically completed; only in detail was it modified or added to thereafter, but the declaration of war and the death of Pius X delayed the promulgation.

It was to Benedict XV that there fell the honour of presenting the new compendium of ecclesiastical legislation to the world under the title of *Codex juris canonici*. Promulgation took place on Whit Sunday, May 27th, 1917, by means of the constitution *Providentissima Mater Ecclesia*. The new provisions came into force on Whit Sunday of the following year, May 19th, 1918.

The new Code represents an immense advance, and, indeed, a veritable innovation in the Church. It is planned on the model of the *Code Napoléon*, which has been adopted by almost all modern States. In this it differs from earlier collections containing the legislation of the Church. It really is a code of laws, and not a collection of solutions of particular cases, the form in which the legislation of the *Corpus juris canonici* was very often presented, the juridical rule shown by means of a concrete case which the pope had resolved. The Code of 1917, on the contrary, gives the juridical rule in an abstract and systematic manner, in a clear and concise formula. Another advantage is its exclusive character; whereas none of the older official collections had claimed to bring together all the laws of the Church and to supersede earlier collections, the new code made all earlier collections void. Thenceforward only the texts contained within it had the force of law; the others, save for a very few clearly defined exceptions, were abrogated. This removed one of the great difficulties with which canonists had had to contend before 1917.

The texts are composed as a whole in excellent classical Latin, which is in general no obstacle to precision. Account is taken of the most recent advances and attainments of juridical science. In certain delicate problems, such as the relations of Church and State or the relations of Catholics with the members of other religious confessions, the draftsmen concerned showed both tact and prudence. In short, despite defects which are amply compensated by its merits, the *Codex juris canonici* is a work of importance, as is best shown by the very favourable reception which it has received—and not only in ecclesiastical and Catholic circles.

The Code contains 2,414 canons, corresponding to the articles of civil codes. Its material is divided into five books. The first book, containing canons 1 to 86, treats of law, custom, the manner of computing the time within which certain obligations must be fulfilled, rescripts, privileges, dispensations—in a word, general principles: *Normae Generales*. The second book, containing canons 87 to 725, is concerned with persons, their obligations and their rights, dealing in turn with clergy, religious and laity: *De Personis*. The third book, containing canons 726 to 1551, includes, under the title *De rebus*, everything that did not find a place in the other four books: the various sacraments, holy times and places, divine worship, the magisterium of the Church, benefices, the temporal goods of the Church. This is the book which has been most criticized, precisely because of this amalgam of dissimilar material. But criticism is easy, and this is an occasion for saying so. Those who drew up the Code were quite certainly better aware than anyone else of the lack of harmony and balance in the material included in this third book. But any other solution would have been still more inappropriate, so they adopted the least bad solution. The fourth book, *De Processibus*, containing canons 1552 to 2194, is devoted to procedure in all its forms: in disputes, criminal processes, marriage processes, ordination processes, causes for beatification and canonization and administrative procedure. The fifth book, *De Delictis et Poenis*, with canons 2195 to 2414, contains the penal law of the Church; here we find in the first place general statements about the conception of a crime, about responsibility and ecclesiastical punishments, and then the penal code properly so-called of the Church; that is, the enumeration of the various breaches of the law for which penalties are provided. To refer to a text in the Code it is enough to cite the number of the canon, and unnecessary to mention the book or the other subdivisions—parts, sections, chapters.

Current editions of the Code contain, after the general table of contents, a long preface by Cardinal Gasparri describing the work of codification, the promulgating constitution *Providentissima Mater Ecclesia*, the *motu proprio* establishing the commission for the interpretation of the Code and the text of the profession of faith; and then come the 2,414 canons, followed by eight documents which define certain points in the law of the Church too difficult fully to expound in the text of the canons; these concern the election of the pope, the appointment of parish priests by competition, the offence of soliciting preferment in the Church, and the marriage of unbelievers. A detailed alphabetical index concludes the volume.

Some editions give footnote references to the old collections used when the Code was being drawn up, and these make it possible to reconstruct the history of most of the canons. For the benefit of students interested in the texts which provided sources for the Code, Cardinal Gasparri undertook the publication of all the documents cited in the footnotes, save only those which were already accessible without difficulty—the *Corpus juris canonici*, the documents from the Council of Trent and the liturgical books. Begun in 1923, publication was completed in 1939, after Gasparri's death, by the Hungarian Cardinal Serédi. The collection comprises eight volumes of documents and one very valuable volume of tables. In addition, the Holy See has decided to publish the successive drafts worked out for each canon by the consultors charged, under Gasparri's direction, with the compilation of the Code; this publication should be very instructive for the interpretation of some of the texts. Publication of these drafts was entrusted to Mgr (now Cardinal) Roberti. It is progressing slowly; one volume had appeared by 1958, containing various preliminary versions of canons 1556 to 1924.

Legislative activity on the part of the central power did not come to an end with the promulgation of the Code; nor will it ever come to an end. Canon law is a living law. In everything that does not concern the divine law, natural or positive, it must adapt itself to the circumstances of human societies. The evolution is more rapid at some times than at others. Every legislator believes that what he is doing will endure, but life goes on thereafter. Gregory IX in 1234 was convinced that his Decretals would be definitive, but before the end of the thirteenth century it had proved necessary to add a sixth book to his collection of five: the *Liber Sextus* of Boniface VIII. And soon a new compendium was necessary to complete these two.

The same danger threatened the Code, for the legislative activity of the Church is perhaps more intense today than it has ever been. But to be aware of a danger is sometimes to be able to avert it. Benedict XV, in the *motu proprio* which appeared on September 15th, 1917, a few months after the Code had been promulgated, did what he could to prevent it from fast becoming obsolete, decreeing the creation of a permanent commission charged to interpret the Code and giving it exclusive competence to declare the authentic meaning and application of canons whose terms might give rise to difficulties. It also falls to this commission to watch over the future of the Code, incorporating in it such modifications as may come to seem necessary, according to the rule laid down by Benedict XV: if a new prescription, contrary to a text in the Code, is promulgated, the commission will draft its terms in the style of the Code and the new text will take the place of the canon thus made null. If the new law deals with a point not covered in the Code, the commission will decide at what place it can conveniently be inserted; but in no case will the numbering of the old canons be changed; the new texts will be added to the canons dealing with similar matters, with paragraphs numbered *bis*, *ter* and so on. As to the work of the Roman congregations, it will so far as possible be restricted to the publication of instructions and decrees which interpret, supplement and apply the provisions of the Code; hence, in their exterior form, texts coming from the Roman congregations would have to take the form of commentaries on the canons rather than of new laws. Thanks to these measures of Benedict XV's the relative permanence of the Code is assured; but the work of adaptation indispensable in times so disturbed as ours was not retarded thereby. To be convinced of this it will be enough to glance at the fruits of the work of the commission for the interpretation of the Code and of the various Roman congregations since 1917.

Ever since its creation the commission for the interpretation of the Code has constantly been replying to those who have consulted it through the bishops, the other local ordinaries and the major superiors of religious institutes; for, to avoid being overwhelmed with requests, it does not reply to questions submitted to it by private persons directly. All the volumes of the *Acta Apostolicae Sedis* from 1917 to today contain replies of the commission, and its decisions have dealt with hundreds of canons.

The various Roman congregations have conformed to the ruling of the *motu proprio* of 1917; but within the framework established by Benedict XV they have been extremely active. Thus the Congregation for the Sacraments has published a series of decrees and instructions on the procedure to be followed in matrimonial causes which are commentaries on canons 1960 to 1992. Two of these instructions amount almost to little codes in themselves; one, of May 7th, 1923, concerning causes for dispensation on the ground of non-consummation, contains a hundred and six articles, and the other, of August 15th, 1936, concerning processes of nullity properly so-called, has two hundred and forty. On June 29th, 1941, the same congregation produced a long commentary on canon 1020, occupying twenty-two pages of an issue of the *Acta*

Apostolicae Sedis: this instruction affects all priests engaged in the parochial ministry, for it goes in great detail into the manner of making pastoral inquiries about engaged people before the celebration of marriage. The position of military chaplains and priests entrusted with pastoral responsibility towards the numerous displaced persons or emigrants has been regulated with care; the Code had made only a brief allusion to this, in canon 451. Various recent instructions have clarified the juridical status of these priests, whose powers have been more or less equated to those of parish priests. The enclosure of nuns has been the subject of new decisions, made necessary both by economic factors and by the pastoral conditions of the mid-twentieth century. The new form of the religious life followed by members of secular institutes has been given a juridical shape. The law of the eucharistic fast has been considerably relaxed. New rules govern the times at which Mass may be celebrated; after some hesitation, evening Masses on Sundays and feast-days have become usual in most towns and cities. We shall be content with these illustrations; the list of the complementary provisions which have been added to the legislation of the Code is much too long to give in full.

The Code itself has not been changed by these numerous decrees and instructions. More than forty years after its promulgation, modifications of detail have been made only in a very few of its canons. A few words have been suppressed in canons 1097, 1099 and 2319; certain terms have been replaced by others in canons 160, 241, 262 and 2330—the alteration being the same in each of these four—as well as in canon 534, par. 1, and canon 1532. All these modifications are later than 1944. Editions of the Code published in 1959 scarcely differ at all, therefore, from the original text promulgated by Benedict XV. However, in order to interpret a law from the Code correctly, account must be taken of all the work done since 1917 by the commission for its interpretation and by the various Roman congregations; work of which the fruits are scattered through the numerous volumes—one for each year—of the *Acta Apostolicae Sedis*. There is no difficulty about looking up these documents, and many writers have greatly eased the labours of those wanting to know about these latest amplifications of the Code, among them such canonists as Bruno, Sartoni, Cimetier, Cance, Matthaeus Conte a Coronata, Regatillo and Mayer, who have undertaken the publication of replies, decrees and instructions, arranging them according to the order of the canons. To look anything up it is enough to have an up-to-date edition of one of these works.

THE CODE FOR THE EASTERN CHURCHES

The law of the Eastern Churches in communion with Rome was in much the same state as that of the Latin Church before 1917; only considerably more so, the multiplicity of rites having led to diversity in legislation. The various Churches, Maronite, Syrian, Coptic, Melkite, Armenian and so on, each had their own special law, in which custom still played an important part. There had never been any attempt to make a collection of the laws common to all these Churches. The Code of 1917 did not concern them; it was only applicable to the Latin Church, apart from a few canons which bound Eastern Catholics as well as Western.

After the codification of the Latin law the Holy See decided to carry out a similar work for the Eastern Churches. The task was both arduous and delicate, for, while endeavouring to achieve a certain unity, it was only right to take account of the individualism characteristic of each Church, and likewise to resist the temptation to Latinise Eastern law.

It is to Pius XI that the credit for this initiative belongs. On his instructions, the Congregation for the Eastern Church addressed a circular letter to all the bishops concerned on January 5th, 1929, informing them of the intention of the Holy See to work out a Code for the whole of the Eastern Church, and inviting them to submit their suggestions. At the end of 1929 the pope set up a commission of cardinals which

5—W.C.L.

he instructed to undertake the work of codification. Cardinal Gasparri was made chairman of it. As early as 1930 a committee of specialists was set to work. This was composed of a representative of each group of Eastern Christians in communion with the Holy See together with a number of Latin canonists. The work of drafting followed the procedures used for the codification of the Latin law. The texts were submitted to the Eastern bishops before being promulgated.

The new Eastern Code was planned on the model of the Latin Code of 1917 and is written in Latin. Those who drew it up were content simply to adopt the text of the Latin Code, when the subject-matter lent itself to this. But the individual characteristics of the Eastern Churches have been safeguarded so far as possible. Many of the canons keep a place for local law and customary law. The uniformity which has been sought has not suppressed all traces of individualism.

Unlike the Latin Code, the Eastern Code was not published all at once; Pius XII promulgated the various parts of it as they were completed. Publication began in 1949 with the law of matrimony, and promulgation took place on February 22nd, 1949, with the decree *Crebrae allatae*; the new Code for marriage came into force on May 2nd, 1949. The arrangement of the subject-matter in this part follows exactly the corresponding section of the Latin Code, so much so that it is easy to compare the two texts. The Latin law of marriage includes 132 canons, and the Eastern law 131, and practically every text in the *Codex juris canonici* has its equivalent in the Eastern Code. Yet although as a whole each was planned according to the same principles, there are numerous differences of detail to be found. What seem to be the most characteristic divergences concern the impediments of consanguinity and affinity; others concern the form of the celebration, the competence of parish priests, and the very wide powers of dispensation which the Eastern Patriarchs enjoy.

The other parts of the Code followed at varying intervals. First came the law of procedure, which was promulgated on January 6th, 1950, by the decree *Sollicitudinem nostram* and

came into force on January 6th, 1951. A third instalment
included the law of religious and of temporal goods and the
definitions of the terms used in Eastern law; this was promulgated on February 9th, 1952, by the decree *Postquam
apostolicis litteris* and came into force on November 21st,
1952. The law of persons aroused more curiosity and interest
than the other parts; this was the most delicate part of the
whole Code, for in it the Holy See had to define, among other
things, the juridical status of the patriarchs and the character
and extent of their jurisdiction, and had to decide the manner
in which the appointments of the various patriarchs, as well
as those of bishops, would be made. The legitimate suscepti-
bilities of the Eastern Churches were in question at so many
points. This part, awaited with the greatest impatience, was
the part for which we had to wait longest. Only in 1957 was
the law of persons promulgated, by the decree *Cleri sanctitati*
of June 2nd; it came into force on March 25th, 1958. It was
favourably received. It dispelled the apprehensions which
some had felt, for in it, avoiding any application to the
Eastern Christians of the principles that have become classic
in the present-day law of the Latin Church, the Holy See,
with great sensitivity, respects the special characteristics of
these Churches, especially with regard to the selection of
patriarchs and bishops, who are still to be appointed by means
of a ballot.

The new Code as a whole, as promulgated up to 1958,
comprises 1,590 canons, divided as follows among the various
parts: for marriage, 131 canons; for procedure, 576; for the
law concerning religious and temporal goods and the definition of terms, 325; for the law of persons, 558.

As in the Latin Church, a commission is charged to watch
over the authentic interpretation of the new texts and to reply
to problems arising out of them submitted to it by the authorities of the various Eastern Churches; this is called the Commission for the Codification of Eastern Canon Law
(*Commissio ad redigendum Codicem juris canonici orientalis*).
Since the appearance of the law of marriage in 1949 the

Commission has given many replies, which have been published in the *Acta Apostolica Sedis* in the same way as the replies concerning the Latin Code. New requests for the clarification of this or that text in the new Code still reach Rome all the time.

At the same time as the codification another work was carried out on the initiative and under the auspices of the Holy See: the collection and publication of the sources of the law of the Eastern Churches. A commission was established for this purpose in 1930, and this and the other commission charged with the work of drafting pursued their labours side by side. Learned men of all the rites were called upon to assist in this work, which is of the highest importance for the knowledge of the law of the Eastern Churches. Most of the texts were scattered through collections that were difficult if not impossible to come by; others existed only in manuscript form and were buried in the archives of some bishopric or monastery. At great expense the Holy See has undertaken the publication of all these sources, the interest of which is not confined to canonists but is shared by historians and theologians also.

The first volume came from the press in 1930. At the time of writing these words the collection of *Fontes codificationis canonicae orientalis* includes some forty volumes, in three series, the first two containing texts of the various systems of Eastern law and the third papal documents concerning the Eastern Churches. The work is not yet complete and the commission is continuing its publication of the sources.

PARTICULAR LEGISLATION

Legislative activity is now much less important at the regional or local level than it used to be in the past. The reason for this lies in the centralization which has become more and more marked in the Church. The Roman authorities lay down rules for ecclesiastical institutions in great detail. There is no longer any room for particular initiative on any major scale. The lower authorities have become, so far as legislation is concerned, primarily executive organs. Their rôle consists mainly in making the law known to the clergy and faithful, in some cases in interpreting it, and in making sure that it is observed.

Plenary councils have become rare. The Holy See does not insist on the regular meeting of these assemblies, bringing together the representatives of several ecclesiastical provinces, and indeed seems not to encourage them. Provincial councils, on the other hand, are supposed to meet every twenty years, according to the prescriptions of the Code of 1917. As we have already said, circumstances have not yet made it possible to judge the importance which these provincial councils will have from a legislative point of view; they are an institution which we have not yet had time to evaluate.

Practically speaking, particular legislative activity is only to be found at the diocesan level. The bishops and similar prelates are, in short, the only effective legislators after the Holy See. They enact their laws either during a synod or at other times. Since the promulgation of the Code synodal assemblies have been regularly convened in every diocese. The first of these to be held after 1917 had an exceptional importance, being the occasion for the bishops to revise their diocesan legislation to bring it into line with the new Code. Between 1919 and 1927, therefore, all dioceses in France (and many in other countries) published new editions of their synodal statutes, amounting in most cases to a book of about a hundred pages although sometimes quite considerably larger. The texts are drawn up along the lines of the canons in the Code, which they are often content simply to reproduce; they are called not canons but articles. The Latin language was still in use in some of the French dioceses after the first world war when these statutes were drawn up, but all the French dioceses have now adopted the national language.

The synods of the second decade after the promulgation of the Code are of less interest; the changes to be noted between 1920 and 1930 had not been such as to make any comprehensive revision of the post-war statutes seem necessary. In most of the dioceses the bishops added a short supplement to the text of the first synod. The war of 1939–45 made it difficult for synods to meet, and nearly all the dioceses waited until it was over. Between 1946 and 1951, therefore, synodal meetings were very numerous, so that in France alone we had six synods in 1946, ten in 1947, seventeen in 1948, twelve in 1949, eight in 1950 and six in 1951. Most of the bishops, in many cases even if it meant a new edition, took the opportunity to adapt their statutes to the new conditions created by the second world war. In 1956 the fourth series of synods began; this time the bishops were content, as during the 1930s, to add supplements to the text of the earlier statutes.

PART II

THE OBJECT OF THE
CHURCH'S LEGISLATION

The Church legislates in a vast and very varied field. Between these modest covers we can do no more than glance briefly at the whole; yet we mean to make our survey complete. Without becoming lost in the detail we shall try to indicate the wide range of the subject-matter of canon law.

There are various ways in which the legislation of the Church can be presented. Before 1917 the text-books used to differ considerably; the subject was not divided according to any definite plan, but each writer adopted the order of his choice. Some still followed the five divisions of the Decretals; others based themselves on the usages of civil law, making the distinction between private law and public law and in public law describing first the constitutional part and then the administrative. A few canonists invented schemes of their own, setting aside the traditional divisions.

Since 1917 all authors expounding canon law have followed the order in which the material is treated in the Code, which is in five books: the general principles of law, the law of persons (clergy, religious and laity), *de rebus* (the sacraments, holy places and times, divine worship, the magisterium, benefices, temporal goods), procedure, and crimes and punishments. The advantages of this plan of work cannot be gainsaid. It makes it possible without any great difficulty to give a complete picture of the universal legislation of the Church;

although there is a danger that a brief account may become too schematic and that some questions may not be kept in proper proportion. We shall try, therefore, in presenting canon law, to remember all the time that the Church is a living reality. We shall follow the way marked out in 1955 by that great master of canonical science, Professor Gabriel Le Bras, in the introductory *Prolégomènes* to his *Histoire du droit et des institutions de l'Eglise en Occident* (Paris, Sirey, pp. 97 et seq.).

The Church has a sociological originality which sharply distinguishes her from other societies; that is, she occupies a place apart among organized associations of men. The purpose which is hers means that she is called upon to make provisions at three levels. In the first place she must regulate the internal order of the society which she constitutes. Then she must look after the position of her members within other societies, and particularly within the State, for she does not live outside time. Finally, since her purpose is to guide the faithful to eternal salvation, she is bound to help them, by appropriate measures, in the pursuit of their end which lies in the next world. In short, the Church is organized at three levels: the internal, the external and the higher. The first is dealt with in her constitutional and administrative law, the second in the relations which she maintains with States, and the third in the order of grace.

It is true that one cannot draw hard and fast lines between these three levels; that water-tight compartments are out of the question. To think in such terms would be to be at odds with life, in which there is always overlapping. Unbreakable bonds unite the essentials at the different levels, as we could illustrate with countless examples. We will cite only the classic case, that of marriage. This is concluded according to human formalities carefully worked out by the Church, and the Church always stresses her competence to do this; but the civil power is also concerned with it in some aspects; and for the couple concerned marriage is a source of graces which help them to attain their supreme end through the married state. The sacrament is nevertheless the primary element in marriage, which is why we do not hesitate to treat of it at what we have called the higher level.

It seems, then, that in adopting the division of the three levels we can give a better picture of the law of the Church than in following the order of the Code. So we shall describe in turn the legislation concerning the internal organization of ecclesiastical society, the relations between the Church and States, and then finally the government, to the extent that that is possible, in the order of grace.

CHAPTER V

THE ORGANIZATION OF THE SOCIETY OF THE CHURCH

The doors of the Church are open to all men, without any distinction of race, language or colour. She requires only that entry into the Church shall be the result of a decision freely taken, in the sense that no adult can be constrained by force to embrace the Catholic Faith. Parents who are members of the Church, however, are obliged to make their children Catholics from the moment of their birth.

Admission into the society of the Church is performed by means of baptism by water, which neither baptism of desire nor baptism of blood (that is to say, martyrdom) can replace; for we are speaking of admission to the visible Church, and not of incorporation into Christ by grace, the accomplishment of which does not come within the competence of law. A human being is a member of the Church as soon as he is validly baptized, enjoying the rights and subject to the duties of a Christian. The step is decisive; return to the unbaptized state is impossible. Once a man has entered the Church he remains a member of it always. It is of course true that a Catholic can break with the Church by denying his faith, renouncing his rights and not fulfilling his obligations; no authority can prevent him from doing this. The Church on her side imposes a kind of *de facto* exclusion on those of the faithful who have been guilty of grave crimes; to bring them to repentance she puts them under the ban of the ecclesiastical society in inflicting the penalty of excommunication upon them. But despite all these attitudes or measures the Catholic remains in law a member of the Church, since the seal of baptism which constitutes the mark of membership in the ecclesiastical society is indestructible. So, after a wilful withdrawal or an exclusion ordered by authority, a baptized person who wishes again to become an obedient member of the Church is not submitted to any new ceremony of admission; he cannot be made to regain something which he has never lost. He has simply been provisionally deprived of rights which every Catholic enjoys from the fact of belonging to the Church. He regains his rights as soon as he shows another disposition again, the sincerity of which the Church reserves it to herself to judge.

THE INDIVIDUAL STATUS OF CATHOLICS

The Church, like every society, defines the juridical status of her members, which is affected by age, place, relationships and rite.

Various rights and obligations presuppose the attainment of a certain age, and canon law accordingly makes a distinction between a person's majority and his minority. The majority is attained at the age of twenty-one completed years. It is required in principle for the full and free exercise of rights, save for the exceptions specified by law, such as marriage, entry into a novitiate, or the choice of a place of burial; to perform these and other actions a Catholic who has not attained his majority is not subject to the authority of parents or guardians. On the other hand, the emancipation of minors is not provided for in ecclesiastical legislation. Minors are classified between those who have and those who have not reached puberty. Legal puberty is fixed at the age of fourteen years for boys and at the age of twelve years for girls. Up to the age of seven years a child is known as an infant and is not deemed to possess the use of reason; it is not until he has left infancy that he becomes subject to the laws of the Church.

For other actions in the religious life a Catholic is more or less bound to a particular place. This is the case, as we have seen, for subjection to particular laws; it is also true to some extent for the formalities of marriage, for ordination, for judicial procedure and above all for the exercise of jurisdiction on the part of the authorities. So it is that canon law distinguishes between places of origin, domicile and quasi-domicile.

For the purposes of canon law a Catholic's place of origin does not mean the place of his birth but the parish in which his parents had their domicile at the time of his birth, or, if they had no domicile, their quasi-domicile. For posthumous or illegitimate children the place of origin is the domicile of the mother, or, if she had none, her quasi-domicile. The place of origin of the children of "vagabonds" (*vagi*) is the place of their birth; that of exposed or abandoned children is the place in which they were found. Children must in principle be baptized in their place of origin and by their parish priest, and it is in principle from the bishop of their place of origin that the clergy receive their ordination.

The notions of domicile and quasi-domicile are of capital importance; they determine upon which bishop and parish priest each of the faithful depends, and to whom therefore he can appeal if the need should arise. It is by domicile and quasi-domicile that the Catholic acquires his own parish priest, and his bishop, and, inversely, it is by domicile and quasi-domicile that the faithful become the subjects of this or that parish priest or bishop. Under the present state of the law domicile is acquired by an effective residence of ten years in one place, or by the simple fact of settling down in a place with the intention of remaining there for the greater part of the year. In the second case the domicile or quasi-domicile is acquired immediately upon arrival in a place to take up residence. The domicile is parochial if the person concerned lives in a parish; it is diocesan if he resides within a diocese while frequently changing his place of residence within it. A married woman has a compulsory or legal domicile, that of her husband; and a minor has the domicile of his parents or guardian. But married women and minors above the age of seven years can acquire a quasi-domicile of their own; the woman legitimately separated from her husband can even acquire a domicile. Catholics who have no domicile or quasi-domicile anywhere, the "vagabonds" or *vagi*, are deemed to reside in the parish in which they are living for the time being. A domicile or quasi-domicile is lost on leaving a place with the intention of never going back to it.

Canon law has its own rules regarding the relationships which people can bear to one another in the light of consanguinity, affinity or spiritual relationship. For the legal relationship resulting from adoption canon law is content to accept the laws in force in each country: the forms of adoption, like the juridical consequences of marriage, are those laid down in the relevant systems of civil law. In England, therefore, adoption creates a diriment impediment which makes marriage invalid.

Consanguinity is the bond which unites persons descended from the same stock. It is reckoned by lines and by degrees, as in all systems of law, with this difference, that since the eighth century canon law has adopted the system of the ancient Germanic law in working out the degrees in the collateral line, whereas some civil legal systems follow the system of Roman law. In canon law the degrees of kinship in the collateral line are included in one single line, and, if the lines are unequal, in that which is longest; in French law, for instance, the degrees of the two lines are added together. By canonical reckoning a brother and a sister are consanguineous in the first degree of the collateral line, first cousins in the second degree and a nephew and his aunt likewise in the second degree (mixed). By the French reckoning a brother and sister are consanguineous in the second degree, first cousins in the fourth degree and a nephew and his aunt in the third.

Consanguinity has juridical consequences: it creates a diriment impediment to marriage within the direct line *ad infinitum* and within the collateral line to the third degree inclusive (second cousins), and various other impediments, some of which we cite. Thus it is forbidden to elevate to the College of Cardinals a prelate who is the brother or first cousin of an existing cardinal (although there have been recent exceptions to this rule, including the creation by John XXIII of the second of the two Cardinals Cicognani). A bishop may not admit his brother or his cousin to the diocesan administrative council, nor make his brother or his nephew vicar general. No one may hold the office of judge, promoter of justice or defender of the bond in cases which concern their kinsmen up to first cousins inclusive.

Affinity, or kinship by marriage, is the bond existing between both parties to a marriage and those who are consanguineous with the other. Under the present state of the law it results only from a valid marriage, and no longer, as in the past, from carnal relations or putative marriage. Affinity is reckoned by lines and degrees in the same way as consanguinity, so that those who are consanguineous with the wife become the relations by marriage of the husband to the same degree and in the same line as they are in kinship by blood with the wife, and *vice versa*: the wife's cousin (consanguineous to the second degree in the collateral line) becomes the relation by marriage of the husband to the second degree in the collateral line; the woman's mother (first degree in the direct line) becomes the relation by marriage of the husband in the first degree in the direct line.

The juridical consequences of affinity are virtually confined to marriage and procedure. Affinity constitutes a diriment impediment to marriage in the direct line *ad infinitum*, and to the second degree in the collateral line; a widower may not marry his deceased wife's first cousin without a dispensation. The *officialis*, the promoter of justice and the de-

fender of the bond are not allowed to exercise their office
in a cause which concerns their relatives by marriage in the
direct line or in a collateral line to the second degree. But this
very rarely arises, since these offices are held by priests; it
can occur in the event of a widower becoming a priest and
being appointed by his bishop to one of the positions in
question. A case more frequently occurring, on the other hand,
concerns the position of witness, which cannot be exercised by
those who are related to the petitioner by marriage in the
direct line or in a collateral line to the first degree, save in
processes concerning marriage or ordination, or any other
processes concerning personal status; this rule applies *a
fortiori*, and within the same limits, to blood relatives of the
petitioner.

Spiritual relationship derives from participation at a validly
conferred baptism or confirmation; under the law as it stands
today this relationship arises in baptism between the baptized
and the baptizer on the one hand and between the baptized
and the godfather on the other. In confirmation it arises only
between the person confirmed and his sponsor. Only the relationship which follows from baptism constitutes a diriment
impediment to marriage.

Because of the diversity of rites, Latin and Eastern, existing
within the Church, the law includes very strict provisions to
prevent arbitrary or impulsive changes from one rite to
another. In the first place it defines the manner of determining
to which rite a person belongs. Baptism is here decisive.
Every Catholic belongs to the rite in which he has been baptized, or in which he ought to have been baptized if for one
reason or another baptism has been administered by someone
of another rite; for infants are supposed to be baptized in the
rite of the father if the father is Catholic and, if he is not,
then in the rite of the mother. A change of rite is permitted
only with the authorization of the Holy See. Married women
alone are not subject to this rule; they can adopt the rite of
their husbands, and can return to their original rite if the
marriage comes to an end.

THE THREE STATES: CLERICAL, RELIGIOUS AND LAY

Those who are baptized form a society in which all are originally equal; the Church knows no privilege of birth. This does not prevent her from becoming a strongly structural and hierarchical society. Her adult members are divided into three states, those of the clergy, religious and laity.

The clergy

The clergy are the governing element in the Church. It was the Founder of the Church, according to Catholic teaching, who desired that there should be a division between the ministers of worship and the great mass of the faithful. The authority which the clergy possess, therefore, does not come to them from below; they are not the delegates of the people. Their powers derive from a delegation from above; they are commissioned by God.

Entry into the clerical state is accomplished by the ceremony of the tonsure, which is simply a sacred rite and not an order properly so-called. But under the provisions of the law as it is today the tonsure is only conferred on those who show the intention of proceeding to the priesthood; it represents only a stage, and the first one, along the road which ought to lead the cleric, if nothing unforeseen occurs, to the priesthood; for nowadays the priesthood is the normal condition of the clergy. Once entered upon the clerical state, the young Levite goes on through the different degrees which lead him to the priesthood. He begins with the minor orders, survivals from ancient offices, which in the Latin Church number four: those of doorkeeper, lector, exorcist and acolyte. Then he commits himself decisively by receiving the major orders: the subdiaconate, the diaconate and the priesthood. Some are called to the episcopate, which is the supreme degree in the hierarchy of Orders.

The conditions of admission to the clerical state are various. In the first place, it is open only to men; women are excluded from it. The reasons which can be brought forward to justify this exclusion derive essentially from tradition. It is a fact that Christ, for all the solicitude for women which he shows throughout the Gospels, chose no woman in ensuring that his work would continue; the Twelve were all men. The times in which Christ lived did not permit the choice of a woman; his Jewish contemporaries would not have understood it. The Apostles, who were true Jews, clearly made no change in this. St Paul, faithful to the Jewish heritage, set strict limits to the part to be played by women in Christian assemblies, and thereafter a very firm tradition was established, reserving the priesthood and even the clerical state as such to men, and setting women apart from it. The institution of deaconesses did not endure for long.

Open to men alone, entry into the clerical state must follow a free decision on the part of the man concerned. The Church threatens with pain of excommunication those who may seek to compel someone to embrace the ecclesiastical state. So that young people may not allow themselves to be influenced by persons animated often by excellent intentions, the Congregation for the Sacraments has taken a very wise precaution, requiring that all candidates shall seek their admission to orders in a written request attesting their full and free desire to receive orders.

In addition to the moral qualities essential for the sacred office, and the necessary intellectual dispositions, the law also requires that candidates for orders shall be of an age appropriate to a commitment of such importance. The Code does not contain any precise indication of the minimum age required for the conferring of the tonsure; it is content to say that the tonsure cannot be conferred before the beginning of theological studies properly so-called. Such studies presuppose the completion of a full secondary education and of one or two years of philosophy; in practice these requirements set the minimum age at seventeen or eighteen years for the most gifted boys. The law is more precise in determining the age required for the reception of the major orders, requiring

6 —W.C.L.

twenty-one completed years for the subdiaconate, twenty-two for the diaconate, and twenty-four for the priesthood. The age of thirty years is required for the episcopate. No one is authorized to receive an order without having passed through the various lower orders, and intervals, known as "interstices", must elapse between the reception of the various orders: a delay of one year is required between the last minor order and the subdiaconate, three months between the subdiaconate and the diaconate, and three months again between the diaconate and the priesthood. It is for the bishop to decide what time shall elapse between the conferment of the tonsure and each of the minor orders.

Out of consideration for the office and the faithful, the Church excludes from the ecclesiastical state persons who are afflicted with certain physical defects and certain diseases, or who are in positions which she judges to be incompatible with the priesthood. Hence the aspirant to the priesthood must not be subject to any canonical impediment. The list of impediments is long; certain impediments are of their nature permanent and can only be lifted by means of a dispensation; they are known as irregularities. Others, called simple impediments, are temporary; they can come to an end of themselves with the passage of time. The principal irregularities are illegitimate birth (unless there has been legitimation or solemn profession), corporal defects (blindness, deafness, deformity, the loss of an arm or leg), diseases (epilepsy, madness), successive bigamy (a widower who has married for a second time in the Church), simultaneous bigamy (a divorced man who remarries in a civil ceremony), *infamia iuris* (a penalty inflicted for certain grave offences), culpable homicide and abortion, mutilation, attempted suicide or the illicit exercise of liturgical functions. The principal simple impediments are birth from non-Catholic parents, the married state, submission to ordinary military service, and *infamia facti*, or loss of good name. These impediments cease as soon as their cause disappears; if it does not disappear then a dispensation must be sought. Children born of non-Catholic parents are admitted to orders as soon as their parents adhere to the Catholic faith or, alternatively, when a dispensation has been granted; a married man as soon as the marriage bond is dissolved by the death of his wife. A young man liable to military service can only receive ordination once this obligation has been discharged; and a man who has had a bad reputation (*infamia facti*) can be ordained when, in the bishop's judgment, he has regained the respect of those around him. In order that possible impediments or irregularities may be disclosed, banns of ordination are published, like the banns of marriage; the names of the future ordinands are read out in their parish church on a Sunday or feast-day, or are posted up at the door of the church. The faithful are obliged to disclose to the parish priest or the bishop any impediment or irregularities they may know about.

Finally, the bishop must only admit to the ranks of the clergy the number of subjects necessary for the service of his diocese, or of a diocese which is short of priests if the bishop of that diocese agrees. This problem rarely arises nowadays, because of the growing need for pastoral clergy and the relatively small numbers of candidates. This does not prevent the number of the clergy from being limited in law; in the last century some dioceses had difficulty in making use of all their priests. Furthermore, the bishop is not authorized to admit to the clerical state subjects whose material subsistence he is not able to guarantee; before he receives the subdiaconate, therefore, each cleric must be able to show a title of ordination—that is, an assurance that he will dispose of the means to provide for his needs. As a general rule this title is provided by the diocese or the mission. The bishop or the vicar apostolic undertakes to employ the cleric in the pastoral work of the diocese or mission, and to provide him in return with enough to live on.

With his admission into the ecclesiastical state the cleric enters a highly organized and hierarchical community. By the conferment of the tonsure he is automatically attached to a diocese or a religious institute; this is known as his incardination. It does not mean that no change is thereafter possible; a cleric has the right to leave his diocese for reasonable motives, but he is only permitted to do so when he finds another bishop to incardinate him permanently and without reservation in his diocese, and when his first bishop gives him, in the same manner, letters of excardination. Instead of approaching a bishop a cleric may also seek admission to a religious institute, when permanent profession in that institute is equivalent to excardination.

Among themselves the clergy are subordinated to one another according to a twofold hierarchy: the hierarchy of Order and the hierarchy of jurisdiction. The first is based upon the power received from ordination and concerns the worship of God, and in particular the eucharistic sacrifice and the administration of the sacraments. It is composed of the bishops—and in the hierarchy of order the pope is no more than a bishop like all other bishops—the priests, and the lower ministers: deacons, subdeacons and those in minor orders. The hierarchy of jurisdiction concerns the government of the Church and the instruction of the faithful; it is based not upon ordination but upon the delegation, known as the canonical mission, received from the higher authority. It comprises the supreme pontificate, the subordinate episcopate and other lower degrees represented in the dioceses by the vicars general, the deans and the parish priests. The pope holds his power immediately from God, and not from the college of cardinals, whose members are of his own choosing. From the moment of his election he possesses supreme authority in the Church. Bishops receive their power immediately from him. Lower authorities receive it either from the pope or from the bishops (and similar prelates), or from those to whom the pope or the bishops have transmitted it. This power is called ordinary if it is attached in law to an office, as for example to the office of vicar general or to the office of parish priest; it is delegated if it is accorded to some cleric or some category of clerics, as is the case with the power accorded to a curate in a parish or to a professor in a seminary. This would also be the case with the power accorded to a parish priest if the power did not form part of the parochial office, as for example the power of dispensing from impediments to marriage in ordinary circumstances.

Clerics have rights and privileges proper to their state; they are also bound by obligations arising from the special character of their office.

So it is that the power of order, the power of jurisdiction and ecclesiastical benefices are exclusively reserved to the clergy; no one else may legitimately lay claim to them. The clergy have a right to the respect of the faithful, and to certain honorary prerogatives in religious assemblies. They have retained some of the numerous and important privileges which they formerly possessed, or at any rate the Church strives to make these respected by the secular authorities. She demands that her ministers shall be judged by ecclesiastical tribunals (privilege of the forum), that they shall be exempt from military service and from obligations unbefitting their state, such as jury service (privilege of personal immunity), and that in the event of judicial distraint clerics who are insolvent shall be able to retain such of their goods as are necessary for decent subsistence (privilege of the competence). Recent Concordats have guaranteed one or another of these privileges.

As to obligations, these are both positive and negative in character. The positive obligations concern piety (frequent confession, and a retreat to be made at least every three years), obedience to the bishop, study (with an annual examination for three years after ordination to the priesthood), life in common (recommended, but obligatory only in certain cases), celibacy (at least in the Latin Church, from the subdiaconate onwards), the daily recital of the breviary, and the wearing of ecclesiastical dress in conformity with the usages of the country. The negative obligations include the many prohibitions that are imposed on clerics, who are forbidden to engage in occupations unbefitting the clerical state, to attend overworldly spectacles or entertainments, to engage in commerce, to accept political commitments without episcopal permission, to be absent from their dioceses for any considerable time, or to enlist in the armed forces.

There is no difficulty about leaving the ecclesiastical state and returning to the lay state so long as a cleric has not received the major orders. Those who have received only the minor orders can renounce the clerical state of their own accord; to do so in correct fashion it is enough that they shall advise the bishop of their decision. They are excluded from office as a consequence of certain acts: abandonment of ecclesiastical dress despite warnings from their superiors, voluntary enlistment in the armed forces, marriage. Finally, the bishop is permitted to exclude them if he judges that their advancement to holy orders would not redound to the credit of the Church.

For clergy who have freely received the major orders the position is no longer the same. From the subdiaconate onwards they have committed themselves to lifelong celibacy, and so are no longer able to renounce the commitment of their own accord and to return to the lay state. It is true that no ecclesiastical authority will be in a position to prevent them from leaving the ranks of the clergy and living in fact as laymen, but in law they will remain bound by the obligations of the clerical state, and notably by the obligation to celibacy. They will not be able to contract a valid marriage; reception of the major orders constitutes an impediment which makes a marriage null. A return to the lay state is only legitimate on the intervention of authority. Subdeacons and deacons can obtain reduction to the lay state, with a dispensation from the obligation to celibacy, without great difficulty. But priests obtain it only with much difficulty, and if they do so it is, with only rare exceptions, without the dispensation from celibacy; they are, therefore, not entitled either to marry or to regularize a matrimonial position in which they may have become involved. On the other hand, reduction to the lay state can be imposed by authority in consequence of extremely grave crimes which the law punishes with degradation. In this event the cleric ceases to be bound to recite the breviary, but he is not released from the obligation of celibacy. In no way can the indelible character received at ordination be lost with a return to the lay state. But readmission to the clergy is only possible with the permission of the Holy See.

Religious

The religious life is a state of perfection open to all the faithful who seek to realize the Christian ideal by the practice of the evangelical counsels under conditions fixed by the Church. The members commit themselves by public vows to the observance of perfect chastity, of poverty and of obedience, in an institute approved by the ecclesiastical authorities. Unlike the clerical state, the religious life is meant for women as well as for men. Among the men who enter it, some proceed to the priesthood and others do not receive any order. The numbers of those in the religious state is not of itself limited, as is theoretically the case with clerics, for the religious life is instituted in the first place for the attainment of individual perfection, whereas the ecclesiastical state has the pastoral ministry as its purpose: the bishop must only admit to the clergy the number of subjects necessary for the needs of the diocese. No limitation of this kind is prescribed for the religious state. Entry into the religious life, withdrawal from it and its interior organization are all carefully regulated.

Admission to the religious state is by stages; the demands of the religious life are such that candidates must have plenty of time before entering upon the commitment which will bind them finally and absolutely. Canon law provides in the first place for a period of initiation, the postulancy, then for a rather longer time of trial, the novitiate, followed by a period of probation, the temporary profession, and then the final commitment through solemn profession.

Postulancy lasts in principle for six full months; it is made under the guidance of an experienced religious in a house of the institute which the candidate intends to join. The postulant becomes familiar with the spirit and the methods of the chosen institute, so as to be able to make up his mind, when the time comes, in full knowledge of what he is doing; the superiors, on their side, use this period to decide whether the candidate meets the demands of the institute. The postulancy ends with an eight-day retreat; then the candidate is admitted to the novitiate, if he expresses the desire and the institute gives its assent. From young girls or women the law demands in addition formal evidence of their absolute freedom; for this reason, at least a month before admission to the novitiate, the bishop or his representative questions the postulants in order to satisfy himself that they are acting in full liberty and are fully aware of what they are doing. This interrogation is required not only before entry into the novitiate but before temporary profession and again before perpetual profession.

The novitiate is served in a house of the institute set aside for this purpose. It lasts one full and unbroken year. An interruption of thirty days renders it invalid; if there is such an interruption the year must be begun all over again. Candidates are not admitted until they are at the age of fifteen completed years. They wear a special habit, which is conferred upon them in a ceremony at the time of entry into the novitiate. The year is devoted almost entirely to spiritual formation under the direction of a novice-master or mistress appointed from among the institute's most capable members.

After the year of the novitiate, which exceptionally can be prolonged by a few months but never by more than six months, the candidate is admitted to profession—that is, to the explicit and public pronouncement of the three vows of religion. But first he must make over the administration of his property to a third party, and in the religious congregations—not in the orders—must make a will to provide for the distribution of his money and property after death, which he is free to dispose of as he chooses. With his profession the novice enters into the religious state properly so-called. The age of sixteen completed years is necessary for the profession to be valid. The commitment which the novice makes with this first profession is, however, not final; the law only permits temporary vows to be taken, so as to leave further time for reflection. The period covered by temporary vows is in principle three years; sometimes it is extended, but as a general rule not beyond six years.

Temporary profession is followed by perpetual profession, which cannot be taken before the age of twenty-one completed years. The professed religious is finally committed to the religious state. The nature of the perpetual vows varies according to whether they are taken in one of the ancient orders, like the Benedictines, the Franciscans and the Dominicans, or in a congregation founded in a more recent period: the vows taken in the ancient orders are known as solemn vows, and the others as simple vows. Conversely, an institute in which solemn vows can be taken is known as an order, and one in which only simple vows can be taken is known as a congregation. The difference lies especially in the question of possessions; religious in solemn vows, whether men or women, who are known as regulars, are not able to possess or to acquire property. Before perpetual profession, therefore, they must renounce all their goods, in favour of anyone they may choose; hence there is no need for those joining an order to make a will, as is required before the temporary profession of candidates for a congregation. Religious in simple vows retain their inherited property, although not its use, and do not lose the capacity to acquire possessions. Moreover, solemn profession constitutes an impediment which invalidates a subsequent marriage, whereas simple profession only renders such a marriage illicit. A nun belonging to a congregation, in simple vows, who leaves her institute and marries, contracts a valid union. But a nun belonging to an order, taking solemn vows, cannot contract a marriage without a dispensation, and any attempt to do so would be invalid and not only illicit.

All male religious, even novices, enjoy in principle the rights and privileges enjoyed by clerics, to the extent that these are compatible with their state; thus it is clear that the exercise of the power of order and of jurisdiction can only be granted to them if they have been ordained to the priesthood.

They also share the common obligations of clerics, and are subject in addition to certain other duties on account of the more perfect life to which they are called by the vows of obedience and poverty.

The internal organization of each institute, of men or of women, is carefully regulated and is democratic in character. Supreme authority in almost all the great institutes is held by the general chapter, which is composed of representatives of all the religious forming the institute. The chapter ordinarily meets every six years and proceeds to elect the superior-general, to whom is entrusted the government of the institute; it likewise elects the council that is charged to assist the superior-general. Institutes of some importance are divided into provinces comprised of local houses. The government of each province is in the hands of a superior known as a provincial, the choice of whom lies, in most modern institutes, with the superior-general. The general and the provincials are called major superiors; in the exempt institutes of priests they have very extensive powers of dispensation from the general laws of the Church. At the head of each separate house there is a local superior who is appointed either by the general or by the provincial. In most of the ancient orders there is a more democratic system, all the superiors being chosen by the votes of their brethren or sisters, even the local superiors. In any case the various superiors are not in principle appointed for life, but must be changed at frequent intervals. The law requires that local superiors shall not remain in office for more than three years; at the most their terms of office may be extended for a further three-year period. The Holy See insists very strongly that the provisions concerning the regular changing of superiors shall be carried out.

Withdrawal from the religious life presents no difficulty for the religious who has taken only temporary vows; after the expiry of the vows he can leave the religious state if he so desires. The superior on his side is empowered to send him away if there are grounds, apart from reasons of health, for judging him unsuited to the religious life of the institute. The novice clearly has the right to leave when it seems to him that he ought to, and the superior can dismiss him at will. Others do not possess the same facilities for abandoning the religious life, nor their superiors for sending them away. Those professed in perpetual vows and those professed in temporary vows which have not expired are not permitted to leave the religious state on their own account. It is true that no authority can prevent them from deserting the institute, but in this case they incur the penalty of excommunication. The sole legal means by which they are able to leave is the indult of secularization which is granted, according to the institute, by the Holy See or the diocesan bishop. A professed religious who is in holy orders clearly remains bound by the obligations of the priesthood; it is not possible for him to return to the lay state. He must find a bishop who will agree to incardinate him among the diocesan clergy. Grave faults may entitle superiors to send away members of their institute and to exclude them from the religious state, but the sending away must be done according to very strict rules laid down by law. A religious who wishes simply to pass from one congregation or order to another must seek permission from Rome; and he will be obliged to begin a new novitiate in the new institute.

In 1947 Pius XII created a new form of the religious life in establishing secular institutes with the constitution *Provida Mater*. He did this in order to meet the requirements of modern life, which are sometimes difficult to fit in with the classic forms of the religious life. He wished to provide for the numerous people who aspire to the ideal of practising the evangelical counsels and profiting from the advantages of the religious life while yet remaining in the world. The secular institutes are groups of people who observe perfect chastity and practise obedience and poverty under the direction of superiors without being bound by public vows and without habitually and necessarily living a community life. Their members are in an intermediate position between religious and lay people, but they are nearer the former than the latter, whose status it now remains for us to examine.

The laity

The Church is in fact made up of the great masses of baptized people who do not belong to either the clerical or the religious state. These are the laity, a word coming from the Greek, *laos*, *laos theou*, meaning "the people of God". Clerics and to some extent religious exist to serve them; and the pope is called the servant of the servants of God, *servus servorum Dei*.

The duties of the laity correspond to the general obligations of the faithful which are the subject-matter of the legislation of the Church in everything that does not exclusively concern the clergy and religious. For this reason the Code of canon law did not find it necessary to devote a special section to the duties of the laity, as it did to the duties of the clergy and religious.

As perfect members of the Church, the laity have a strict right to the spiritual wealth which the ecclesiastical society is called upon to dispense in the name of its Founder: the teaching of the truth, and the sacraments. In addition, every baptized person can demand, in justice, all the benefits and advantages which are not peculiar to the clergy and religious: a share in the prayers of the Church and in the indulgences, blessings and dispensations, assistance at liturgical functions, the honours of ecclesiastical burial. The perpetration of a crime or an exceptionally grave sin alone permits the authority to deprive the layman who is culpable of the enjoyment of these rights; and this will only be on a temporary basis, so that the offender may be brought to a better frame of mind.

Canon law provides for and favours pious associations of lay people, the purposes of which can be various and the organization of which is not rigidly defined. Some pursue the perfection of individuals, taking their inspiration from the ideals of the great religious founders: these are the third orders, of which the best known are the Franciscan and the Dominican. Members of the third orders secular do not take vows and do not lead a community life; they are content to live as fully as is compatible with their lay status in the spirit of the order with which they are associated. The confraternities, of which the origins go very far back into history, tend nowadays to be exclusively concerned with the advancement of public worship. Women are excluded from them for this reason, for active participation in the liturgical ceremonies of the Church is in principle reserved to men; women are only admitted to the confraternities as so to say passive members, in the sense that they are able to belong to them in order to gain the indulgences and to share in the other spiritual favours bestowed upon them. The best-known of the confraternities, in the present sense of the term, is that of the Most Blessed Sacrament. Other associations, called sodalities, are occupied with works of charity or piety. They are governed by rules that are less strict than those of the third orders and the confraternities, and in principle they do not possess juridical personality. All associations, whatever they may be, must have a title and statutes which have received the approval of the Holy See, or at least of a bishop or similar prelate, and they are subject to the jurisdiction and the supervision of the local ordinary.

In recent decades a new factor has arisen in favour of the laity, of which the Code of 1917 took no account. Pius XI and Pius XII, in founding Catholic Action, insisted upon a more intensive participation of the laity in the work of the Church. It is still too early to determine the exact status of this new form of the apostolate, which is as yet only in its beginnings. It may be that one day we shall see the laity participating in the power of jurisdiction (we are careful to say jurisdiction, and not order), which meanwhile remains an exclusive right of the clergy. It is difficult to say what the future will bring. All depends upon the circumstances in which the Church is called upon to transmit the message of

Christ. Recent attempts to give a new value to certain of the minor orders spring from similar preoccupations.

Composed of these three categories of members, clergy, religious and laity, the Catholic Church forms a society of more than four hundred millions of faithful, spread through the entire world. All races and all languages are represented in her. The multitude of her subjects, their geographical distribution and their variety tend inevitably to create centres of separatism within the Church; if this does not lead to schism, national or even regional or local particularities must at least be ceaselessly watched. In order to safeguard unity, the Church must constantly resist latent tendencies towards separatism. She does this in drawing up her organization at different levels, subordinated one to another: the central level, the regional level and the local level. The three pillars of the society of the Church are the Holy See, the diocese and the parish. We shall examine these in turn, and so shall be led to study in turn the machinery of the central power, of diocesan administration and of parochial organization.

THE CENTRAL POWER

The Catholic Church is organized on the model of the monarchies; supreme power, in all its forms, is concentrated in a single person. It is true that authority in the Church is held by the episcopal body as a whole and belongs to the bishops as the successors of the apostles. But the only person to possess this authority in its plenitude is the pope, the successor of St Peter, the chief of the apostles.

The pope is at the same time Bishop of Rome, Archbishop and Metropolitan of the Roman Province, Primate of Italy, Patriarch of the West, Successor of the Prince of the Apostles, Sovereign Pontiff of the Universal Church, and Head of the Vatican City State. These titles appear under the pope's name in the official year-book of the Holy See, the *Annuario Pontificio*.

The pope is chosen by voting. Since 1179 the college of

cardinals has held the exclusive right of electing the Sovereign Pontiff, and since the end of the thirteenth century the election has taken place in conclave, to protect the electors from external influences and to compel them to make their choice speedily. The procedures of the election have been specified in many pontifical documents; Pius XII made the last revisions of them on December 8th, 1945 with the constitution *Vacantis Apostolicae Sedis*, which was applied for the first time in 1958 at the election of John XXIII.

The conclave begins at the earliest fifteen days and at the latest eighteen days after the death of the pope. The choice can fall on any person who is not excluded by divine law or the law of the Church, but in fact, since the end of the fourteenth century, the Sovereign Pontiff has always been chosen from among members of the electoral college. The last pope who was not a cardinal at the time of his election was Urban VI (1378–89). No law, of course, makes it necessary to choose an Italian, but since Adrian VI (1522–23), who was Dutch, there have only been Italian popes; and it is still thought best today to choose an Italian, although the Italians no longer have a majority in the electoral college. The ballots begin the day after the entry into the conclave and continue, at the rate of two sessions a day and two ballots a session, until one candidate obtains two-thirds plus one of the votes of the electors present. It was Pius XII who introduced the rule requiring two-thirds plus one of the votes, and he did so in order to simplify the balloting. In fact, for the validity of the election, a candidate must receive two-thirds of the votes, by a rule going back to Alexander III in the twelfth century. But the vote of the candidate elected must not be included in this two-thirds and, as a result, before Pius XII's reform, every time a candidate had received exactly two-thirds it was necessary to proceed to a scrutiny of the ballot-papers in order to make sure that he had not voted for himself. This made a complicated system of ballot-papers necessary; it had to be possible to discover, if the need should arise, for whom the elected candidate had cast his vote, while safe-guarding the secrecy of the ballot so far as the other electors were concerned. To remedy this inconvenience, Pius XII decreed that for the future, in order to be elected, a candidate must receive a majority of two-thirds plus one of the votes. If by chance the candidate elected had cast his vote in his own favour, his action would not impair the validity of the election; even without his own vote he would command the necessary majority. No longer can any civil power interfere in the election; the right of veto claimed since the sixteenth century by the three great Catholic powers, France, Spain and Austria, was abolished by Pius X in 1904.

As soon as a candidate has obtained the required number of votes and has given his assent, the part of the electoral college is ended. He who has been elected immediately becomes Sovereign Pontiff in the Church. He then makes known the new name which he is adopting. The custom of taking a new name goes back to the tenth century; to be precise, to 956, when John XII began this tradition. If the new pope is not already a bishop he receives episcopal consecration from the dean of the cardinals. On the day of the coronation, which takes place with magnificent ceremony in the basilica of St Peter's at the Vatican, the senior cardinal deacon places the tiara on the head of the new pope.

The supreme power with which the pope is invested from the moment of his acceptance of the Sovereign Pontificate extends into all fields; faith and morals as well as the government of the universal Church are subject to his competence. In addition, canon 218 of the Code of canon law recognizes his immediate authority over each particular Church; over the ministers, bishops and priests, as well as over the faithful. The pope can therefore intervene directly in the administration of a diocese, as we have already indicated, without the local bishop being able to resist him in any way. In short, he unites in his person the supreme authority, legislative, judicial and executive or coercive, as much in the universal Church as in each local Church; and in matters of faith and morals he even enjoys infallibility in certain circumstances.

The pope is assisted in the central government of the Church by the cardinals, who are his immediate collaborators and who constitute the Sacred College. When complete, the college of cardinals used to contain seventy members until the reform introduced in November 1958 by John XXIII, who increased their number to seventy-five. About fifteen of them reside in Rome, at the pontifical court, or curia, for which reason they are known as curial cardinals, and the others are distributed throughout Christendom, governing particular dioceses or exercising other functions.

After the mass elevations by Pius XII on January 12th, 1953, the Sacred College was complete, which rarely happens. It then included seventy members, of whom twenty-six were Italian, seven French, four American, four Spanish, three Brazilian, two Portuguese, two German, two Argentine and two Canadian. There was one Englishman, one Austrian, one Belgian, one Dutchman, one Hungarian, one Irishman, one Pole, one Yugoslav, one Cuban, one Colombian, one Chilean, one Ecuadorean, one Peruvian, one Syrian, one Armenian, one Indian, one Australian and one Chinese. The Italian cardinals no longer represented more than a small minority, with twenty-six out of the seventy, although in the past they had formed a comfortable majority. In 1853, among seventy cardinals, there were fifty-four Italians and sixteen non-Italians, and only eight countries were represented; in 1953 twenty-six countries were represented. By the multiplicity and diversity of the countries represented in it the Sacred College was to present, in the intention of Pius XII, "a living image of the personality of the Church".

The successor of Pius XII is continuing the policy of his predecessor in the choice of cardinals, as could be seen in the appointments which he announced on November 17th, 1958. It is true that, of the twenty-three names in that list, thirteen were those of Italians, but Italians remained a minority in the Sacred College, and of the other ten two were French, two were American, and one each came from England, Germany, Austria, Spain, Mexico and Uruguay.

The members of the Sacred College are divided into three orders, those of the cardinal priests, the cardinal bishops and the cardinal deacons. The distinction between these is based on historical survivals, and is purely formal, for nowadays almost all cardinals have received episcopal consecration. Occasionally cardinals in the curia have received only the priesthood; there were two in 1958. Since the beginning of the twentieth century no cardinals have been only deacons and not priests.

The cardinal bishops, six in number, reside in Rome or its immediate neighbourhood. They are the successors of the bishops who used in former times to occupy episcopal sees in little places near Rome—Ostia, Albano, Frascati and Palestrina among others. The cardinal priests represent the presbyterial college of Rome; that is, the priests who from the earliest Christian times administered the parish churches of Rome, which were called titles, *tituli*. Hence to this very day the pope allocates a Roman church to each cardinal priest, so that, for example, Cardinal Gerlier, the archbishop of Lyons, is cardinal priest of the title—that is, of the church—of the Santissima Trinità al Monte Pincio. Similarly Cardinal Spellman is cardinal priest of the title of Santi Giovanni e Paolo, and Cardinal Godfrey of the title of Santi Nereo ed Achilleo. The cardinal deacons constitute the third and last order; they are the successors of the seven Roman deacons of whom we have evidence since the middle of the third century, and who represented, in the Church of Rome, the seven deacons instituted by the apostles in the earliest Christian Community in Jerusalem (Acts 7. 1–6). In the eleventh century their number was increased to fourteen. To each of them also a Roman church, known as a deaconry, is allocated.

The selection and appointment of the cardinals lies exclusively within the competence of the pope. Nobody has the right to interfere in elevations to the college of cardinals, and the

Sovereign Pontiff is not bound to take the advice of anyone at all; he appoints them in complete freedom. The proclamation of new cardinals takes place during a consistory.

The cardinals rank first in the Church, having precedence over bishops, archbishops, primates and even patriarchs. They are subject only to the pope. Through the functions which they fulfil at the pontifical court they participate in the government of the universal Church. It is to them that the pope entrusts the direction or the supervision of the various administrative and judicial bodies charged with the central government of the Church which constitute the Roman curia.

For a long time the business of the Church used to be conducted by the pontifical chancery. The ceaselessly increasing volume of that business however, and its complexity, made the creation of specialized bodies necessary. The system of the Roman congregations, which to some extent correspond to the ministries of a modern state, goes back to the sixteenth century, but their present organization is governed by Pius X's constitution *Sapienti Consilio* of June 29th, 1908. The chief merit of the reorganization carried out by Pius X lay in making a clear distinction between the administrative and the judicial spheres, entrusting the administration to special bodies, the Roman congregations proper, and justice to other bodies, the Roman tribunals.

Since Pius X's reorganization and the Code of 1917 the central government of the Church has been carried out in the legislative and administrative sphere by eleven congregations; and in the judicial sphere by three tribunals. To these two categories of well defined bodies five offices are added, corresponding to the secretariats which are found in our modern states.

The congregations, then, are the bodies of an administrative and legislative order; it must be recalled that in the Church the administrative and legislative spheres are not so sharply separated as they are in our democratic states. We give the list of the congregations in the order found in the Code of 1917:

1. The Holy Office watches over doctrine and morals and is responsible for the Index. Everything concerning marriages contracted between a Catholic and a non-Catholic comes within its competence.

2. The Consistorial Congregation is the governing body upon which depend almost all the bishops of the Latin Church; it nominates most of the bishops, and supervises their administration with the help of the reports which they must make every five years; since 1952, the pastoral care of displaced persons has also depended upon it.

3. The Congregation for the Sacraments is concerned with everything to do not with sacramental doctrine or liturgy but with legislation in regard to them: for example the sacraments of marriage (dispensations from impediments, validization), of the Eucharist (dispensations from the eucharistic fast, celebration of Mass under other than normal conditions), or holy Orders (authorizing priests to carry out ceremonies that are normally reserved to bishops).

4. The Congregation for the Council works in a very wide field, its competence including everything that concerns the discipline of the faithful and the clergy, apart from the bishops who come under the Consistorial Congregation.

5. The Congregation for Religious examines and resolves all problems regarding the life, constitutions, vows, property, studies and privileges of religious.

6. The Congregation for Propaganda is responsible for the direction of the missions, supervising the training of missionary priests and the selection of missionary bishops, defining the boundaries of missionary territories and providing financial assistance for the missions.

7. The Congregation for Rites is responsible for publishing the liturgical books, for the rules concerning the celebration of the offices of the Church and the administration of the sacraments, and for causes of beatification and canonization.

8. The Congregation for Ceremonial looks after the solem-

nities of the pontifical *cappella* and the pontifical court and diplomatic receptions and visits; its activity is confined to Rome.

9. The Congregation for Extraordinary Ecclesiastical Affairs deals with questions in which the civil power is concerned: the delimitation of dioceses and the appointment of bishops in countries where the government enjoys certain rights in these matters.

10. The Congregation for Seminaries and Universities rules and controls centres of higher education which depend directly upon the Holy See.

11. The Congregation for the Eastern Church has competence over all the Churches of Eastern rite that are in communion with Rome, whether persons, discipline or the liturgy are concerned.

Each congregation is presided over by a cardinal who bears the title of prefect, save three in which the presidency is reserved to the pope personally: the Holy Office, the Consistorial Congregation and the Congregation for the Eastern Church. The cardinal prefect is assisted by a secretary, an under-secretary and a numerous secretarial staff working in a research department, a documentary service, a financial department and an executive department. In the three congregations of which the pope is prefect the effective direction lies with a cardinal secretary, assisted by an assessor, a *sostituto*, and under them, as in the other congregations, a full staff.

The congregations proper work in the administrative sphere and to some extent in the legislative and doctrinal spheres. Judicial matters are for the tribunals, which are three in number.

The Sacred Penitentiary, with the Grand Penitentiary at its head appointed by the pope, judges actions which concern the internal forum, or the conscience. It also remits certain very grave canonical punishments from which absolution or dispensation is withdrawn from lower tribunals and reserved to the Holy See.

The Rota and the Apostolic Segnatura are the ordinary

tribunals of the Roman curia for causes *in foro externo*; we shall have an opportunity to say something of their respective characteristics at the end of this chapter, when we deal with canonical procedure. Lastly, it should be noted that the Holy Office is sometimes called upon to act as a tribunal; it judges criminal cases of exceptional gravity which do not come within the normal jurisdictions.

Alongside these congregations and tribunals we find a third group, of administrative bodies with various functions; secretariats of a kind known as offices, which are five in number:

1. The Apostolic Chancery is charged with drawing up and despatching bulls—that is, pontifical documents drawn up in solemn form—dealing with such matters as episcopal appointments, the proclamation of holy years or the creation and delimitation of dioceses and ecclesiastical provinces.

2. The Datary delivers letters of appointment to lower ecclesiastical posts which are withdrawn from the competence of the bishops and reserved to the Holy See.

3. The Apostolic Camera, under the Cardinal Camerlengo, is less important than it used to be; it is concerned with the temporal goods of the Roman Church during a vacancy of the pontifical see; in normal times the temporal affairs of the Holy See are managed by a commission of three cardinals with the help of lay experts.

The Secretariat of State, on the other hand, is a very important body, with a large staff, and with the Cardinal Secretary of State at its head. It directs papal policy; upon it depend the nuncios and internuncios accredited to the various governments, and the ambassadors and ministers plenipotentiary or *chargés d'affaires* which the states maintain at the Holy See address themselves to it.

5. The Secretariats of Briefs to Princes and of Latin Letters draw up in solemn form missives intended for official personages.

Finally, for the sake of completeness, we should add a series of permanent commissions concerned with the most widely-ranging questions—the interpretation of the Code, biblical studies, sacred archaeology, historical sciences, the moral supervision of the cinema, radio and television, the pontifical work of social service, and so on.

Such are the institutions of which the central power of the Catholic Church normally disposes. The supreme authority lies in the hands of the pope, who has complete freedom in appointing the heads of all these bodies, and who through them exercises uninterrupted control over the conduct of the Church's affairs. Contact between the Holy See and the local Churches scattered throughout the world is maintained by the bishops.

DIOCESAN ADMINISTRATION

The territory of the Church is divided into dioceses, the real basis of the local organization of the Church, at any rate in countries which have been Catholic for a long time. In those known as missionary countries the first step is the establishment of prefectures and then of vicariates apostolic, and when the organization is sufficiently advanced the vicariate is made into a diocese. A great many vicariates and prefectures apostolic have been raised to the status of dioceses in Africa and Asia in recent years, the Holy See desiring by this means to make it clear to the native Christian populations that it does not regard them as inferior to the European and American populations. In addition, there are certain occasional parts of the territory of the Church outside the diocesan organization, forming little autonomous and independent enclaves within the dioceses and including one or more parishes; these are a kind of miniature diocese, governed by the abbot of a monastery or a prelate and known as the case may be as abbacies *nullius* or prelatures *nullius*; the word *dioecesis* being understood and the phrase showing that they do not depend upon any diocese. According to the *Annuario Pontificio* for 1959, the Church included on December 31st, 1958, 316 residential metropolitan sees, 42 residential archiepiscopal but not metropolitan sees, 1,283 residential episcopal sees, 85 prelatures and abbacies *nullius,* 216 vicariates apostolic, and 115 prefectures apostolic. In short, the diocese represents the normal territorial division and administrative unit, while the vicariates and prefectures are destined to become dioceses and the abbacies and prelatures are small and relatively unimportant.

The number and importance of the dioceses varies from one country to another, historical factors accounting for the contrasts. Italy has nearly three hundred of them, whereas France has eighty-seven for a much greater area although a total population that is about the same. Germany, western and eastern together, has only twenty-four. The dioceses, apart from a few exceptions, are grouped in ecclesiastical provinces, each governed by a metropolitan who bears the title of archbishop; but it should be noted that not all archbishops have metropolitan rank, for in certain cases the title of archbishop is only an honorary one.

The division into provinces has no more than a secondary importance; the powers of a metropolitan over his suffragan bishops, as they are called, are very limited, and amount to no more than honorary prerogatives, and rights of supervising and deputizing. The real administrative unit is the diocese. The Holy See deals directly with each bishop; the Roman congregations do not in principle approach the bishops through their metropolitans. Each bishop on his side is in direct touch with the Roman Curia, without using the metropolitan as his intermediary. Hence the importance of those appointed to the government of the dioceses and the care which the Holy See takes in their choice.

According to canon 329 of the Code of 1917, the pope freely appoints the bishops throughout the Latin Church. However, with variations in its application, the ancient right of election reserved to the titular canons of the cathedral church survives in some countries, notably in Switzerland for the dioceses of Coire, Basle and Saint-Gall, in Austria for the diocese of Salzburg, and in all the dioceses of Germany save those in Bavaria. In fact the freedom of choice is restricted to three candidates: the Holy See presents three names to the electoral college, and it is from these three candidates that the canons choose the bishop. In certain countries, more and more exceptionally, the right of nominating the bishops belongs to the head of the state. In former times concordats frequently recognized the right of sovereigns to nominate the bishops; this was one of the privileges most coveted by the civil authorities on account of the influence which the bishops exercised on the people. Today the only states in which the government can still by right nominate bishops are France, by virtue of the concordat of 1801, for the dioceses of Metz and Strasbourg; the republic of Haiti, in the West Indies, by virtue of a concordat concluded in 1860; Peru, by virtue of a special favour granted by Pius IX on March 5th, 1875; the principality of Monaco by virtue of the bull *Quemadmodum* of March 15th, 1887; and finally Spain, by virtue of the agreement of June 7th, 1941, confirmed by the concordat of 1953. But the rights recognized in the head of the Spanish state and the prince of Monaco are very limited.

Rome, nowadays, is reluctant to recognize the right of a civil power to nominate bishops, and the practice finds no favour either with pontifical diplomacy or with the present state of canon law. But the Holy See readily understands that the secular authority cannot be uninterested in the choice of men so influential as bishops and willingly grants a right of consultation to a government that asks for it. Under such an agreement the Holy See undertakes to make known to the civil power the name of the candidate whom it proposes to raise to the episcopate, and authorizes the government to express, if need be, any objections of a political order which it may be able to bring against the nomination. This prerogative has been recognized in various countries, including France, Italy, Portugal, Germany and Poland. But whatever the means used in the nomination of the candidates, it is within the exclusive competence of the Holy See to confer the episcopal powers, properly so called, of order and jurisdiction.

A bishop has wide powers and rights. Thanks to the plenitude of the priesthood with which he is endowed, he can confer
orders and conduct all consecrations. He is master in his
diocese, under the authority of the pope, and has legislative,
judicial and coercive power within the limits laid down by the
law, of which we have already spoken. The importance of
the office imposes equally grave obligations. The bishop must
watch over the well-being of the faithful entrusted to him, in
doctrine, religious life and morals. He is responsible for the
pastoral care of his diocese. Finally, he provides the link
between the central power and the individual Catholic. It is
through the bishops that the Holy See exercises its authority
over every one of the faithful. It is not surprising, therefore,
that canon law requires the bishops to maintain very close
relations with Rome; the visits *ad limina* and five-yearly reports are the principal means by which they do so.

Every bishop, at fixed times, must make a journey to Rome,
called the visit *ad limina apostolorum*, literally to "the
thresholds of the apostles", that is to the tombs of St Peter
and St Paul, in order to make contact with the Sovereign
Pontiff and the various Roman congregations. This journey is
required every five years for the European bishops and every
ten years for the bishops of the other continents. In addition,
each bishop is bound to send to Rome every five years a
written report, supported by a detailed questionnaire covering
all aspects of the religious life of the diocese: faith and
worship, the organization of the diocesan curia, statistics of
the clergy, ordinations, religious practice, works of the apostolate, the cooperation of the religious orders and so on. These
five-yearly reports are studied by the Consistorial Congregation. The Holy See has at its disposal, therefore, comprehensive information about the state of the Catholic world
which is all the time being brought up to date.

To help him in his administrative work the Bishop is
assisted by a body called the diocesan or episcopal curia,
the members of which include one or more vicars general, a
chancellor, secretaries and an archivist. Judicial affairs are

entrusted to the members of the diocesan tribunal, the composition of which we shall indicate later on, when dealing
with canonical procedure. The cathedral chapter, composed of
a given number of canons, constitutes the council which the
bishop must consult in certain matters; in dioceses where there
is no chapter the canons are replaced by priests appointed
by the bishop who bear the title of diocesan consultors. The
chapter has lost a great part of the importance which it used
to enjoy in the past. The Code of 1917 diminished its rôle
still further, and nowadays the bishop is only very occasionally
bound to obtain the chapter's agreement; most of the time
it is enough for him to seek the opinion of his council, without
being bound to follow it. The chapter comes into its own
again, although only for a short time, the moment the diocese
becomes vacant with the death of the bishop, or his translation
elsewhere or resignation. The law of the Church then makes
the chapter responsible for the administration of the diocese,
with the obligation to appoint a vicar capitular within eight
days. As soon as he is appointed the vicar capitular takes over
the administration of the diocese, which he retains until a
new bishop takes possession of the see, and the chapter
returns to its former position.

In large dioceses the bishop is assisted in his pastoral
work by one or even several coadjutors, who have received
episcopal consecration and so may deputize for the bishop of
the diocese at ordinations and especially at confirmations.
The Holy See also often gives a coadjutor to an aged or sick
bishop, and sometimes accords to this coadjutor the right of
succeeding the bishop whom he assists in the administration
of the diocese. In canonical language it is usual to reserve
the title of auxiliary for coadjutor bishops who have no right
of succession.

PAROCHIAL ORGANIZATION

Dioceses are subdivided into smaller administrative areas;
these are the parishes, of which the number and the size

vary; in the towns they include a large population and a small territory, whereas the reverse is usually the case in the country-side. For the Catholic, the parish is the spiritual centre *par excellence*. It is within the framework of the parish that the real pastoral work is done, and that the faithful carry out their religious duties.

Responsibility for the parishes is entrusted to parish priests. There is only one parish priest at the head of each parish, just as there is only one bishop at the head of each diocese. The parish priest can be assisted in his work by other priests, generally known as curates. In ordinary law the selection and appointment of parish priests and curates lies with the bishop, although in some dioceses in Germany and central Europe the ancient right of patronage survives. By virtue of this prerogative, either individuals—the descendant of a noble family, for instance—or bodies—such as a chapter or a township—are entitled to present candidates to the bishop when the parishes in which they have the right of patronage fall vacant. The bishop is obliged to bestow the parish on the priest presented if he fulfills the conditions which the law demands. In some districts of Switzerland the people of the parish similarly enjoy the right of choosing the parish priest, and if the priest they choose satisfies the necessary conditions the bishop cannot refuse him canonical investiture. But such cases are relics of the past. The right of patronage and the right of choice find no favour in the present state of canon law, and will gradually disappear even in those few places where for one reason or another they survived after 1917.

When he has received his letters of appointment, the parish priest makes his profession of faith and takes possession of the parish in a ceremony of varying solemnity. As soon as he has taken possession of it he is entitled to exercise the powers attached to the office of a parish priest and is bound by the obligations which derive from them. The rights of the parish priest are not even relatively comparable to those of the bishop; he has no legislative, judicial or coercive power. The Church only recognizes in him a sort of dominative or paternal power. He can give orders to those subject to him, but not jurisdictional precepts, and in no case is he authorized to inflict canonical punishments. On the other hand, a whole series of pastoral and liturgical functions are reserved to him, to the extent that other priests may not perform them in the parish without his permission: the administration of solemn baptism and extreme unction, the public carrying of holy communion and the viaticum, assistance at marriage, the nuptial blessing, the blessing of the baptismal font and so on. The parish priest can absolve his own parishioners from their sins anywhere in the world; he can dispense them everywhere from fasting, abstinence and the law requiring assistance at Mass, as well as from that requiring abstention from manual work on Sundays and holy days. He has the same powers in regard to all travellers passing through his parish. We have already noted the powers of dispensation from impediments to marriage which the Code allows to parish priests in urgent cases or when there is danger of death.

The obligations which the law imposes on a parish priest arise from concern for the good of the souls in his care: he must reside in the parish, he must preach, he must teach the catechism, administer the sacraments and look after the sick and the dying; he must offer the sacrifice of the Mass for his parishioners on Sundays and holy days. In addition, much administrative work falls upon a parish priest: he must keep registers of baptisms, confirmations, marriages and burials; he must keep records of his parishioners, he must make the necessary inquiries when people want to get married; he must administer the temporal goods of the church and of the parish in collaboration with the members of his parish council, if he has one.

The work of parish priests and the condition of the parishes are under the constant and regular control of the diocesan administration. The bishop is bound to visit every parish in his diocese every five years, in person or through a representative. It is with the data collected in the course of his parochial visitations that he draws up the five-yearly report on the condition of the diocese required by the Holy See. So it is that, through the bishops, the central authority knows the state of affairs in every local Church down to the least detail.

THE SETTLEMENT OF DISPUTES AND THE PUNISHMENT OF CRIME

The ecclesiastical society is not composed of saints but of men who combine many faults with their good qualities. Conflicts and quarrels between its members are inevitable. Good organization can prevent many disputes but will never be able to prevent them all. It is necessary, therefore, to provide for their settlement. Hence the Church, like civil society, has a procedural law and the penal law which normally and necessarily goes with it. We shall explain the essential elements of these two parts of the legal system of the Church, beginning with procedure.

Canonical procedure

The Church, as we have several times had occasion to say, knows no separation of powers. The Sovereign Pontiff combines judicial power in the universal Church with legislative and coercive power. The residential bishops are invested with precisely the same powers in their dioceses, and so also are the other ordinaries—vicars and prefects apostolic, abbots and prelates *nullius*, superiors general and provincials of the exempt religious institutes of priests—in their respective territories or in regard to the persons depending upon them. As a general rule these various authorities do not themselves exercise judicial power; they entrust the office of judge to subordinates to whom they delegate their power. But the responsibility lies with them, and nothing can prevent them from presiding at any time over the tribunal which derives from their jurisdiction.

For reasons which we have already seen, the judicial power of the Church is only exercised over those who have been baptized, for only they are the subjects of the Church and

so have recourse to her tribunals. It happens only exceptionally that an unbaptized person is called upon to appear
before an ecclesiastical tribunal and the ecclesiastical judge
is empowered to assist him. This sometimes occurs in matrimonial cases. Two unbaptized persons, for example, have
contracted a marriage of which the nullity is afterwards established on account of a civil impediment or a manifest lack of
consent. The couple separate, and one of them wishes to
marry a Catholic. The Church will only authorize the second
union after the first marriage has been declared null, and will
require the nullity to be recognized by her tribunal. Apart
from these very rare cases the judicial system of the Church
is intended only for those who have been baptized, but she
clearly does not claim an exclusive right over them. The
Church has no intention at all of replacing secular justice.
The rights which she claims are restricted to certain spheres
and to certain persons. Thus the Church reserves to her tribunals cases concerned with matters of a strictly spiritual
order, such as the sacraments and preaching, or of a temporal
order when spiritual issues are involved, concerning such
matters as ecclesiastical benefices, religious funerals or church
furnishings. She also claims her own exclusive competence in
deciding when canon law has been violated and in judging
persons who enjoy the privilege of the tribunal—that is, clerics
and members of religious institutes. Hence it is in principle
forbidden to make these persons appear before State tribunals;
but the law is flexible enough at the present time to leave un-
troubled the consciences of Catholic judges who might find
themselves obliged to summon a cleric or religious. It is
enough to seek the permission of the ecclesiastical authority;
and in urgent cases permission may even be presumed.

The judicial organization of the Church is relatively simple;
the procedure itself is more complex.

The Code of 1917 provides for three degrees of jurisdiction:
the tribunals of the first instance, those of the second instance,

and then those of the third instance which are in principle the Roman tribunals.

The bishop's tribunal is the first instance, or, in missionary countries, that of the vicar or prefect apostolic; in the exempt congregations of priests and in the religious orders it is the tribunal of the provincial superior or of the local abbot of an independent monastery. For the purposes of this account we shall deal only with the diocesan tribunal; what we shall have to say can be implied, *mutatis mutandis*, to the other tribunals of the first instance.

Every bishop has his tribunal, although in some countries nowadays several dioceses combine to establish a single common tribunal; this they do for practical reasons, and it is a practice which the Holy See encourages. But this arrangement does not affect the principle and does not in any way diminish the right of each bishop. It is before the diocesan tribunal that all the legal disputes of persons coming in one way or another within the bishop's judicial competence must be brought in the first instance. The only exceptions are the cases of individual or corporate persons whom the law reserves to the Sovereign Pontiff (heads of state and their families, cardinals, legates, bishops in criminal cases) or to the tribunals of the Holy See (bishops in non-criminal disputes, dioceses, exempt religious institutes), and those which the pope summons to his own tribunal on his own initiative or at the request of those concerned; for every one of the faithful can demand that his case shall be introduced directly in a Roman court, without passing through those of lower instance. The competence of the episcopal tribunal is determined in principle by the domicile or quasi-domicile of the defendant party; in certain cases other factors may be taken into consideration, as for example the place where a contract was made, or where the object of litigation is situated, or where an offence was committed.

The diocesan tribunal is composed of a presiding judge, known as the *officialis*, to whom the bishop confides his powers; it is only for some quite exceptional reason that the bishop presides over his tribunal in person. But the bishop and the *officialis*, who must not be the vicar general, form only one single tribunal, so that it is not possible to appeal from one to the other. A certain number of judges are available as well as the *officialis*, for certain cases, notably matrimonial cases, can only be judged by a collegiate tribunal composed of three judges; for others the law requires as many as five judges. Hence every bishop must appoint, in addition to the *officialis*, some priests who are specialists in canon law —four at the least and twelve at the most—to carry out the duties of judges in his tribunal. These are appointed during a synod, the bishop submitting their names to the approval of the assembly, whence the name of synodal judges sometimes borne by the advisers of the *officialis*. The diocesan tribunal also includes an auditor, whose duty it is to examine the process, and a notary or clerk who must write, or at least sign, all the proceedings, without which they are null and void. The office of auditor is very often filled by the *officialis* himself, or by a synodal judge. The prosecution is undertaken by the *promotor justitiae* in criminal cases and certain contentious cases, and by the *defensor vinculi*, the defender of the bond, in marriage and ordination cases. The parties concerned may be represented by a procurator and their interests are defended by an advocate; generally the same person serves both as advocate and procurator. The advocates are clerics, sometimes laymen, but the approval of the bishop is necessary before they are admitted to plead.

The second instance of the diocesan tribunal is constituted in principle by the tribunal of the metropolitan archbishop; the suffragan bishops of an ecclesiastical province must address themselves to the tribunal of their own metropolitan. So for example cases judged in the first instance by the diocesan tribunals of Bayeux, Coutances, Evreux and Sées pass in the second instance before the tribunal of Rouen. The second instance for the metropolitan tribunal is provided by the tribunal of the suffragan bishop whom the archbishop has appointed for this purpose on a permanent basis, with the approval of the Holy See. Evreux provides an appeal tribunal for cases judged in the first instance at Rouen. Archbishops who have no suffragans, and bishops immediately subject to Rome, send their cases in the second instance to the metropolitan tribunal of the province where they have chosen to take part in the provincial council (see chapter II of this book), provided that the Holy See has not decided otherwise. The rule is applied to the tribunal of Marseilles; attending the provincial council of Aix-en-Provence, the Archbishop of Marseilles sends to the tribunal of the same metropolitan see the cases judged by his tribunal in the first instance. The Holy See has itself designated the appeal tribunal of the courts of the first instance of Metz and Strasbourg; this is not the metropolitan tribunal of the province chosen for the provincial council; under instructions from Rome, each of these two diocesan courts serves as a court of the second instance for the other, Metz for Strasbourg and Strasbourg for Metz. For exempt religious priests the appeal tribunal in cases judged in the first instance by a provincial or a local abbot is the tribunal of the superior-general of the institute or monastic congregation. The composition of the tribunal of the second instance is on the same lines as that of the first instance; the same persons take part and in the same way. The procedure is identical.

Cases are judged in the third instance by the Roman Rota. Only in a few countries, like Germany and Spain, does the Holy See permit local tribunals to judge in the third instance. For a very long time Spain has had the privilege of possessing a tribunal organized on the model of the Roman tribunal: the Spanish Rota, the rights of which were confirmed by Rome on April 7th, 1947. In Germany certain diocesan tribunals serve reciprocally as courts of the third instance by special permission of the Holy See. Thus the tribunal of Munich receives in the third instance cases judged in the second instance by the metropolitan tribunal of Bamberg, and *vice versa*; the tribunal of Cologne performs the same service for the metropolitan tribunal of Freiburg im Breisgau. But these are exceptions.

In the third instance cases are normally sent to the Holy See, which has two ordinary tribunals, the Rota and the Apostolic Segnatura.

The Rota is, by definition, an appeal tribunal for the metropolitan and diocesan tribunals; it is only exceptionally that it judges in the first instance. It likewise receives cases which it has itself already considered, so that it is its own appeal tribunal; there is no difficulty about this, for it works by rotation, and the same case will therefore not be heard again by the same judges. The tribunal of the Rota is composed of twelve judges, called auditors, who belong to different countries; by tradition there are two Spaniards, one Frenchman and one German among them, and in recent years Britain and the United States have also been represented; indeed, a Scottish auditor became dean of the Rota when John XXIII elevated Cardinal Jullien to the sacred college. The judges are assisted by a large subordinate staff, and a considerable body of approved advocates, both priests and laymen, argue cases before the Rota, which at the present time judges more than two hundred and fifty cases every year.

The Apostolic Segnatura is the supreme tribunal of the Holy See. It judges, among others, appeals brought against sentences pronounced by the Rota in matrimonial cases, when the Rota declines to give them a further hearing, pronouncing on petitions for nullity or for "restitution" (*restitutio in integrum*) when these are brought against sentences of the Rota. It is also the Segnatura that settles disputes about competence if these should arise between lower tribunals. The judges, six or seven in number, are cardinals, and the staff consists of a secretary, a notary and a college of *prelati votanti* and *prelati referendari* who do the preliminary work for the judges.

Canonical procedure as such presents certain features which differentiate it from the procedure of most contemporary states. It is secret, without publicity for its arguments. All trials take place behind closed doors, in the sense that the only people admitted are the contending parties, their representatives, the prosecutor and his staff, and any persons whose presence the judge may deem useful in examining the case. Further, the procedure is written: the pleadings of the advocates, the replies of the *defensor vinculi* or the *promotor justitiae* are made not *viva voce* but in the form of memoranda; sometimes a short oral explanation on the part of an advocate is allowed by the judge. Lastly, certain cases are never finally closed; that is to say that they cannot become the subject of irrevocable judgment; it is possible to re-open them even after ten or twenty years or more, if new evidence has been discovered. In these same cases the decision taken by the judges is only enforceable after two concurring sentences have been passed. The rule is applied to cases which concern personal status: marriage, ordination or religious profession. A judgment of nullity in marriage becomes enforceable only after a second tribunal has decided in the same sense; and nothing prevents the *defensor vinculi* from taking the case to the third instance. On the other hand, a couple whose marriage has been declared invalid by a first tribunal and valid by a second may not remarry. But they have the right to submit the case to a third instance, and even to other successive instances, if they are in a position to produce new arguments in favour of the nullity. There is no rule in cases of this kind; so also it is possible to open a trial of nullity in marriage after twenty years of married life. These cases are not fanciful.

There are three procedures known to canon law: the criminal procedure, the contentious procedure, and the administrative procedure. The first, the criminal or penal procedure, is concerned with the pursuit and repression of public crimes. It can only be set in motion by the public prosecutor, that is, the *promotor justitiae*, to whom the bringing of criminal charges is reserved. Any one of the faithful, however, can denounce those who are guilty of them to the ecclesiastical authorities, who conduct a private inquiry before handing the matter over to the *promotor justitiae* if it should be deemed appropriate to do so; for the ecclesiastical authorities will usually avoid a penal trial. In the majority of cases, in fact, the law permits the bishop to inflict a judicial reprimand on the delinquent who admits his fault. It is only when this step is unsuccessful or if circumstances or the law make strong action unavoidable that the dossier will be forwarded to the *promotor justitiae*. From that moment justice will take its normal course: the *promotor justitiae* draws up the act of indictment and sends it to the judge, who summons the accused and proceeds to the inquiry into the dispute and the solemn administration of the evidence. When the evidence and the documents have been assembled the judge decrees the publication of the dossier, then the closure of the inquiry; the advocate presents his pleading, the *promotor justitiae* his replies and the judge pronounces sentence, against which the normal ways of appeal are open within the lapse of time for which the law provides.

The procedure in disputes—that is, contentious procedure—is designed to define rights. It has two forms: the regular or normal, and the special form which follows from special rules and which is compulsory in trials of marriage and ordination cases. We leave on one side the beatification and canonization causes, in which a strict procedure related to the judicial trial is used, for which reason the rules enacted for beatifications and canonizations appear in the fourth book of the Code among the canons devoted to trials. But it seems more appropriate to leave this question for the chapter in which we shall treat of the Church's relations with the next world.

Nor shall we delay here to examine the regular procedure in disputes; the course of a normal trial of this kind before an ecclesiastical tribunal does not differ very much from the course followed in cases of the same kind in secular tribunals. The special procedure presents more interest, for the ecclesiastical tribunals have above all to pronounce on matrimonial cases, which are subject to particular rules; on the other hand they are very rarely occupied with cases seeking to declare an ordination invalid or to prove that the person concerned is not subject to the duties—of celibacy, of reciting the breviary and so on—of ordination received under the influence of grave fear. These cases are moreover dealt with under a procedure which borrows nearly all its features from the laws governing trials of nullity in marriage. It is, then, the procedure used in matrimonial cases that deserves our attention.

In this, it is well clearly to distinguish the reasons which lead the contending parties to have recourse to ecclesiastical authority to resolve the difficulties arising from their union. If the parties invoke non-consummation they can obtain not the annulment of the marriage but dispensation from the bond. A marriage which has not been consummated is valid if it has been contracted according to the provisions of the law, so that it is not possible to pronounce its nullity. But for a very long time the Church has been accustomed in these cases to grant a dispensation from the bond and to authorize each of the parties to contract a new union. This is not a question of a right but of a favour which the Church accords to her subjects. The procedure followed when this happens is therefore not of a judicial but of an administrative order. It is not the diocesan tribunal or the Rota which is competent but an administrative body: the Congregation of the Sacraments. The diocesan tribunal is simply charged to examine the case in order to furnish proof of non-consummation, and to transmit the dossier to the Holy See with the written opinion of the *defensor vinculi* and of the bishop. The Congregation of the Sacraments decides whether the proofs are sufficient and whether it is possible to ask the pope to dispense the bond. There is no appeal against the decision of the congregation, for we are in the administrative field. So as soon as the dispensation is granted the couple can remarry in accordance with the instructions given by the Holy See; it often happens that the party who has been the cause of the non-consummation is not authorized to make a second marriage without the permission of the Congregation of the Sacraments.

Cases in which it is sought to obtain a dispensation from

the bond by virtue of the Pauline privilege or the privilege of the faith are of the same order; they come to the Congregation of the Holy Office and are not within the competence of the ordinary tribunals since what is in question is the granting of a favour and not the recognition of a right. The partner in a marriage contracted outside the faith who is later baptized is allowed to marry a second time to a Catholic partner if the first partner refuses to be converted or at least to cohabit in peace. This is the application of a measure taken by St Paul and described in the First Epistle to the Corinthians (7. 15) in favour of married pagans who were converted to Christianity; whence the name of the Pauline privilege. The dispensation from the bond is granted by the Sovereign Pontiff by virtue of what has come to be called the privilege of the faith, for the favour is never accorded to a married person who was baptized at the time of his marriage; it is available only to one who was married while still unbaptized and who received baptism subsequently. The favour is granted to him to reward his fidelity to the Christian teaching which he has lately embraced, whence the name of privilege of the faith. All these cases which are not of a strictly judicial order come within the competence of the Holy Office, the diocesan tribunals being required simply to draw up the dossier and send it to Rome.

True marriage trials are for the declaration of the nullity of unions contracted under irregular conditions. The Church does not do a favour to the couple concerned in proclaiming the invalidity of their marriage, if it is found to be invalid; they have a right to the declaration of this nullity, if proof of it can be provided. The procedure used in establishing it is of a strictly judicial order, and responsibility for it rests with the tribunals.

Nullity can be caused by one of the three following reasons: a defect of form in the celebration of the marriage, a lack of consent—grave fear, a condition contrary to the nature of marriage; the rejection of children, of the unity, of the indissolubility at the time of the marriage—or the presence of a diriment impediment. The right of introducing a case in nullity is reserved to the parties concerned or to the *promotor jus-titiae*; no other person is entitled to come forward as the plaintiff in these cases. Contrary to the rule followed in other trials, the nearest members of the family and relatives by marriage are admitted to give evidence, for the one strong and simple reason that they know better than others the intimate state of the married life of the parties concerned, which often provides the most valuable information on which to base the inquiry. The *defensor vinculi* plays a very impor-tant part; it is for him to bring out the significance of every-thing that is in favour of the validity. Hence he must be summoned to the interrogation of the parties, of the witnesses, of experts; he has the right to consult the documents in the case at any time.

The case itself is introduced by a written document before the ecclesiastical tribunal of the place where the marriage was celebrated or where the defendant party has domicile or, if absolutely necessary, a quasi-domicile. If the document is ad-mitted the tribunal proceeds, in the presence of the parties, to the discussion of the issue, which describes the exact ground of the nullity which will be argued. From this moment the legal process commences; it is pursued by the inquiry which seeks to assemble the proofs by interrogating the parties, the wit-nesses, the experts. When the case appears to have been examined sufficiently, the *officialis* authorizes those concerned to examine the dossier; this is the publication of the proceed-ings. Then he decrees the closure of the preliminary investiga-tion. The advocate presents his case, the *defensor vinculi* replies; the advocate can bring forward a further elaboration of his case if he wishes, but the *defensor vinculi* always has the last word. The tribunal, composed of three judges, gives a majority verdict. If the judgment is favourable to the nullity the *defensor vinculi* must put in an appeal within ten days to the higher instance; otherwise it is for the parties concerned to ask for the case to be re-examined before the appeal tri-bunal. In any event the parties can only contract new unions

after two sentences in favour of the nullity have been pronounced. It is true that these trials make the parties liable
for fees, especially advocates' fees, but their significance
should not be exaggerated, and it should not be forgotten that
those who are not very well off are given the advantage of
legal aid which may cover part or even the whole of the
amount. Legal aid is given in almost half the cases judged
by the Rota, and the proportion is about the same in the
diocesan and metropolitan tribunals.

There are cases where all this complicated judicial
machinery seems superfluous, inasmuch as the nullity of the
marriage seems to be obvious. So a summary procedure, which
is nevertheless of a judicial order, has been provided for. The
law permits it to be used when the invalidity of the marriage
arises from the existence of one of the following impediments:
disparity of cult, orders, a solemn vow, marriage, consanguinity, affinity and spiritual relationship; the law also requires certainty that a dispensation was not granted at the
time of the marriage. The bishop then declares the nullity
without any other formality; it is enough for him to hear the
defensor vinculi, who on his side is not obliged to appeal to a
second instance, if the bishop's decision seems to him
justified.

Lastly, canon law provides an administrative procedure
which makes it possible to settle some affairs and even to
inflict sanctions without recourse to judicial procedure
properly speaking, whether contentious or criminal; but this
procedure, greatly simplified, is only used in cases concerning
ecclesiastics, and its use is only permitted in matters strictly
defined by the law. Its purpose is to protect the public good
of the ecclesiastical society. It makes it possible for the
ecclesiastical authority to substitute more suitable priests for
parish priests whose ministry has become unprofitable, without this necessarily being due to any fault of theirs, as the
result perhaps of old age or infirmity or unpopularity among
their parishioners or incapacity; for parish priests enjoy
security of tenure guaranteed by the law. The bishop cannot

replace them as he pleases, as he does for example curates, chaplains or seminary professors. This security is greater or less according to the nature of the parishes; the parish priests who enjoy the greatest security are called in English rectors (or in French *curés inamovibles*, as distinguished from *curés amovibles*). The former, generally speaking, have parishes in the towns and more important centres. This same procedure likewise permits the ecclesiastical authority to inflict penalties upon ecclesiastics who show themselves negligent in carrying out their duties or who prejudice the community of the faithful by their conduct.

The bishop examines and judges in administrative processes. He is assisted by a notary or clerk and must generally take the opinion of two synodal examiners and sometimes of two parish priests appointed to serve as consultors. The person concerned cannot appeal to the tribunal of the second instance against the final decree of the bishop, for the affair is in the administrative sphere; if he thinks himself wronged he can have recourse to the Holy See. Administrative procedure is provided for the settlement of seven cases, of which the first three are contentious in character and the remaining four are penal: the dismissal of rectors, the dismissal of other parish priests, the transfer of parish priests, the calling to order, followed, it may be, by sanctions, of clerics failing to observe the law of residence, of clerics suspect of bad conduct, of parish priests who are negligent in their pastoral office, and the infliction of the suspension called *ex informata conscientia* for secret or, occasionally, public offences.

The penal law

The Church recognizes in herself the power of inflicting punishments. She enforces certain laws with sanctions which are essentially of a spiritual order, but she does not exclude temporal punishments such as fines, or the confiscation of the revenues attached to an ecclesiastical office. In short, the Church has a penal law, like every perfect society, *societas perfecta*; she is obliged to fashion her institutions along juridical lines, as a consequence of her roots in historical time. And law without the opportunity of invoking sanctions if need be would often be ineffective; those who have been baptized remain dependent upon their human state.

Clearly the Church has authority to inflict punishment only on those who are her subjects; she has no coercive power over those who have not been baptized. In practice the exercise of this power is reserved to the authorities which hold the legislative power: the pope and certain bodies in the Roman curia in the universal Church, the bishop in his diocese, the vicar and prefect apostolic, the abbot and prelate *nullius* in their respective territories, the major superiors of exempt institutes of priests in regard to those who are subject to their jurisdiction. Vicars general cannot inflict punishments without a special mandate from their bishops, and the competence of the *officialis*, the ecclesiastical judge, is limited to the application of the sanctions for which the law provides; any other initiative in a penal matter is in principle forbidden to him.

Alongside elements common to the law of civil societies, the penal law of the Church presents special features of its own which derive from the special character of the ecclesiastical society. Those who hold coercive authority must never at any time forget that they are the representatives of God, who is good. The Gospels counsel gentleness and mercy towards the weak, whoever they may be, and Christ was severe only to the proud. This was not forgotten when the Code of Canon Law was drawn up, when the section *De poenis in genere* was prefaced with a quotation along these lines from the Council of Trent (canon 2214, paragraph 2). But it is above all in the nature of the punishments and the way they are inflicted and remitted that the ecclesiastical penal law is distinguished from the law of secular societies.

Practically speaking the Church disposes only of spiritual sanctions; those of a temporal order are very rarely used. The different punishments for which present-day canon law provides are divided into two great categories according to their purpose: "medicinal" punishments (*poenae medicinales*), known as censures, and "vindicative" punishments. As the name suggests, the former are above all designed to correct the guilty person; they are inflicted to lead the offender to a better frame of mind and therefore presuppose contumacy. They are therefore never inflicted for a determined time; their duration depends upon the attitude of the person concerned. As soon as he has made amends he is entitled to the remission of the punishment, which is given under the form of absolution. But to give greater weight to the punishment the law withholds the power to give absolution from most censures from simple priests, parish priests and confessors, reserving it for higher authorities. Thus certain censures are reserved to the diocesan authorities or their equivalents (bishops or other ordinaries), while others are reserved to the Holy See; and reservation to the Holy See includes three degrees which make the absolution more difficult: simple reservation, special reservation and very special reservation. According to the kind of reservation, absolution from the punishment must be sought either from the diocese or from Rome, and as a general rule this will be done through the confessor or the parish priest, who has authority in urgent cases to give the absolution on the spot, with recourse afterwards to the competent authority.

Medicinal punishments are three in number: excommunication, interdict and suspension. Excommunication is the most severe of the canonical punishments; the Catholic upon whom it is inflicted is so to speak placed outside the community of the faithful and is deprived of all the rights which had been conferred upon him by virtue of his membership of the Church: the sacraments, burial by the Church, participation in the services of the Church and the benefits of public prayers. This punishment is of such gravity that the Church never uses it as a vindicative punishment, inflicting it for a definite period such as six months or a year. Excommunication can only be used as a medicinal punishment; that is to say, the duration of the punishment depends solely on the offender. It is enough that one who has been excommunicated shows dispositions of repentance for him to be able in strict justice at once to claim absolution from the punishment and full readmission to the communion of the Church.

The interdict is a punishment of a special kind, which can have a local and not only a personal character. The local interdict, placed on a church or on a parish, means that it is forbidden to carry out the external solemnities of worship there. The personal interdict deprives offenders of certain spiritual benefits without excluding them from the communion of the faithful. Frequently used in the Middle Ages, the local interdict has become a very rare punishment nowadays.

Suspension can be imposed only on clerics, and deprives them, in whole or in part, of their rights and powers. Thus the ecclesiastical authority can forbid a cleric to celebrate Mass, to hear confessions, or to collect the revenues of his benefice, and this is partial suspension. Total suspension forbids all use of the power of orders and jurisdiction.

Vindicative punishments are intended in the first place to obtain the expiation of the crime and the punishment of the person who has committed it; their object is the good of society, whereas the object of censures is first and foremost the good of the individual. Their duration, therefore, does not depend upon the will of the offender, but on the decision of the competent authority. A person upon whom a vindicative punishment has been inflicted is not entitled to the remission of the punishment until he has been corrected. He must wait until the time decided upon has expired, at any rate unless his conduct leads his superior to judge it appropriate to dispense him from carrying out a part of the punishment. Contrary to the case with censures, there is no absolution from a vindicative punishment, but there can be dispensation, and the dispensation is not a right but a favour which the superior is not obliged to grant.

Vindicative punishments are more numerous and more various than censures. Some can be inflicted only on clerics, and others upon any member of the Church. Among the punishments to which all Catholics are liable are deprivation of the burial of the Church, deprivation of the sacraments, exclusion from legitimate ecclesiastical actions (which include in particular standing as godfather or sponsor at baptism or confirmation), ineligibility for certain favours or responsibilities open to the laity (such as those of cantor or sacristan), *infamia juris*, a fine, and, lastly, the local and collective interdict, for, unlike excommunication, the two other forms of censure, interdict and suspension, can be used as vindicative and not only as medicinal punishments. The vindicative punishments imposed only on clerics are, among others, suspension, penal transfer to a less important position, penal deprivation of office, a prohibition against residing in a stated place or compulsory residence in a stated place, temporary or permanent deprivation of the ecclesiastical habit, deposition and degradation.

As well as punishments properly so-called, canon law also disposes of milder sanctions. Some are in the nature of cautions or warnings when crimes have been committed; these are the penal remedies, four in number: the admonition, the rebuke, the precept, the placing under supervision. Others enable the ecclesiastical authority not to inflict a true punishment at once, or to compensate for the remission of a punishment: these are penances, usually consisting of prayers to recite, a pilgrimage to be carried out, a fast, alms to be given or a retreat to be made.

In the manner of inflicting punishments the penal law of the Church shows one special characteristic which is not met in any other legal system. Certain punishments are incurred by the offenders without any intervention on the part of authority; the simple perpetration of the crime gives effect to the punishment. Infliction is automatic, if the offender fulfils all the conditions for which the law provides. It is not necessary for a judge to pronounce a sentence of condemnation; the sentence has been imposed by the very fact of the perpetration of the crime, whence the term, *latae sententiae*, by which these punishments are known in contrast with those of which the infliction requires a sentence of condemnation, known as punishments *ferendae sententiae*. Many canonical punishments are inflicted in this way; they are easily recognized from the terms of the law in which they are the sanctions: *ipso facto, latae sententiae*, using the present and not the future tense.

Not all the laws of the Church have a penal character; only some of them carry punishments as their sanctions. The penal laws in force throughout the Latin Church appear in the last hundred and one canons of the Code of 1917: canons 2314 to 2414. To complete the picture we give the list of the principal crimes punished with excommunication *latae sententiae*. Those who are guilty of any of the following crimes automatically incur an excommunication reserved to the Holy See:

1. Reserved in a very special manner: profanation of the consecrated species, violation of the secrecy of the confessional.

2. Reserved in a special manner: apostasy, heresy, schism, the summoning of a bishop before a state tribunal, the false denunciation of a confessor.

3. Reserved in a simple manner: trafficking in indulgences, joining freemasonry or a similar sect, the violation of the enclosure of enclosed monks or nuns, duelling, the usurpation of the goods of the Church.

An excommunication reserved to the Ordinary (bishop, vicar general, etc.) is provided for abortion, the action of a Catholic contracting a marriage before a non-Catholic minister or in baptizing children outside the Catholic religion.

An unreserved excommunication punishes the alienation of the goods of the Church without authorization from the Holy See or constraint exercised against a person to make him or her enter the ecclesiastical or religious state.

We have seen something of the internal structure of the Church—her constitutional, administrative and penal law, and her procedure. We have seen that the Church is a strongly organized and hierarchical society. She undoubtedly bears the marks of a highly developed centralization, but the lower instances dispose of the necessary powers in urgent cases, and especially when there is danger of death. In these circumstances the good of souls comes before all considerations of an administrative order; when a person's eternal salvation is at stake the Roman authority delegates to the least minister in the scale of the hierarchy all the powers that in normal times it reserves to the higher instances.

CHAPTER VI

THE RELATIONS OF
CHURCH AND STATE

The Church does not live outside time. Her members are the citizens of a state which also imposes its obligations upon them. The Church defends the interests of the heavenly city, the state those of the terrestrial city. The Church must be vigilant to see that the civil power does not make excessive demands which might be incompatible with the spiritual end of the faithful or might seriously imperil it. The temporal interests for which the secular power is responsible often are or seem to be in conflict with the spiritual interests, so that there is frequently a latent tension between the two powers. In the absence of a compromise arrangement there is a danger that they will deteriorate into violent crisis. The Church has everything to gain from a harmonious relationship with the secular power, and states are not less interested in a good understanding. The Church is a power which it is better for a state to count among its friends than among its enemies. Many states are well aware of this; this is why they strive to maintain straightforward diplomatic relations with the Church, leading in many cases to agreements known as concordats. In other countries conflict has broken out; the postwar years provide many examples of it, especially in the countries of Central Europe.

We have no intention of attempting a history of concordats and clashes, or of the theory of the relationship between the

9—W.C.L.

two powers. We propose simply to indicate what attitude the Catholic Church adopts towards the civil power, and how the secular authority behaves towards the Church, not in theory but in practice. For this purpose it seems useful first of all to describe the juridical position given to or recognized in the Holy See and the Catholic Church in international law. Then we shall describe the effective relations with the different states which have not entirely declined to entertain relations with her.

THE HOLY SEE AND THE CATHOLIC CHURCH IN INTERNATIONAL LAW

In the person of the pope who represents it, the Holy See enjoys a twofold sovereignty: territorial sovereignty as representing the Vatican City State, and personal authority as representing the Catholic and Universal Church. The territorial sovereignty is of secondary importance, but it is not to be despised, for it permits the free exercise of the personal sovereignty. We shall briefly sketch the characteristics of this twofold sovereignty with which the Holy See is invested in the person of its representative, the pope.

The pope is temporal sovereign of the little state known as the Vatican City. This position is the result of the agreements signed in Rome at the Lateran Palace on February 11th, 1929 by Cardinal Gasparri, the Secretary of State of Pius XI, on behalf of the Holy See, and by Mussolini, head of the Italian Government, on behalf of Italy. Since the entry of Italian troops into Rome on September 20th, 1870, the old temporal power of the popes, created in the eighth century by Pepin the Short, had ceased to exist. But Pius IX and his successors refused to accept the *fait accompli*, supported by an Italian law known as the Law of Guarantees, recognizing the independence and extra-territorial status of the Vatican. Thereafter, in protest against the occupation of Rome, the Sovereign Pontiffs refused to leave the Vatican. The Lateran Agreements in 1929 put an end to this tension by settling the celebrated "Roman Question". Those agreements comprise a treaty and a concordat which form a juridical whole, inter-dependent and complementary to each other.

By the treaty Italy recognizes the Holy See's full rights of property, exclusive and absolute power, as well as sovereign jurisdiction over the Vatican, with all the rights of legation, active and passive: the Holy See is authorized to accredit Nuncios to the different states, and the various governments can maintain permanent representatives at the pontifical court. The diplomatic envoys at the Vatican, even if they reside on Italian territory, enjoy all the immunities recognized by international law. Moreover, Italy recognizes that the Holy See has full property rights, with the immunities recognized in international law for the residences of diplomatic envoys, over certain churches and buildings situated on Italian terri-tory in Rome or its immediate neighbourhood; these include the patriarchal basilicas of St John Lateran, St Mary Major and St Paul's outside the Walls, the papal summer villa at Castelgandolfo and the palaces of the Apostolic Chancery, of Propaganda and of the Holy Office. The most complete free-dom of communication with the rest of the world is guaran-teed to the Vatican City State. In short, this miniature state of little more than a hundred and ten acres, with about a thousand inhabitants, is no more than the realization in the international field of the essential conditions of freedom which the pope deems indispensable for the fulfillment of his office. Thanks to the existence of this sovereign city state, the Roman Pontiff is as independent of all secular power as in the time when he was the ruler of the Papal States. In return, the Holy See undertakes to preserve a strict neutrality in inter-national rivalries of a temporal order, and not to take part in international conferences called to settle differences of that order at least unless the members of an international assembly invite it to do so or appeal to its mediation. But in any event the Holy See reserves the right to make its moral and spiritual authority felt in the international field.

The concordat with Italy which was signed at the same

time as the Lateran Treaty defines the relations between the Catholic Church in Italy and the civil power. It guarantees the free exercise of the Catholic religion in Italy. The Church is thereby freed from the control of the state whether through the administration of ecclesiastical property or through the appointment of bishops; the government no longer has more than a right of consultation in the choice of bishops, renouncing the exercise of the old royal *placet* or *exequatur*. Religious marriage is recognized by the civil power.

As representative of the Vatican City State the pope is a temporal sovereign; by virtue of this the Holy See enjoys territorial sovereignty. But there are other and more important things about it, for the smallness of the Vatican City State would alone hardly give the Vatican City State much standing in the eyes of other states with territorial sovereignty. What state would accredit an ambassador to the sovereign of a territory of a hundred and ten acres, or what government would conclude solemn conventions under international law with such a sovereign? The territorial sovereignty of the Vatican City State is only one aspect of the pontifical authority.

The pope and the Holy See represent the universal Catholic Church. And the Catholic Church in its universality has the character of a supra-national institution. There is nothing, therefore, to prevent the recognition of international personality in it, which confers a real sovereignty upon it, even though one of another order than territorial sovereignty. This way of looking upon the Catholic Church is fully in line with the development of modern international law. Supra-national bodies are increasing in remarkable fashion these days, on account of the worldwide character of numerous problems which it is no longer possible to solve within a single state. This is a new phenomenon. International personality is attributed to them, so that, while not possessing territorial sovereignty, these bodies are able to conclude agreements with states whose sovereignty is of a territorial order. The classic institution of this kind is the United Nations Organization, and there are many others—NATO, UNESCO and so forth. It is in this category of new juridical institutions of a supra-national character that most contemporary writers place the Holy See. M. le Roy, professor in the faculty of law at Lille and in the Institut d'Études Politiques in Paris, recently wrote: "The universal Church is not a state, but an international institution. . . . For the jurist the United Nations and the Holy See, the pope and the secretary-general of the United Nations Organization, belong to the same juridical categories." (*Annuaire de l'École des législations religieuses de l'Institut catholique de Paris*, 1952, pp. 45–6.)

So personal sovereignty is added to the territorial sove-reignty which the Holy See enjoys on account of the Vatican City State. As representing the universal Church, the Holy See is placed in the category of international institutions and is made, for this reason, a normal person in the law of nations. As a result, if a state accredits a diplomatic envoy to the pontifical court, or if it concludes a concordat with the Holy See, it sees in the person of the pope not the temporal sovereign, not the representative of the Vatican City State, but the head of the universal Catholic Church. It is for this reason also that concordats have the character of international agree-ments and not of simple contracts made between the state and an organism of the same state; such a contract would concern internal public law and not the law of nations. The Portuguese concordat signed in 1940, for instance, was not concluded between the Portuguese Government and the Catholic Church in Portugal, but between the Portuguese government and the universal Catholic Church, represented by the pope and the Holy See, to govern the juridical position of the Catholic Church in Portugal. It is the same with all concordats.

Such is the international juridical position of the Catholic Church which the pope and the Holy See represent. We must now see how it is expressed in the relations with the various states. The diplomatic relations and concordats are the essen-tial manifestations of it.

DIPLOMATIC RELATIONS

The Holy See maintains relations with a considerable number of states by means of diplomatic representation. The practice of having a permanent and reciprocal representation between the pontifical court and secular governments goes back to the sixteenth century; the Middle Ages only knew envoys sent on temporary and limited missions.

The pope's permanent representatives with states bear the title of nuncios or internuncios, depending partly on the importance of the post and partly on the readiness or refusal of the government concerned to allow the pope's representative to serve as doyen of the diplomatic corps. Ambassadors accredited by their governments to the Holy See are usually the opposite numbers of nuncios, and ministers plenipotentiary of internuncios. Nuncios are nowadays always the doyens of the diplomatic corps accredited the various powers: thus the nuncio in Paris serves as doyen of all the foreign diplomatists entrusted with missions to the French government, and as such speaks for all the diplomatic corps in Paris in, for example, offering new year wishes to the President of the Republic.

On January 1st, 1959, the Holy See was in diplomatic relations with forty-two states, being represented by a nuncio in thirty-two of them and by an internuncio in ten. Of the thirty-two nunciatures, eleven are in Europe, two in Asia, and nineteen in Latin America. In Europe a nuncio is accredited to the following states, which we give in alphabetical order: Austria, Belgium, France, Germany, Holland, Ireland, Italy, Luxembourg, Portugal, Spain and Switzerland. France and the Holy See are the only countries which can be represented in Switzerland by a diplomatic envoy having the rank of an ambassador; all other states have simple legations in Switzerland, and not embassies. Historical reasons lie behind this discrimination on the part of the Swiss in favour of France and the Holy See. In Asia the Holy See is represented in only two countries by a nuncio, the Lebanon and the Philippines.

On the other hand we find a nunciature in almost every country of central and southern America: Argentina, Bolivia, Brazil, Chile, Colombia, Costa Rica, Cuba, the Dominican Republic, Ecuador, Guatemala, Haiti, Honduras, Nicaragua, Panama, Paraguay, Peru, Salvador, Uruguay and Venezuela. All these countries which we have named have their ambassadors at the Holy See, with the exception of Switzerland, which has no official representative at the Vatican—a paradoxical position, explained by history and internal politics.

The Holy See maintains an internunciature in the following ten countries: China, Egypt, Ethiopia (since 1957), India, Indonesia, Iran, Japan, Liberia, Pakistan, and Syria; the first of these is of course in Formosa, at the seat of the Nationalist government, the Chinese Communists having long ago severed all relations with the Vatican. These countries in their turn are represented at the Holy See by ministers plenipotentiary, with the exception of Iran, whose representative has the title of ambassador. And, as may be imagined, the nunciatures or internunciatures in the Communist-dominated countries of Europe—Czechoslovakia, Esthonia, Hungary, Latvia, Lithuania, Poland, Rumania and Yugoslavia—are vacant.

In other countries again the Holy See is represented only by an apostolic delegate who has no diplomatic status. An apostolic delegate is a simple intermediary between the Sovereign Pontiff and the bishops of the country or territory (known as the apostolic delegation) to which he is sent; his functions are defined in an instruction of the Secretariat of State at the Vatican dated May 8th, 1916. At the present time Rome has about fifteen apostolic delegates scattered through the world. Some delegations go back to the last century, but most of them are of recent date. We give the list in the order of their establishment, beginning with the most recent: Thailand and Malaya (1957), Korea (1949), Palestine and Jerusalem with Cyprus and Jordan (1948), French West' Africa, or Dakar (1948), Great Britain (1938), British East and West Africa (1930), the Belgian Congo and Ruanda-Urundi (1930), Indochina (1925), South Africa (1922), Australia with

New Zealand and Oceania (1914), Mexico (1904), Canada (1899), the United States (1893), Turkey (1868), and Iraq, with Arabia (1832).

As the list shows, the Holy See is represented in Britain only by an apostolic delegate, without diplomatic status, although the British government accredits a minister plenipotentiary at the pontifical court. For historical reasons it is still not thought possible to receive on British soil an envoy of the Holy See with diplomatic status. The case is the opposite to that in Switzerland, which for similar reasons refuses to send a representative to the pontifical court but receives a nuncio in Berne. Finland, where the Holy See is not represented, maintains a minister plenipotentiary at the Vatican; so it is also with the little principalities of Monaco and San Marino. President Roosevelt sent a personal delegate to the pope, with the rank of ambassador, who was at the Vatican all through the second world war, and President Truman afterwards continued this arrangement. When Mr Myron Taylor asked to be relieved of this office he was not replaced, from consideration for Protestant sentiment in the United States. Lastly, we should note the importance which the Arab states have been attaching, these recent years, to having good relations with the Vatican. Most of the sovereign states of Islam now maintain diplomatic relations with the Holy See; those which are exceptions in this—Saudi Arabia, the Yemen, Libya, Afghanistan—have hardly any diplomatic relations with other states. Egypt was the first Moslem state to establish diplomatic relations with the Holy See, apart from the Lebanon, which, while wanting to be thought of as an Arab state, is not really a Moslem state since half its population is Christian. The first Egyptian minister plenipotentiary presented his letters of credence to Pius XII in October 1947, when all the Arab press commented at length on the event. Other Moslem states soon followed the Egyptian example. The first was Indonesia; as soon as its sovereignty had been recognized by the Vatican Indonesia proposed that diplomatic relations should be established, and in April 1950 a minister plenipotentiary was accredited at the Holy See and an internuncio with the Indonesian government. In 1953 the Syrian minister plenipotentiary presented his letters of credence to the pope, and Iran and Pakistan in their turn lost no time in exchanging diplomatic representatives with the Holy See.

CONCORDATS

A concordat is a convention concluded between the Holy See and the civil power of a country in order to define the relationship between the Catholic Church and the state in matters in which both are concerned. The government, as we have already noted, does not treat with the Catholic Church in its country, but with the universal Catholic Church represented by the Holy See, so that a concordat comes into the category of international conventions: it is concluded between two powers each possessing sovereignty, as would not be the case if the government treated with the local ecclesiastical authorities.

The institution of concordats does not date from the modern or contemporary period; since the end of the eleventh century the Church has been in the habit of settling her relationships with the secular powers by means of conventions of this kind, and the first of these agreements dates from the year 1098. The list is long, of the concordats and conventions which the Holy See signed with different states between that time and the beginning of the first world war: there were seventy-four of them altogether. The extensive changes in the map of Europe after 1918 inevitably involved the revision of the concordats made by the Holy See with monarchs who had by then been dethroned. The Vatican signed new agreements, therefore, with the Succession States created by the break-up of the Austro-Hungarian Empire, but also with other states both in Europe and elsewhere. In no period have concordats been so prolific as in ours. We give for reference the chronological list of concordats from 1919 until the present, with the dates of signature: Latvia (May 30th,

1922), Bavaria (March 29th, 1924), Poland (February 10th, 1925), Rumania (May 10th, 1927), Lithuania (September 27th, 1927), Italy (February 11th, 1929), Prussia (June 14th, 1929), Baden (October 10th, 1932), Austria (June 5th, 1933), the German Reich (July 20th, 1933, this concordat not replacing the separate conventions signed with Bavaria, Baden and Prussia), Portugal (May 7th, 1940), Spain (August 27th, 1953) and the Dominican Republic (June 16th, 1954). To these thirteen concordats properly so-called should be added a number of important but less solemn agreements over questions of detail, like that made with France in 1926 over the liturgical honours to be paid to the representatives of France in the countries of the Near East, and those signed with Colombia in 1928 on the subject of the missions, with Portugal in the same year concerning the delimitation of dioceses and the appointment of bishops in the Portuguese colonies, and with Argentina in 1957 concerning military chaplains. There were twenty-six conventions of this kind in the forty years between 1919 and 1959, in addition to the thirteen concordats. The text of all these diplomatic agreements was published by the late Mgr Angelo Mercati in two volumes entitled *Raccolta di concordati su materie ecclesiastiche, tra la Santa Sede e le Autorità civili* (Rome, 1954); the first volume includes the texts of concordats and agreements from 1098 to 1914 and the second of those between 1915 and 1954.

Some of the concordats signed between the two world wars were unilaterally denounced after 1944 in central and eastern Europe. The Communist provisional government of Poland denounced the Polish concordat on September 14th, 1945; new negotiations led, on December 31st, 1956, to an internal *modus vivendi* between the government and the Church in Poland. On July 19th, 1949, the Communist government in Bucharest similarly denounced the Rumanian concordat; and it should be noted that this unilateral denunciation was legal and in conformity with the rules of international law, for article 23 of that concordat had stipulated that "the two parties reserve to themselves the right of denouncing the present concordat if six months' notice is given". The concordats with Latvia and Lithuania, as may be imagined, suffered the fate of those two countries, which was to disappear.

Almost all modern concordats deal with the same questions, the settlement varying according to the country concerned and the circumstances. The subjects of agreement include elevations to the episcopate and other appointments to important ecclesiastical offices, canonical marriage, religious instruction in the schools, the freedom of the religious orders, the freedom of the Church to hold property, and the exemption of the clergy from armed military service. Regarded as a whole, the concordats concluded after 1918 are more favourable to the Catholic Church than were those of the last century, the difference arising from the fact that at the end of the eighteenth century and the beginning of the nineteenth the Church was very weak; she needed the support of the civil power, which took advantage of this to impose its conditions. After the first world war the Holy See enjoyed an increased prestige and some of the new states were glad to be able to rely upon her support.

It is worth noting in conclusion that the signature of a concordat provides no basis for an estimate of the attitude of the government in question towards the Catholic Church. The concordat governs relations of a purely juridical order, defining the reciprocal rights and duties of the contracting parties. That is all. The Holy See on its side, in treating with a state, does not in any way imply approval of the actions or the form of its government, but seeks only the spiritual good of the members of the Catholic Church in the country concerned.

CHAPTER VII

THE ORDER OF GRACE

The Church must guide men to heaven: that is her purpose and the reason for her existence. All her activities converge towards this end, even if it is not always easy to perceive the connection between certain matters which preoccupy the Church and the "one thing necessary", which is the salvation of her members. The elements of the law which we have analysed so far provide the Church with the exterior structure necessary for carrying out her work; it is in an indirect fashion that it assists the individual Catholic to attain his destiny. Other institutions, on the other hand, have the direct and immediate purpose of bringing men into contact with God. They constitute what we have agreed to term the higher level, or the order of grace, which it now remains to consider. The part played by canon law is even more in the background in this field than in others; it may even be asked how it is possible to introduce supernatural institutions such as the sacraments into a juridical setting. The difficulty is only apparent. Canon law in no way seeks to trespass upon ground which it recognizes as sacrosanct and which is the preserve of theology and secondarily of morals and of the liturgy. Its part is no more than that of facilitating the use of the supernatural means which, through the Church, God has placed at the disposal of men. It does this in prescribing the conditions of their use, so that abuses and also negligence may be avoided; for man, even regenerated by baptism, is still beset by the power of evil.

We shall see how canon law has its place in the regulation

of the sources of supernatural life which are the sacraments, in the homage paid to God in worship, and lastly in the beatification and canonization of outstandingly meritorious members of the Church.

THE SOURCES OF SUPERNATURAL LIFE: THE SACRAMENTS

The Church gives every Catholic her unfailing attention from his birth to his death, and even thereafter. She confers particular benefits to mark the principal stages in his life, and through the various sacraments she helps him to meet the pitfalls which men encounter in the course of their earthly existence. Baptism, which is the sign that he belongs to the ecclesiastical society, in infusing divine life into him, makes a man a member of the Kingdom of God here below. Confirmation gives him strength to remain firm in the faith. The Eucharist nourishes and sustains the divine life received at baptism, and penance makes it possible to recover that life in all its splendour when a Catholic has stained or lost it through his base actions and failings. On the day a man establishes a home the Church is again present; through the sacrament of marriage she heaps upon him the graces necessary for the grave responsibility which he is at that moment assuming.

If a man desires to devote his life to the service of God the Church will show herself particularly solicitous for him, helping him to ascend through the different degrees which lead to the priesthood and making him another Christ, an *alter Christus*. Finally, through extreme unction, the Church sustains all her children in the last and difficult stage which brings life on earth to an end and opens the way to the next world.

The sacraments clearly depend, as we have said, upon theology. Canon Law is content to determine who shall administer and who shall receive them, and the conditions—the place and time—of their administration.

Baptism

The ordinary minister of solemn baptism is a priest, with the parish priest having the first right to perform this service. The extraordinary minister of it is a deacon. Baptism can be conferred in private form, without ceremony, when it is conditionally given for a second time; in this same form any person can confer it when there is danger of death. One god-father at least, or one godmother, if two are not available, is required at a solemn baptism. The law makes certain conditions for the valid and licit exercise of the function of a god-parent, excluding, among others, persons belonging to a non-Catholic religion. These persons may assist at the baptism and sign the register as witnesses, but not as godparents properly speaking. Baptism must be conferred on children born of Catholic parents within a few days of the birth, and if possible in the parish church. The name of the baptized child or person is at once entered in the parish register of baptisms; alongside the record of the baptism the parish priest will later note the confirmation and marriage of the person concerned or, it may be, the reception of the subdiaconate, or solemn profession in the religious life.

Confirmation

In the Latin Church children receive confirmation about the age of seven. Its administration is in principle reserved to the bishop; and by a concession, for which the law provides, vicars and prefects apostolic and abbots and prelates *nullius* who have not received episcopal consecration can confirm within their territories. Lastly, since 1947, parish priests have the faculty of confirming those who are in danger of death.

The Eucharist

The law regards the Eucharist under the twofold aspect of the Mass and Holy Communion. On the subject of the Mass it lays down that each priest is authorized to offer the holy sacrifice only once a day, save on Christmas Day and All Souls Day, November 2nd, when he is permitted to celebrate

three Masses. Priests engaged in the parochial ministry receive
indults permitting them to say two Masses, or even three, on
Sundays and holidays of obligation. The celebration of Mass
must not begin more than one hour before dawn or more than
one hour after noon; although in recent years very wide faculties have been granted to the bishops to authorize afternoon
or evening Mass from four o'clock onwards whenever they
judge it to be for the general good of the faithful. The holy
sacrifice must be offered on a consecrated altar stone and
within a place of worship; the celebration of Mass outside a
place of worship is only permitted to priests who have the
privilege of using a portable altar.

The law recommends the frequent reception of holy communion, and makes it obligatory, at least once a year at
Eastertime, for all the faithful who have attained the age of
reason. A state of grace is required for the reception of holy
communion, and the law requires abstention for three hours
beforehand from all solid food and alcohol and for one hour
beforehand from all other liquid save water, which does not
break the eucharistic fast. The minister of holy communion is
a priest or, exceptionally, a deacon. Communion can be given
on all days of the year, but in principle, save for the sick and
dying, only at the times when it is permitted to celebrate Mass.

Penance

The administration of the sacrament of penance requires,
on the part of the minister, the priesthood and a delegation
of the power of government, called power of jurisdiction.
Hence the priesthood, while indispensable, is not enough
for absolving the penitent faithful from their sins; it is necessary also to have the jurisdiction which the bishop and the
vicars general confer within the diocese, even on religious
who wish to hear confessions outside their religious houses.
The law concedes jurisdiction to all priests when there is
danger of death and authorizes them validly and licitly to
absolve the penitent from all his sins and to remit all canonical

censures, in whatever way they may be reserved. For the Catholic who has attained the age of reason, confession once a year is obligatory. The administration of the sacrament of penance in principle takes place in the confessional in a church or chapel or in a place adjacent to a church; it is strictly required for women, save in the case of illness; the law is much more tolerant about the confession of men, which is permitted in any place at all for a reasonable motive.

Order

The sacrament of order confers the power of offering the sacrifice of the Mass and administering the sacraments. It includes degrees, of which the three highest are of divine institution: the diaconate, the priesthood and the episcopate. The others are of ecclesiastical institution: the four minor orders and the subdiaconate. The tonsure is properly speaking not an order. In describing the status of clerics we have indicated the qualifications required of candidates for orders, and there is no need to do so again here. The ordinary minister of the sacrament of order is the consecrated bishop; with an indult or by virtue of a special provision of the law certain priests—vicars and prefects apostolic who are not bishops, abbots and prelates *nullius*, regular abbots—can confer the tonsure and the minor orders. Episcopal consecration is reserved to the pope; a bishop can licitly consecrate only with an apostolic mandate, under pain of the very grave canonical sanctions which have been incurred in 1958 and 1959 by certain bishops in China. The tonsure may be conferred on any day of the year, the minor orders on Sundays and all double feasts. The holy orders (subdiaconate, diaconate and priesthood) can in principle only be conferred on Ember Saturdays, the day before Passion Sunday, or Holy Saturday. Episcopal consecration takes place, unless there is a special indult, on a Sunday or the feast of an apostle. The names of the ordinands and of the minister are entered in a special register; ordination to the subdiaconate must appear in the parish register alongside the record of baptism.

Marriage

The sacrament of marriage is the subject of numerous and detailed provisions of canon law. The Church claims exclusive competence in laying down the law of marriage properly so-called, in such matters as impediments, the exchange of consent, its effects and the causes of nullity. She recognizes in the state only the right to decide about the purely civil effects, in the law of property for example. The Church makes these claims because according to Catholic teaching the contract and the sacrament are not separable. The two contracting parties are themselves the ministers of the marriage; they confer the sacrament upon themselves in exchanging the matrimonial consent in the forms prescribed by canon law. The priest who is assisting plays the part of an official witness, but does not administer the sacrament of marriage.

In principle, every human person who has the physical and moral qualifications required for a valid exchange of consents has the right to marry. In the interests of society or of individuals, however, the Church has defined a certain number of impediments which limit this freedom. These impediments are of two kinds: some render null the marriage contracted in defiance of the prohibition, and are called diriment impediments, others simply render the marriage illicit and are called prohibiting impediments.

The law of the Church as it is today knows thirteen diriment impediments: being under age (fourteen years for girls, sixteen for boys); impotence; an earlier marriage, however long ago, if it has not been dissolved by the death of the other partner or a dispensation, or declared null by the sentence of an ecclesiastical tribunal; disparity of cult (marriage between a person baptized in the Catholic Church and an unbaptized person being forbidden); holy orders from the subdiaconate onwards; solemn vows as taken in the older religious orders; rape; crime (adultery accompanied by a promise of marriage, or conjugicide); consanguinity (in the direct line and to the third degree in the collateral line— second cousins); affinity (in the direct line and to the second degree in the collateral line); public propriety (forbidding the marriage of a man with a forebear or descendant of his concubine or mistress, and *vice versa*); spiritual relationship (the result of baptism, preventing the baptized person from marrying his godfather or godmother, or the minister of the sacrament); legal kinship (resulting from adoption in countries where the civil law makes legal kinship a diriment impediment).

The prohibiting impediments are simple vows, mixed religion (marriage being forbidden between a baptized person belonging to the Catholic Church and a baptized person belonging to another religious confession), and legal kinship (resulting from adoption in countries like France where the civil law regards legal kinship as a simple prohibiting impediment).

Some impediments express the divine law, natural or positive, and so do not admit of dispensation; such are impotence, an earlier marriage and kinship in the direct line and to the first degree in the collateral line. Others have been instituted by the Church and can be lifted by the authority which established them—that is, by the Holy See, which often delegates its powers to lower authorities.

Before marriage the engaged couple's parish priest subjects them to a detailed inquiry to assure himself that they are not subject to any impediment, that they know the essentials of the Christian doctrine of marriage, and that they are prepared to give their consent in full freedom and knowledge of what they are doing. The findings of this inquiry are written down and signed by the couple, the documents being preserved in the parish archives.

The exchange of consent normally takes place, under pain of invalidity, in the presence of two witnesses and of the qualified witness, the parish priest of the parish in which the marriage is celebrated; the parish priest can delegate his power to any other priest, but his competence is strictly territorial and does not go outside the boundaries of his parish. Local ordinaries (bishops and vicars general) have the same powers as the parish priest within the diocesan boundaries. In danger of death the engaged couple are entitled to exchange their consent before two ordinary witnesses; the law concedes the same facilities to them if they find themselves in circumstances which make it impossible without great inconvenience for a qualified priest to come to them or for them to go to a qualified priest, if these circumstances are likely to continue as long as a month. All Catholics, but only Catholics, are bound to observe these formalities, whether they are marrying among themselves or with persons belonging to other religious confessions. Failure to observe the canonical form leads to the nullity of the marriage.

The exchange of consent before the required witnesses is enough to create the indissoluble bond, and it also confers the graces of the sacrament upon those who are properly disposed. Hence the care of the Church to prepare them for it. She advises in addition that the marriage should be accompanied by certain liturgical rites: the blessing of the rings, the solemn blessing of those who are marrying, and the nuptial Mass.

Extreme Unction

This sacrament is administered to persons who are in danger of death as the result of illness or old age. It may be repeated, but not in the course of the same illness; the person must have fallen gravely ill for a second time after recovering his health. The ordinary minister is the parish priest of the sick person, or, with his permission at least presumed, any other priest.

DIVINE WORSHIP

God showers his goodness upon men through the sacraments. It is just that in return men shall show gratitude to God and give him proof of their worship and submission. The Church encourages and assists her members to render to God the homage due to him by organizing public worship and discreetly supervising private worship.

Theology, liturgy and law all have their parts to play in the organization of divine worship. It is for theology and liturgy to guide the faithful to the authentic sources of piety and to provide them with the elements of a worship which will be appropriate to the dignity of God while at the same time meeting the deepest aspirations of the human heart. They lay the foundations of the practices of worship. The part of canon law lies in deciding the exterior conditions of the services in which God is worshipped. To this end the Code of 1917 contains detailed legislation, laying down first of all the conditions for the places intended for the regular worship of God: churches and oratories. The law defines with great precision the authority qualified to permit the construction of a church, the ceremonies required before the building may be used for worship, the causes of violation and desecration, the persons responsible for the upkeep.

Oratories are erected to serve as places of worship for particular groups and not, like churches, for all the faithful. The law distinguishes three kinds; public oratories, which are open to everyone at the times of the services, even though they have been built for a limited group; semi-public oratories, which only serve a community and are closed to the public; and domestic or private oratories, which are established in private houses for the use of an individual family. No permission is necessary to furnish a room in a private dwelling as an oratory in which a family can pray or make meditations, but the celebration of Mass is permitted only with an apostolic indult.

The altar receives special attention in canon law, by reason of its eminent dignity, for it is upon the altar that the sacrifice of the Mass is carried out, the central act of worship in the Catholic religion. It must be of natural stone, and cannot be used for the celebration of Mass until it has been consecrated by a bishop. It contains relics of at least one saint, and of several if possible, preferably those of a martyr. If the stone is large and attached to the ground by supports of the same material the altar is said to be fixed or immovable; but if the consecrated stone is small and rests on a table the altar is said to be portable or movable. The law requires that there shall be at least one fixed altar in every consecrated church, but permits a portable altar alone in churches and public and semi-public oratories which have been blessed but not consecrated. Fixed altars are forbidden in private oratories.

Many and various things are needed in carrying out the worship of the Church, especially for the celebration of the Mass and the administration of the sacraments: chalices, ciboria, liturgical ornaments, altar candles, altar cloths and linen, the crucifix, the sanctuary lamp. The law lays down in detail which things must be consecrated (the chalice and paten, for example) and which must simply be blessed (the corporal, pall, altar cloths, chasuble, stole, maniple, amice, cincture). For other things blessing is recommended but is not obligatory. It stipulates also upon whom the responsibility falls for buying the sacred furnishings and for looking after their maintenance, as well as after the maintenance of all other ecclesiastical buildings and furnishings. The administration of temporal property belonging to particular churches is subject to very strict rules. The parish priest is assisted in the administration of the property of the parish by a body called the council of maintenance (*consilium fabricae ecclesiae*). The bishop, who is responsible for the control of particular administrations, looks after the property of his see and of the diocese; he also is assisted by a council of maintenance, composed of men competent in temporal affairs. Severe provisions govern the alienation of ecclesiastical property: the authority of the Holy See is required for the alienation of what are known as major relics and of precious images, as well as of anything, whether building or furnishing, of which the value exceeds a certain fixed sum; the bishop can give authority for the disposal of property of which the value does not exceed that sum, but he must have the agreement of his cathedral chapter and his council of maintenance. He is only authorized to act without their consent if the value of the property is less than a certain fixed sum.

10—W.C.L.

As may be imagined, canon law pays no less attention to the conservation of spiritual goods than to that of temporal goods. It requires the ecclesiastical authorities to be vigilant over all literary productions which concern worship, faith or morals. To this end it requires that all books treating of these subjects, as well as all pious images that are not traditional presented for the veneration of the faithful, shall first be submitted to the censorship of the competent authorities. It claims the power of forbidding the exposition of non-traditional pious images in places of worship and the reading of writings which do not conform to the holy teaching of the Church. Lastly the veneration of the saints is contained within narrow limits; any public cult is nowadays strictly reserved to servants of God who have received the honours of the altar as the result of a minutely regulated procedure whose course it now remains for us to study.

THE PROCEDURE OF BEATIFICATION AND CANONIZATION

According to the present dispositions of the law, causes for beatification and canonization fall within the exclusive competence of the Holy See. For a long time bishops and local councils used to authorize the faithful to practise the public cultus of any person no longer living who had been outstanding during his lifetime for particularly exemplary conduct; to say nothing of the martyrs of the first centuries whose cultus had been so to say spontaneous. Authorizations of cultus granted by bishops or councils used to amount to a kind of beatification or canonization. But this procedure gave rise to certain abuses. Hence, in the second half of the twelfth century, Alexander III sought to reserve these causes to the Roman authority, although he did not succeed in withdrawing all initiative in this field from the lower authorities. It was Urban VIII (1623–44) who finally forbade the bishops to accord the honours of the altar to one who had died and instituted a new procedure for beatification and canonization.

After certain modifications introduced by Benedict XIV and other popes, Urban VIII's procedure was adopted by the Code of 1917, where it is the subject of canons 1999 to 2141. The examination of these causes is entrusted to the Congregation for Rites.

A twofold procedure, ordinary and extraordinary, is provided for. The extraordinary procedure is only used for servants of God who died before the prescriptions of Urban VIII came into force and who have been the object of a traditional cultus. For others the ordinary procedure is observed, comprised of the diocesan processes and the apostolic processes.

The bishop is charged to inquire into the writings of the servant of God for whom the honours of public cultus are sought, so that the doctrinal purity of his thought may be proved. He must then ascertain that the reputation for sanctity which the person concerned enjoys, or the reality of his martyrdom, is well established, and that he has not been the object of any public cult already. The record and the documents of the diocesan process are sent to the Congregation for Rites, which submits them to close examination. If the result is favourable the pope signs the decree officially introducing the cause for beatification. Then the apostolic processes begin. The tribunal first discusses the virtues of the servant of God, or the reality of his martyrdom. If the examination leads to a positive conclusion a pontifical decree proclaims the heroicity of the virtues or the reality of the martyrdom of the person concerned. Next comes the examination of the miracles. Two, three, or even four miracles are required, according to the quality of the witnesses who attest them. If the experts recognize the miraculous character of the facts advanced, the decree of beatification is signed by the pope. Beati—those who have been beatified—have the right to a limited public cult, while those not yet beatified cannot be the object of any manifestation of public cult.

Two miracles occurring after beatification make it possible to reopen the cause with a view to canonization. After the new miracles have been recognized a pontifical decree, announced in a consistory, decides that the canonization may safely be proceeded with. The solemn ceremony of canonization is carried out in St Peter's basilica amid magnificent ceremonial, the pope himself singing the Mass and, after the gospel, reading the bull of canonization, which is an infallible decree. In principle saints have the right to a public cultus throughout Christendom.

The Congregation for Rites is constantly receiving new requests for beatification. Its archives contain so many dossiers that very many years would be needed to deal with them all, quite apart from the new requests which are arriving all the time. By way of illustration, consider the number of causes which led to some partial result in the course of 1955 alone. At the request of the Congregation for Rites the pope signed in that year six decrees introducing new causes for beatification, four proclaiming the heroicity of virtues, one approving miracles in a cause for beatification, and five decrees of beatification.

CONCLUSION

THE FUTURE OF CANON

LAW

We cannot close this brief study without saying something about the future of canon law. Has it any future, or are we talking about a dead system of law which no longer has more than an historical interest? No hesitation is possible: canon law today presents all the signs of a system of law that is very much alive, with more than four hundred million people subject to it at the present time. It is perfectly true that its rôle is no longer so important as it was for example in the Middle Ages, when it penetrated far beyond the setting of the religious society. Until the twelfth century canon law had constantly extended the range of its action, and in some departments of life it took the place of or competed with the secular law. From the thirteenth century onwards it has had one by one to yield positions gained and to retreat to strictly ecclesiastical ground. But in the setting of the religious society which is its proper field canon law can be seen to be full of vigour at the present time. Many signs give proof of this: the legislative activity of the Church, the interest shown in the study of canon law, the foundation of new reviews and institutions.

The promulgation of the Code did not put an end to the legislative activity of the Church. As we have already pointed out, numerous provisions have been published to complete or adapt the texts of 1917; and they are appearing with ever increasing frequency. To realize this it is enough to compare

the volumes of the *Acta Apostolicae Sedis*, the official journal
of the Holy See, thirty or forty years ago and now; their size
has considerably increased in recent years. It is true that in
the volumes of recent years the many discourses of Pius XII
take up a great deal of the space, but it is none the less true
that the apostolic constitutions and instructions of the various
Roman congregations are growing in number, for the Church
has all the time to deal with a great number of problems. The
work of the Roman and diocesan tribunals is increasing at an
alarming rate. The Rota gave final judgments in fifty-six cases
in 1926, in eighty-five in 1936, and in two hundred and sixty-
one in 1956. Certain diocesan tribunals which before 1940 had
received two or three requests each year for a declaration
of nullity in marriage judge perhaps a score of cases each
year now. The Church is caught in the wheels of the times;
whether she wants to or not she follows the movement of civil
society, of which the administration is assuming larger and
larger proportions in all departments.

The increased legislative activity of the Church that has
been discernible for the last half-century is accompanied by
a revival of studies in canon law, which fell to a very low
level in the last century. The subject used to occupy only a
very small space in the teaching given in the seminaries; it
found no favour with the bishops. As a significant illustration
of the mentality prevailing at that time, the faculty of theology
at the Institut Catholique in Paris originally made no provision for a professor of canon law; only in 1880 was it endowed with a chair of canon law, and this was given to a
foreigner, Pietro Gasparri, who was to become the moving
spirit, the linch-pin, in the codification of the canon law of
the Latin Church. Thanks to that very distinguished professor,
the teaching of the subject aroused such interest at the Institut
Catholique that a department of canon law was founded there
in 1882; young canonists like Boudinhon and Many were soon
working with Gasparri, and in 1895 the department was replaced by a full faculty of canon law. Some years later, in
1899, another faculty was erected at Toulouse. The plans for

codification and finally the promulgation of the Code in 1917 brought about the full development of canon law studies.

Foundations of faculties and institutes of canon law followed one another: at Strasbourg in 1920, at Washington in 1922, at Lublin, in Poland, in 1923, at Lyons in 1935, at Munich in 1947; nor is this catalogue complete. New reviews wholly devoted to canon law appeared in many countries to swell the numbers of those already existing: the *Commentarium pro religiosis et missionariis* was founded in Rome in 1920, the *Jus Pontificium* in Rome in 1921, *Apollinaris* in Rome in 1928, *The Jurist* in Washington in 1941, *Ephemerides juris canonici* in Rome in 1945, the *Revista Española de Derecho Canonico* in Madrid in 1950, the *Oesterreichisches Archiv für Kirchenrecht* in Vienna in 1950, the *Revue de droit canonique* at Strasbourg in 1951, the *Année canonique* at Paris in 1952. Since 1952 conferences of those concerned in the study of canon law have been held every two years in Paris, bringing professors and practitioners together for three days' deliberations. Conferences of the same kind also take place in the United States, Austria and Spain. Books on canon law have become legion. Commentaries on the Code, in several volumes, have appeared in great numbers, and most of them have already run through several editions. The monographs on specialized canonical problems can no longer be counted. A large encyclopaedia of canon law is in course of preparation. Published series of doctoral theses are attaining impressive proportions; that of the faculty of canon law in the Catholic University of Washington already runs to more than three hundred volumes.

We have been speaking only of the present state of canonical studies, but this revival has gone hand in hand with a perhaps even more striking revival in historical studies in which laymen have been particularly prominent. In the second half of the nineteenth century such men as Maassen, Friedberg, Schulte, Philipps, Sohm and Hinschius, in Germany, rewrote the history of canon law, and their work drew the attention of historians to a subject of which the significance was no longer understood. French universities were not slow to follow this movement, and even to take the lead in it during the first half of the twentieth century. The leaders of this revival in France were, among others, Adhémar Esmein, who died in 1913; Robert Génestal, who died in 1931; Paul Fournier, who died in 1935; and above all M. Gabriel Le Bras, professor in the faculty of law at Paris, at the École des Hautes Études (the Sorbonne) and at the Institut de droit canonique at Strasbourg. These masters were not satisfied with being scholars; they awakened vocations to canonical studies among theological students and those reading Roman law and the history of law. Thanks to them France has today a body of young historians of canon law which any country could envy, who are going to bring out, during the next few years, an *Histoire du droit et des institutions de l'Église en Occident* in at least twelve volumes. M. Le Bras, the man behind this great undertaking, has written the introductory volume, entitled *Prolégomènes* (Paris, Sirey, 1955). In the United States Dr Stephan Kuttner, professor in the faculty of canon law at Washington, is engaged in a still more ambitious task: in 1955 he founded an Institute of Research and Study of Medieval Canon Law, and this is proposing to place at the disposal of the historians of canon law the immense riches, known and unknown, which are buried away in libraries and archives. Its immediate purpose is to make a catalogue and to publish a critical edition of the works of those who made collections of decrees and decretals, as well as a new edition of the Decretum of Gratian.

These few remarks are enough to show what interest in canon law there is in our time. It is far from a dead science. Historians examine the law and the institutions of the Church in order to find there an essential part of any full history of medieval civilization. Churchmen give their attention to the law as it is today, which they must constantly adapt to meet the conditions of the time. This does not prevent them from also being interested in the past; on the contrary, if they are aware of the importance of their work, they consult history in order to draw lessons for the present from it.

Canon law is a living law; how could it be otherwise, when its course is bound to the life of the Church? We have seen that alongside the law of the Latin Church there is the law of the Eastern Church. Is it far-fetched to foresee, in a future that may or may not be remote, an African canon law, or a Japanese canon law? We think not. The Gospel is not a monopoly of the west. It is true that the Mediterranean basin was the cradle of Christianity, but all parts of the world have a right to the truth, and no part of the world is excluded from it by the Church: she opens her doors to all nations, all races and all civilizations. The law of the Church is flexible enough to adapt itself to all historical contingencies, so long as the divine law, natural or positive, is respected.

SELECT BIBLIOGRAPHY

ABBO, J., and HANNAN, J.: *The Sacred Canons*, St Louis, Herder, 1957.

AUGUSTINE, Charles, O.S.B.: *A Commentary on the New Code of Canon Law*, eight Volumes, London and St Louis, Herder, 1929.

BOUSCAREN, T. L., S.J.: *The Canon Law Digest*, four Volumes, Milwaukee, Bruce, 1943–54.

BOUSCAREN, T. L., S.J., and ELLIS, A. C., S.J.: *Canon Law, A Text and Commentary*, Milwaukee, Bruce, 1957.

CICOGNANI, A. G.: *Canon Law*, Westminster, Md, Newman Press, 1935.

CONWAY, W. D.: *Problems in Canon Law*, Dublin, Browne and Nolan, 1958, Westminster, Md, Newman Press, 1957.

CREUSEN, J., S.J.: *Religious Men and Women in Church Law*, Milwaukee, Bruce, 1934.

DAVIS, H., S.J.: *Moral and Pastoral Theology*, 4th edn, four Volumes, London and New York, Sheed and Ward, 1958.

GUY, R. E., O.S.B.: *The Westminster Synods in English*, Stratford-on-Avon, 1886.

JONE, Heribert, O.F.M.Cap.: *Moral Theology*, Westminster, Md, Newman Press, 1952.

JOYCE, George H., S.J.: *Christian Marriage*, London and New York, Sheed and Ward, 1954.

MAHONEY, E. J.: *Questions and Answers*. Volume I, *The Sacraments*, Volume II, *Precepts*. London, Burns Oates, 1946, 1949.

MAHONEY, E. J., and McREAVY, L.: *Priests' Problems*, London, Burns Oates, 1958.

PRÜMMER, Dominic M., O.P.: *Handbook of Moral Theology*, Cork, Mercier Press, 1956, and New York, Kenedy, 1957.

WOYWOOD, S., O.F.M., and SMITH, C., O.F.M.: *A Practical Commentary on the Code of Canon Law*, revised edn, New York, Benziger, 1957.